Hoover Institution Publications

One Germany or Two

ONE GERMANY OR TWO

The Struggle at the Heart of Europe

By Eleanor Lansing Dulles

HOOVER INSTITUTION PRESS
Stanford University • Stanford, California

The Hoover Institution on War, Revolution and Peace, founde
at Stanford University in 1919 by the late President Herbe
Hoover, is a center for advanced study and research on public ar
international affairs in the twentieth century. The views expresse
in its publications are entirely those of the authors and do n
necessarily reflect the views of the Hoover Institution.

Hoover Institution Publications 86
Standard Book Number 8179–1861–2
Library of Congress Card Number 70–96725
Printed in the United States of America

To my son David and my daughter Ann

Contents

Tables

Preface

The dust of the West German general election of September 1969 will not settle for many months. The assumption of the chancellorship by the Social Democrat Willy Brandt marks the first transfer of power from the Christian Democrats since Konrad Adenauer was elected chancellor in 1949. The fact that the coalition of the Social Democratic party with the small Free Democratic party has only two votes more than the required majority in the *Bundestag* indicates the skill and reasonableness which must characterize the leadership in the years ahead. A serious shock to either partner would bring the risk of a breakup of the coalition and a new election. Such a possibility is the more imminent since the Free Democratic party lost a large percentage of its following in the September election.

The election results were as follows:

Party	*Percentage of Vote*	*Seats Won*
CDU/CSU	46.1	242
SPD	42.7	224
FDP	5.8	30
NPD	4.3	0
ADF (DFU)	.6	0
Other	.5	0

On October 21 President Gustav Heinemann sent Brandt's name to the *Bundestag* where he was elected chancellor by 251 votes, 2 more than the majority required. A new government was quickly formed.

The significant failure of the National Democratic party, frequently referred to as the neo-Nazi party, to gain the minimum of 5 per cent required for representation in the *Bundestag* has borne out the forecasts of some of the more thoughtful German commentators and confounded some of the newsmen abroad. Many also have welcomed the trend toward a two-party system. Both parties in the coalition are moderate and pro-Western, although the Social Democratic party is likely to seek new ways of contact and communication with Eastern Europe. Any such new approaches will still have to be within the limits described in this text.

The new government's dealings with the Kremlin and its relations with East Germany will excite the interest of policymakers everywhere. There have been, however, in the weeks following the election no dependable signs of a softer line in Moscow or of a yielding on any substantive point by Ulbricht. The new efforts may prove to have more influence on domestic issues than on foreign policy.

Since the election the financial leadership in the Federal Republic has responded to the change in Bonn by freeing the *Deutsche Mark* from the pegged limits and permitting it to float on the foreign exchanges for a brief period. Its value rose beyond the 6 per cent above par that had been rumored as the probable rate, and on October 24 it was set at a new level of 8.5 per cent above par—27.3224 cents per Mark. Meanwhile the restrictions on exports have been lightened in harmony with the new financial adjustment. In these matters as in others the new chancellor and his cabinet are mindful of the narrow margin in the *Bundestag.*

Six months from now the meaning of the election for foreign policy, finance, commerce, defense, education, and other aspects of German life will have become at least partially apparent. Present forecasts must depend on those basic and continuing factors which have created the strength of the Federal Republic in the last twenty years: the productivity of industry, wide participation in elections, the will to maintain close relations with the NATO countries, cooperation with the European community. These and other constructive elements which have been observed in the past will remain dependable aspects of the German situation. So also will the struggle to play a significant role in Eastern and Western Europe. This effort cannot disrupt in the foreseeable future the close alliance with the West. A poll recently taken in the Federal

Republic showed that 81 per cent wished to have closer relations with the United States. This attitude is not likely to change unless reasonable German interests are rebuffed in Washington or in the other main capitals of the Western world.

The next few years, which will determine progress toward a two-party system and acceptance of a law for voting reform, will be characterized by increasing leadership on the part of the Federal Republic among the nations of the West. This book has been written to explain how the Germans have arrived at this point in their postwar recovery and to indicate the likely future direction of policy. It emphasizes the many instances of cooperation with the United States and other free-world powers. It states the importance of understanding and collaboration to reach mutually accepted goals. It discusses the frustration caused by the division of Germany as a limiting factor in the attainment of stability and lasting peace. Regrettably, it makes no prognostication as to how and when reunification will be achieved. This writer cannot foresee the future and has been forced to settle for a serious attempt to understand the recent past and the present. The struggle will go on long after this book has been published.

In the search for accepted values and developing trends I interviewed many scores of persons. To these persons I owe a special debt of gratitude, for it is on the basis of my conversations with them that this text has been written. The footnotes and bibliographical listing have been added not so much to give sources for the statements made in the text as to serve as guides to students who may wish to push their studies of the various problems in new directions.

I have considered carefully how I could satisfactorily express my appreciation of the help I have received. I conclude that this is a practical impossibility. The list is too long, and the basis on which help has been given has varied from the discreet comments of those who speak with reserve to the more emphatic statements of various newsmen and younger radicals. In this difficult position I have chosen arbitrarily a few names to include here. I first thank W. Glenn Campbell, director of the Hoover Institution, and his associates who made it possible for me to spend some months at

Stanford and to travel to Germany twice to renew old contacts there. Of my other friends at the Hoover Institution I mention at this time only Bertram Wolfe, Agnes Peterson, Carole Norton, and Crone Kernke; and Catherine Berry who was given the hard task of editing the manuscript. Others too in Stanford I would like to mention specifically, but do not. In Washington I wish to name two in particular, my friends Elwood Williams and Martha Mautner, both in the Department of State. Of literally hundreds of persons in Germany who have been generous with their time and assistance I name only Willy Brandt, Klaus Schuetz, Wolfgang Wagner, and Klaus Mehnert. How can I express my appreciation to the many others who should be listed? My American companion on my trip to East Germany, Marc Catudal, has been diligent in checking details, in reading proof, and in making useful suggestions.

If I had taken full advantage of all this help, I would have written a longer book, perhaps a better book; but it must stand as it is. It has been written in the hope that those who read it will gain a better understanding of important issues.

November 1, 1969

ELEANOR LANSING DULLES

CHAPTER 1

The Struggle

There is a struggle at the heart of Europe. It is not new, and it will not soon end. The problems involved are essentially political, but they are also economic, social, and ideological. They concern man's role in government, his freedom to express his will, his function in the economy, and the systems he should adopt to maintain order and produce the goods to strengthen his society.

The European center of this worldwide conflict is Germany. Other European countries are however caught up in it. Recent Czechoslovakian strivings for a democratic communism, Romania's increasing independence, Yugoslavia's freedom from Moscow's dictates, and East Germany's inability to reconcile capitalist traditions with oppressive new systems are all aspects of this struggle. But because of their common racial, social, and historical heritage, the two parts of Germany offer the most striking example of the contrast between the opposing systems. All Europe will be affected by the outcome, and the United States is deeply concerned.

Two main questions now confronting Washington and Bonn are: How can freedom and democracy develop in areas controlled by communism? How can the opposing systems—particularly the economic systems—be brought into better working relations? There are possibilities of a serious clash between the two incompatible systems on German soil. There are also possibilities of accommodation.

The Evolving Situation

There are as yet few signs that there will be a demand for more freedom in the German Democratic Republic (GDR); but the situation there is not the same as it was a year or two ago, and it is changing daily. The pressures on Walter Ulbricht, chairman of the State Council and unquestioned head of the GDR, have mounted since the West German government and Romania exchanged ambassadors in 1967. In 1968 the early successes of Alexander Dubcek in Czechoslovakia and Bonn's renewal of diplomatic relations with Belgrade greatly intensified the threat to the rigid position of the East German leaders. A few years earlier there had been talk in Bonn of "isolating the Zone." Recently public emphasis on this has ceased, but the trend toward economic decentralization and the Western contacts with Eastern Europe have affected a partial isolation. Ulbricht has reacted angrily to these developments. He objected to Romania's links with the Federal Republic, was concerned with the threat of change at the time of the Dresden meeting in March 1968, and was a co-signer of the harsh letter written by five Warsaw Pact nations[1] to Dubcek in July. He has thus put himself in the forefront of those who oppose the East European trend to democratization.

The Germans, East and West, wish to avoid open strife. Both are keenly interested in recent developments. After their ill-fated spontaneous revolt in June 1953, however, the East Germans have shown little appetite for protest. And after the Berlin Wall hemmed in the workers and kept the labor force under control they made great strides forward and have been busy with their administrative and economic problems. Even the students have looked on their education as a means of personal advancement and have failed to show the restlessness of students in scores of other countries. Soon however the external pressures on Ulbricht are likely to be paralleled by internal demands. His dilemma will then become more obvious and inescapable. He will be forced either to adopt a more repressive policy or to grant a measure of freedom that will ultimately change the character of his regime. Time, which earlier seemed to be in his favor, is now running against him. In the near future a new situation may develop.

How to deal with these changes is the problem that the West Germans face. At each new stage of emerging conditions they must decide what they can do to accelerate the liberalizing process that is inexorably at work. They believe that if it continues along present lines it could make possible a constructive association of

[1] USSR, Poland, Hungary, Bulgaria, and the GDR.

the two parts of Germany. The limits to West German action are less rigid than in the past; but the stakes continue to be high. A false move could set back the cause of cooperation between the nations of Central Europe and retard the developing trend toward democratization. The Germans are not unduly optimistic; many of them indeed are cynical about their prospects. The last twenty-five years have worn down their will and dimmed their hopes for a united Germany.

The West German goal is a strong and unified Germany in a Europe whose eastern and western regions cooperate. There is no expectation in the Federal Republic (FRG) of the revival of a greater Germany. Revanchism in the traditional sense is dead. There will be no "new Rapallo"[2] turning Germany away from the West. The West German moves for contacts with Eastern Europe during the last few years have been measured and largely successful. Bonn has exerted an influence in Czechoslovakia through friendly and mainly informal interchanges. Its activities elsewhere have been in a low key but have helped to dispel the hostility inherited from the years of Hitler and the war. It now has to weigh with extreme care the possibilities of giving economic help to the nations of Eastern Europe without creating in the Kremlin a belligerent and dangerous mood. The fact that this course of action has received the understanding and support of the NATO countries, particularly the United States, has made Bonn's path easier. Until recently however rapprochement has been slow. The months ahead will show whether it will accelerate.

The United States also is faced with the problem that overt acts and financial assistance might retard rather than advance the movement toward rapprochement. There is little that Washington can do without seeming to intervene in a manner that would be objectionable to the USSR. Yet the situation in Central Europe is of crucial importance to the United States. It is the key not only to Germany's future but also to the security of Europe and hence of

[2] The Rapallo Treaty of 1922 between Germany and the Soviets, often given too much weight, was held to signify a German choice for relations with the East as contrasted with reliance on the West. At that time the United States had largely withdrawn from Europe.

the United States. The interaction of the two parts of Germany, cooperation between the Warsaw Pact states and Western Europe, and the increasing independence of the nations of Eastern Europe may in the months to come lessen tensions and prevent potential conflict between the two systems. During the past twenty years NATO has saved Europe from being overrun. Seen as a symbol of Western cooperation, it has profoundly affected Russian policy since Moscow's position without its satellites would be precarious. The existence of NATO has dictated caution and intensified Soviet efforts to retain the allegiance of the nations of Eastern Europe.

At this critical juncture Washington's task remains that of nourishing and strengthening the confidence of the Germans in American concern for their future. The mutual trust which has been a cornerstone of the American policy in Europe is essential to the forward movement that is now possible. During recent years errors in tactics have sometimes ruffled relations between Germany and the United States and given rise to political attitudes within West Germany that have been somewhat disturbed by Washington's diplomacy. There has been criticism of the handling of the proposal in 1963 for a multilateral nuclear force, of the request for financial help under the Offset Agreement,[3] and of the way in which the early phases of the nuclear non-proliferation treaty were negotiated with the Soviets. The Germans have been acutely sensitive to Washington's words and actions, and their distress and frustration have at times been reflected in the heat of internal debate. Few Germans fear that the United States will completely retire from Europe, but the issue of troop withdrawal has been disturbing. Recent discussions in the U.S. Senate, in particular the statements of Senators Stuart Symington and Mike Mansfield, have raised fears of drastic cuts. Several Germans have stated that the reduction could go below 200,000 men without destroying the credibility of the U.S. position but that somewhere below that figure there would be a danger point which could not be passed without general anxiety. Few question the continued firmness of America's commitment to Berlin or to the doctrine of German

[3] This agreement, made in 1960, called for the purchase of dollars to finance the procurement in the United States of military equipment for the German army.

reunification through self-determination. Between the United States and West Germany there is basic agreement on all important European matters. Even so, this mutual understanding cannot be taken for granted. Its maintenance is an essential task of American policy.

As the Soviets look at their allies, as they see the contagion of new ideas and the restlessness of youth in many countries, they must perforce reconsider their position. Among other things, they must calculate the cost of holding the GDR on a tight rein. They may, if the pressures that are now building up increase, formulate significant changes in their European policy. Such a new formulation may come in the next year or two, or it may be more remote. The steady gravitational pull of tradition, history, and familiar economic methods renders a permanent division of Germany unnatural. This pull, though not always recognized, is at work in both East and West Germany. In addition, Ulbricht and the Kremlin face a problem that is aggravated by the GDR's improved standard of living and increasing educational opportunities, and by the difficulty of sealing off a region that borders on more independent states. They are also concerned with America's attitude toward Central Europe. Washington is well aware of the importance of not offering the Soviets any direct challenge and of not restricting the room to maneuver. The Soviets on their side, in spite of their unsuccessful propaganda effort to show that the CIA had a hand in the Czechoslovakian action in July 1968, realize that there has been no attempt to intervene in this delicate situation.

The Long Haul

The struggle to resolve the problems of Europe is far from won. As recent developments have shown, the way ahead is long. It will be years before any cooperative system that would include aspects of both communism and capitalism can be expected; yet this is the alternative to destructive conflict. Small steps toward mutual adjustment now may have large consequences later. Any estimates of progress must be based on a factual review of past development and present conditions and must take into account shifts in popular opinion and the varying strength of political leaders and parties. Trends are hard to assess when knowledge is incomplete. There is no clear information, for example, on the prevailing attitudes in the GDR toward Ulbricht, toward the emerging leaders, or toward the young. It is not certain how far production will meet the demands of consumers. Even after the Wall, Berlin remains a constant reminder of the differences between East and West. It is not clear how much the United States can do to promote East-West interchanges. Many Germans hope that the Americans will be able to follow a more active policy in Europe as their obligations in the Far East grow less demanding. Opinions on the relative importance of Vietnam and Europe are strongly expressed.

The chapters that follow reflect dozens of conversations the writer had in Germany and elsewhere on the subject of American-German relations. The views expressed are based on personal contacts and discussions in the course of many trips to Germany. Though supported by documents and published studies, they are not advanced as the basis for any blueprint of the future. They do not go to the core of the strategic problems of European security. They do however reflect vital aspects of changing opinion in various parties, cities, and age groups. They indicate new drives which cannot be repressed and suggest future changes both in the East and in the West even more momentous than the changes of the past. No one writer can give a definitive summary of all the significant facets of the problems facing Germany or the United States. The present survey is restricted to issues now in the foreground. Its contents are offered as benchmarks for the use of others.

Changes in the troubled area in the center of Europe will affect the future of Germany, of the Atlantic Community, and of American security. In considering the prospects of one Germany or two and the related unsettled problems, the writer has found many questions but few answers. No one can say to what extent revolution is receding from the hearts and minds of Russians, Czechs, Poles, Hungarians, or Romanians. No one can measure the potential for independence in Eastern Europe. We can only watch and wait, and seek to influence the answer of history for better and not for worse. In any case, the problem is a painful one as long as there is a wall between the two halves of the great nation at the heart of Europe.

CHAPTER 2

West Germany's Room to Maneuver

Bonn now has a limited range of choice in foreign affairs and little room to maneuver. At the same time West German desire for action is increasing. This potentially dangerous situation makes advisable some consideration of the limits that restrict Bonn's foreign policy. In the past years the attitudes of West German political leaders and the hopes of the Germans have undergone many variations; but there has been little room for political measures to fulfill these hopes.

Most of the limits on West German action in foreign affairs are the result of external factors largely beyond German control. For some years after World War II it was the Western powers that appeared responsible for these factors. More recently these limitations have become minor, and the only barriers of importance are those erected by communist policy. For the past few years the external limits on Bonn's foreign policy have been set by the East. Some limits, however, were imposed by internal political pressures.

INTERNAL LIMITS

The internal conditions which influenced and to some extent circumscribed Bonn's efforts to establish relations with the countries of Eastern Europe were largely the result of a natural reluctance to accept the consequences of defeat in World War II. More than ten million people had been removed from their homes in Prussia, Poland, East Germany, and Czechoslovakia. Many held strong ideas of recapturing the past and regaining their former positions and hereditary homes. For more than ten years these uprooted persons complicated official attitudes toward the Sudetenland, East Prussia, and East Germany. Their antagonisms toward the Russians and bitter memories of war-time suffering made them easy prey to unrealistic plans and demagogic pressures. Other groups, particularly the Social Democrats, caused problems by their expressed pacifism. To a weak nation, whose economic and military strength had not yet been restored, such pacifism was a potential danger. These various groups hampered Bonn officials in their dealings with hostile governments.

The inevitable result of these postwar factors was that the leaders of the majority party[1] came to place their reliance on the West and gave up any inclination to reach out in the opposite direction. Any attempt to cultivate friends in the East seemed to offer little hope of success while running considerable risk of exciting misunderstanding. Under the communist threat the United States, West Germany's main ally, had made a defensive NATO strategy the principal plank of its European policy. In these circumstances Bonn could not develop any eclectic pragmatic policy of its own. During the first fifteen postwar years adjustment to and cooperation in the Western community absorbed almost all the energies of the Federal Republic.

With the passage of time considerations of domestic policy lost some of their urgency. The influence of the expellees and refugees grew less. The divisive pacifist factions came to recognize the dangers of a vacuum in Central Europe and to acquiesce in a limited participation in NATO's defense plans. Renunciation of atomic, bacteriological, and chemical (ABC) weapons was accepted as a proper accommodation to the prevailing conditions.[2] Industrial expansion and rising living standards gradually induced a feeling of independence and confidence in the capacity of the West Germans to develop their own foreign policy. The rejection of communism, the difficult struggle for reunification, the vulnerability of Berlin, the unsettled status of the eastern borders, and the fear of subversive infiltration affected but did not dominate the developing aims and tactics of the Bonn government. By 1964 the post-Adenauer era was in being, and new issues came to the fore.

[1] The Christian Democrats (CDU/CSU).

[2] Under the Brussels Agreement, which was later made a part of the contractual agreements, Germany renounced the ownership, production, and use of atomic, bacteriological and chemical weapons. See Protocol No. III On the Control of Armaments, modifying and completing the Brussels Treaty, Paris, October 23, 1954 (U.S. Department of State, *Documents on Germany, 1944–1959*, pp. 132, 133).

LIMITS SET BY WESTERN POLICY

During the years immediately following the war the West exerted considerable influence on West Germany to assure close association with the Atlantic program. After the Soviet refusal to cooperate in German reconstruction and after the Berlin blockade, West Germany's own choice was not in serious question. Membership in NATO imposed certain obligations on Bonn, but these did not exceed responsibilities which the leaders in the Federal Republic were anxious to accept; the resulting cooperation involved no distortion of West German policy. A responsible attitude of this type is a part of the accepted pattern of behavior among the Western democracies and includes the renunciation of force as a means of achieving national aims.

In any case the commitment to NATO does not deprive Bonn of economic and diplomatic relations with Eastern Europe, nor does it preclude efforts toward a general relaxation of East-West relations. Moscow's 1956 rejection of the Stalinist era opened the door to change. A new situation has come into being with the post-Cuba assumptions concerning American-Soviet relations[3] and with the widespread, perhaps naive, assumption that Russia no longer seeks to spread its political creed far beyond its borders. The Nuclear Test Ban Treaty, the Soviet-American agreement on the nuclear non-proliferation treaty, and the view that NATO has already accomplished its purpose have given rise to a new set of assumptions. President Johnson's speech on October 7, 1966, brought a new emphasis. The President called for new attitudes; he reaffirmed the position that German unity in a restored Europe remained a vital goal but said this could be achieved only "through a growing reconciliation because there is no short cut." This gave whatever American support was necessary for the eastern policy (*Ostpolitik*) of the Federal Republic whose government was by this time in the hands of the Grand Coalition of the Christian Democrats, Christian Socialists, and Social Democrats.

The Western powers do not fear a "new Rapallo." This phrase,

[3] See chapter 9.

which still has a certain currency in the West, ignores all major events and developments since 1941. Neither Russia nor West Germany has any appetite for the kind of alliance that might be a provocation to the Western democracies. The conditions of modern war and the prevailing hopes for peace are potent influences against any pact aimed at upsetting the present hard-won balance in Europe. Europe, both East and West, is—and will continue to be—keenly aware of America's strength and of American commitments to Europe. The involvement of the United States is an effective guarantee that Germany will not be lured away from cooperation with her Western neighbors.

Western observers have viewed with interest and sympathy the efforts of the Federal Republic to extend its foreign policy to include dealings with communist countries. They recognize the obstacles in the path of any dramatic action, but they have supported the recent attempts to pierce the Iron Curtain. Experience will reveal the points at which resistance will be encountered as well as the dangers besetting satellites who go beyond the limits set by Moscow. Any threat to Russian hegemony in Eastern Europe impinges on Soviet vital interests.

LIMITS SET BY THE SOVIETS

What limits does Soviet policy impose on West German diplomacy? As one of the parties to the surrender and occupation arrangements, the USSR has had a hand in the legal and political restrictions which were imposed in 1945 and, in the absence of a treaty, are still in force.[4] Bonn's actions are therefore limited by the attitude of the Soviet leaders, the absence of settled national boundaries, and its own exclusion from membership in the United Nations Organization. Even had Soviet policy with regard to Germany been other than it is, West Germany would have had to renounce the use of force in its pursuit of reunification. Had the international atmosphere been more friendly, however, Bonn could have used less restrictive caution in its dealings with its neighbors.

Clearly Soviet policy directly and indirectly narrows the area of

[4] See chapter 8 for further comments on the evolution of Soviet policy.

feasible German action. Anxious to prevent any erosion of its extended influence and any loss of its hold over the nations it dominates, the Kremlin keeps a keen and watchful eye on the expansion of trade between these countries and the capitalist world —a development that offers it both advantages and disadvantages. It seeks to have first call on the production of Czechoslovakia, Romania, and the other Warsaw Pact nations.[5] It wishes to have Warsaw made aware that the Soviets are the defenders of the Polish borders. It seeks to prevent any increase of diplomatic independence in nations that form its western bulwark against capitalist influence. It considers Ulbricht's strength a deterrent to revolt in East Germany. It holds the Warsaw Pact to be essential to the integration of policy and tactics and to be a restraining influence on the critics and diversionists on its side of the Iron Curtain. Finally, the Kremlin sees in Berlin at once a sign of its own limitations, a means of enforcing its will by harassment, and, should the Western powers ever weaken or forget where their interests lie, a potential means of blackmail. Continued sway over its satellites and the prevention of any increase in Germany's strength are vital interests of the Soviet Union. Its capacity to protect these interests, though not absolute, continues; in recent years, however, it has in many ways grown less.

The test of the Soviets' policy will be the ability of their economic system to compete with that of the West, and their success in intimidating the governments under their influence into accepting the Soviet road to socialism or, should these governments insist on following their own road, into adherence to the basic tenets of Marxism-Leninism. The threats to Soviet policy are the spirit of nationalism, now on the increase in several satellites, and the obvious need for greater production. It is generally assumed that a speedy increase in production can be effected only through exchanges with the capitalist countries.

In the intellectual world also there are stirrings that cannot be ignored. Their inability to keep art and science in leading strings,

[5] The Warsaw Pact, signed on May 14, 1955, is a cooperative military agreement between the USSR and Bulgaria, Czechoslovakia, East Germany, Hungary, Poland, and Romania.

to control writers, and to prevent the "poison" of free thinking has raised serious difficulties for the communist leaders. In this growing problem West German penetration of the Iron Curtain has already played a part.

At the meeting in February and April 1967, after agreement on the diplomatic exchanges between Romania and the Federal Republic, the Soviets endeavored to set barriers against further extension of Bonn's *Ostpolitik*. They laid down rigid and impossible conditions to be met by Bonn before Moscow would sanction further dealings of the Warsaw Pact countries with the Federal Republic. Yugoslavia which is not a member of the Warsaw Pact or of the Council for Mutual Economic Assistance (Comecon)[6] was not directly affected by these conditions. There was however no direct restraint on closer economic relations.

In 1969 the Soviet aims are definite and unmistakable, but their application is not immutable. The kinds of pressures the Soviets exert are illustrated by the visits of their leaders to various capitals, the cancellation of credits to Romania, and their propaganda. The leaders in the various Warsaw Pact nations are still mainly dependent on the Kremlin for support and thus have to restrain their party functionaries and keep down independence. Soviet repression fails where the changed atmosphere enables the head of the party to act more or less on his own. In such cases the weapons at hand are far more limited than they were when economic hardship was widespread and the party apparatus in the various capitals was weak.

Moscow could exert little influence on Bonn by means of a direct approach to remind the government there of the vulnerable position of West Berlin, the increased strength of Ulbricht, or Soviet power and German guilt. Bonn's ability to resist threats has grown with its awareness of Western support, with its rearmament and membership in the European community, and with Soviet failure to act on threats over NATO. The West Germans now accept the fact that Russian aggression would bring NATO retaliation and are free of the inhibitions that might otherwise have hampered their *Ostpolitik*.

[6] The organization for mutual economic cooperation of the Warsaw Pact nations.

Thus the main limit that the Soviets can set to West Germany's room to maneuver is the restraint they can exert on the Communist party leaders in their satellites, including East Germany. This restraint will change with the changing nature of Soviet worldwide interests and will vary with the degree to which the Kremlin dominates the foreign policy of the various countries.

POSSIBILITIES OF ACTION

What then can Bonn do? Its capabilities would appear to be far greater in the sphere of economics than in that of politics. It has established trade missions in Czechoslovakia and Poland, and its arrangements with Romania and Yugoslavia predicate their establishment in those countries also. The interzonal trade agreements negotiated by Heinz Behrendt, Ulbricht's specialist, and Willy Kleindienst, who represents the Federal Republic in West Berlin, keep the two parts of Germany in contact. What more Bonn can do will depend on two factors: (1) the amount of credit that the Federal Republic decides it can afford to extend, and (2) the degree of the risk (as Bonn sees it) that, failing such special credits, East Germany will be able to reduce its relations with capitalist countries. In any case commerce offers further opportunities for Bonn's *Ostpolitik*.

Cultural exchanges and tourism sometimes contribute considerably to the expansion of common interests. They may prove to be one means of lessening the fear and suspicion which have persisted in Central Europe for two decades. Attitudes in Czechoslovakia, Romania, Yugoslavia, and even Poland have shown signs of improvement. This is partly the result of the widely held view that the threat to international security, whether from Russia or from Germany, has declined. Partly also it may be attributed to the economic achievement of West Germany. And partly it is due to the restraint imposed on Germany by membership in NATO and to Germany's success in reconstructing her political system. There is reason to think that further progress can be made in East-West relations along these lines.

Since the diplomatic exchanges between Romania and the Federal Republic, Bonn's room to maneuver in regard to the Warsaw

Pact nations has been, as mentioned earlier in this chapter, severely curtailed. The only hope of further progress lies in patient and skillful exploitation of economic, cultural, and other relations. Opportunities for relations with the GDR are particularly limited; most experts consider that as long as Ulbricht remains in power it will not be possible to loosen the present restraint on contacts to any appreciable extent or to lower the barriers; and many think that his successor is likely, at least for a few years, to pursue an equally hard line.[7] Since 1966 all efforts to initiate debates, secure travel passes, or expand practical dealings have been futile. The East Germans show fewer signs of restlessness and less desire for new economic relations than the people of Czechoslovakia and some other Warsaw Pact countries. Partly because of their substantial economic progress since 1961 and partly because of their skills, standards of production, and inherited characteristics, they have as yet no urgent need to press for an expansion of commerce. Ulbricht, frequently called the last Stalinist, has no present intention of compromising for the sake of economic gains.[8]

Bonn's attempts to close the gap which has opened up between the two halves of Germany have taken the form of *little steps* and *contacts*. In 1964 and 1965 considerable optimism had been felt in Berlin and elsewhere, particularly by those who regarded American policy as a major deterrent and thought that, with their growing independence, Germans would be able to approach Germans in a reasonable way. These hopes were dashed later in 1966 when Albert Norden, secretary of the Central Committee of the Socialist Unity Party (the communist SED), reversed the tentative agreement for debates, and when requests for passes (*Passierscheine*) for West Berliners to visit relatives in East Berlin were refused.[9] There is little that can now be done to bring people in the two areas together. West German businessmen can still visit the GDR, but their dealings are severely limited and apolitical. The communist attitude toward West Berlin has not softened, and little change

[7] Erich Honecker is one of the leaders frequently spoken of as Ulbricht's successor.

[8] See chapter 4.

[9] Eleanor Lansing Dulles, *Berlin*, pp. 93–96. On several occasions the GDR granted large numbers of passes to visit East Berlin.

can be expected in the coming months or even years. The limits to maneuver are rigorous and imposed not by the Soviets alone but also by German communists and others.

Even declarations with regard to the Oder-Neisse line[10] that might help stabilize West German relations with Poland and with East Germany cannot receive official endorsement. When in 1968 Foreign Minister Willy Brandt agreed that the line should be recognized as a permanent border, he was reminded that no decision on this matter could be made without a peace treaty to which the Four Powers were parties. The declaration that the Munich Agreement of 1938 was null and void may have gratified the Czech government, but it has failed so far to satisfy the Warsaw Pact countries since it did not state that the agreement had *never* been valid.

In a recent article Dr. Alard von Schack gave it as his opinion that the Federal Republic should concede to the GDR a separate identity. He stated that the Federal Republic was prepared to enter into a variety of arrangements with the GDR and its government. He considered that conceding more status to the representatives of the GDR would improve the possibility of technological exchanges and that this would give the East German people a better basis for judging where their interests lie when practical opportunities might, at some later date, open the way to reunification. He stated that the people of Germany realize that a unified German state can be achieved only as part of a gradual, comprehensive rearrangement of European relations:

> People in this country also realise that restoration of the unity of Germany as a state will take a long time and can only be achieved as a part of a rearrangement of Europe and with the consent of all neighbouring countries and opponents in the Second World War. It could possibly be achieved step by step.[11]

[10] The Oder-Neisse line follows the rivers of these names. It was established by the Soviets and was not officially recognized by the Western Allies. It assigned to Poland former German territory and was the effective boundary between Poland and East Germany.

[11] Alard von Schack, "The Next Stage in Federal Republic Eastern Policy," *German Tribune* May 4, 1968. This article, which originally appeared in *Aussenpolitik* February 1968, by a retired judge and freelance writer in

He overlooked the fact that, in the opinion of most of the experts, Ulbricht has made full recognition the price for any dealings, thus cutting off the small steps.

Somewhat earlier, in 1967, Dr. Eberhard Schulz had explored many facets of the relations of the Federal Republic to the GDR.[12] His emphasis was on a realistic approach and more normal relations. While he admitted the dangers in formal recognition, he anticipated a trend toward acceptance of the regime in East Germany. He advocated a flexible and pragmatic policy which would include more dealings with the GDR than are now carried on. He urged that more attention be paid to people as a guide to action and, even if reunification were postponed, to the interdependence of the German populations. He did not think the three major powers could or should hold back the Federal Republic from pursuing a more liberal policy. He pleaded for more realism and also for more innovation. In his view, inaction would be more apt to confirm the present division than action along the lines that, given a degree of compromise, are still possible.

Rethinking German Policy, recently published by the Society of Germany Indivisible, endeavored to escape from dead-end efforts and worn-out ideas by proposing that a draft peace treaty be drawn up and that this should be followed by a peace conference. The writer, Wilhelm W. Schuetz, stated optimistically, "There are many ways to achieve a peace conference," and went on to say that it could be done by using old machinery such as the Council of Deputy Foreign Ministers or the Disarmament Commission, or under the United Nations.[13] He urged that as the only way to make progress is in connection with world security, a broadly based conference would be the most effective. A security system in which all Germany would be included[14] and by which European unity would

---

Bonn was considered sufficiently important to be translated into English for the *German Tribune* and thus reflects widely held official opinion.

[12] Eberhard Schulz, *An Ulbricht fuehrt kein Weg mehr vorbei*, pp. 187, 217, 248–56. Dr. Schulz is one of the leading experts in the *Deutsche Gesellschaft fuer Auswaertige Politik*.

[13] Wilhelm W. Schuetz, *Rethinking German Policy*, p. 113.

[14] The term "all Germany" is not used to include the former eastern provinces, now administered by Poland.

be achieved would appeal to the interests of all nations. The establishment of an international control system would be an essential part of his proposal. He stressed the need of keeping the present equilibrium substantially unchanged.

These and other writers have advocated action within existing limits. None of them have succeeded in recommending acceptable new courses of action. New ideas and approaches however are there for the finding by those who are prepared to expand their horizons and look beyond present limits.

CHAPTER 3

West Germany's Eastern Policy

POSTWAR RELATIONS

Only after the Federal Republic of Germany (FRG) had joined the Western community of nations and was well on the way to economic reconstruction did it start to show active concern in a policy toward nations in Eastern Europe. There were many obstacles to diplomatic progress in this direction. These were mainly the result of the war and the bitter legacy of the Hitler years. They were accentuated by the fact that in the minds of many there were now not one but two German states. There could be no quick or easy restoration of the fabric of international relations, but the importance of moving ahead became increasingly evident in the second postwar decade.

Varied contacts with the West were firmly established in the first decade. Although Germany could not become a member of the United Nations because of the failure to achieve a peace treaty, the FRG was a member of many multilateral economic organizations and an active participant in the North Atlantic Treaty Organization (NATO). Relations with the United States became steadily closer after American aid to recovery had become evident in the early postwar years. The United Kingdom shared in planning and in administrative arrangements. Contacts with France improved continuously, especially after the agreement in October 1956 to return the Saar to the FRG and the later development of close personal relations between Chancellor Konrad Adenauer and President Charles de Gaulle.

Leaders in Bonn played a constructive part in planning for the European community. By the end of the 1950s the Federal Republic had added important contingents to NATO and was an active member of the European Economic Community (EEC), the International Monetary Fund (IMF), and other cooperative organizations. The lines of communication were by this time firmly joined, fruitful, and comprehensive. The Republic's continuing alignment with the democracies in the West was unquestioned, and its influence on foreign affairs was vigorous.

In Eastern Europe on the contrary, cut off as it was by the Iron Curtain, the Federal Republic faced serious obstacles. At the very start of his independent course of action in foreign affairs, Chancellor Adenauer had proved by his visit to Moscow in September 1955 that he was looking both East and West. But the obstacles to relations with Eastern Europe became more restrictive as relations with East Germany became frozen. In 1961 communications were still further reduced by the building of the Berlin Wall. This abnormal situation heightened the Federal Republic's sense of frustration, the more so as West German capacity and interests in the West were expanding.

East Germany

In the Soviet Occupied Zone the Socialist Unity Party (SED) had the nominal right to carry on foreign policy in the name of the People's Chamber (*Volkskammer*). From 1949 on, it had attempted to create diplomatic relations that were for the most part confined to representation and stopped short of full power. The German Democratic Republic (GDR), as the Zone later came to be named, joined the Council for Mutual Economic Assistance (Comecon) in 1950, the year after its foundation.

Relations with the satellite countries, while not truly comparable to diplomatic agreements with other countries, included recognition and various types of cooperation in scientific, cultural, and economic matters. Albania, Bulgaria, Poland, Romania, Czechoslovakia, and Hungary recognized the GDR in 1949, the Soviet Union on October 15 of that year. Table 1 gives the schedule of East German establishment of diplomatic relations with various countries from 1949 on.

In March 1954 the Soviet government, cognizant of the Paris Agreements, issued a statement purporting to grant to East Germany status as a sovereign republic, thus creating new fears in Bonn. Immediately afterward the East German authorities announced that agents of the Four Power Control Council, set up after the German surrender, would have to accredit themselves to

Table 1
Establishment of Diplomatic Relations Between the GDR and Other Countries

			Country	Type of Relation
1949	October	15	USSR	Recognition
	October	17	Bulgaria	Recognition
	October	18	Hungary	Recognition
	October	18	Czechoslovakia	Recognition
	October	18	Romania	Recognition
	October	18	Poland	Recognition
	October	25	China	Recognition
	November	6	Korea (North)	Recognition
	December	2	Albania	Recognition
1950	April	13	Mongolian Socialist Republic	Recognition
1954	December	16	Vietnam (North)	Recognition
1957	October	10	Yugoslavia	Agreement to exchange diplomats
1960	August	20	Indonesia	General consulate
	August	26	Burma	General consulate
1962	October	5	Yemen	Recognition by East Germany
1963	January	12	Cuba	Agreement for full diplomatic recognition
	October	28	Yemen	General consulate
1964	January	29	Zanzibar(later Tanzania)	Recognition
	February	12	Ceylon	General consulate
	February	12	Yugoslavia	Consular agreement
1965	February	19	Tanzania	General consulate
1967	March	13	Cambodia	Verbal agreement to take u consular relations
1969	April	30	Iraq	Recognition
	May	8	Cambodia	Recognition
		25	Sudan	Recognition
	June	5	Syria	Recognition
		30	People's Republic of South Yemen	Recognition
	July	9	United Arab Republic	Recognition

Sources: Zusammenstellung der von der "Deutschen Demokratischen Republik" se deren Gruendung, 7. Oktober 1949, abgeschlossenen internationalen Vertraege und Verei barungen, comp. Lothar Kapsa; U.S. Department of State.

and be approved by the East German authorities.[1] This attempt to establish the GDR as a separate nation met with little success in the diplomatic field. In May 1955 the Warsaw Pact, designed to give its members more power in international relations, was concluded between the USSR and Albania,[2] Bulgaria, Czechoslovakia, East Germany, Hungary, Poland, and Romania. This was shortly after the Federal Republic had become a member of NATO. New arrangements between the GDR and the USSR for bolshevization and integration into the Eastern bloc were negotiated in Moscow.

The general intent of these steps was to increase the prestige of the GDR without substantially lessening its dependence on the USSR and thus to bar the Federal Republic from expansion eastward. The aim was to prevent the development of an effective *Ostpolitik* before any such policy could emerge. The result was a situation in which the Hallstein Doctrine became imperative.

THE HALLSTEIN DOCTRINE

The GDR was precluded from any genuinely independent foreign policy by the fact of its continued occupation—which mere words could not terminate—and by its legal status under the Potsdam Protocol of August 1945 and earlier agreements. Yet it was succeeding in implanting in world consciousness the appearance of a national entity. In April 1954 therefore the Federal Parliament (*Bundestag*) adopted a resolution "withholding recognition of 'sovereignty' granted to the East German regime," and the three Western powers issued statements to the same effect.

In a further attempt to stem the growing tide of acceptance the Federal Republic a little later developed the Hallstein Doctrine,[3] named after Walter Hallstein who was state secretary at that time. Foreign Secretary Heinrich von Brentano in December 1955 announced to a conference of a dozen or more ambassadors meeting

[1] U.S. Department of State, *Documents on Germany, 1944–1959*, pp. 482, 483.

[2] Albania came into conflict with the USSR in 1961, withdrew from the pact, and from then on was not invited to participate in the meetings.

[3] *Bulletin Bonn* No. 181, June 29, 1956 (cited in *The German Question*, ed. Walther Hubatsch et al., pp. 80–81); Eleanor Lansing Dulles, *Berlin*, p. 208.

in Bonn that the Federal Republic would sever diplomatic relations with any nation that recognized the government of the Soviet Occupation Zone. In a later statement he underscored the importance of this position in these words:

> This is a matter of tremendous political importance: recognition of the GDR in terms of international law signifies recognition of the division of Germany into two states. Thus reunification is no longer the elimination of a temporary disturbance in the organism of our all-German state, but is transformed into the task of unifying two different German states. The unity of Germany as a state has not been destroyed from a legal point of view.[4]

The application of this doctrine may be studied in the history of Bonn's diplomatic relations with Yugoslavia. This case is of particular interest because, with the exception of the USSR, Yugoslavia was the first communist nation to which Bonn sent an ambassador and the only communist nation with which it subsequently broke relations. Here, as on other occasions, Tito's changes of policy surprised and puzzled the world. Yugoslav bitterness over the war was still operative, and Tito walked a tightrope as he shifted from sympathetic support for Imre Nagy in Hungary in 1956 to recognition of the GDR in 1957 and maintained relations with Moscow while accepting financial help from the United States.

If the world did not understand Tito, he for his part did not understand Germany, or at least, according to Eberhard Schulz, not the Hallstein Doctrine.[5] Bonn's rupture of diplomatic relations following Tito's recognition of the GDR came as a shock.[6] It was more than ten years before diplomatic relations between Belgrade and Bonn were resumed. Meanwhile this, the first concrete application of the Hallstein Doctrine, had been noted by interested capitals elsewhere.

The resumption of relations in 1968 was generally taken to mean that the doctrine had been eroded—or was being applied with greater flexibility. The press was divided as to the meaning of this

[4] Walther Hubatsch et al., *The German Question*, pp. 80–81.

[5] Eberhard Schulz, *An Ulbricht fuehrt kein Weg mehr vorbei*, pp. 115–20

[6] According to Dr. Schulz, Ambassador Karl-Georg Pfleiderer's death in Bonn on his return from Belgrade may have been occasioned by the difficulties he experienced in his dealings with the unyielding von Brentano.

action. *Die Zeit* referred to "the burial of a dogma." The *Deutsche Welle* on February 1, 1968, emphasized that it would be "wrong to assume that, after establishing diplomatic relations with Yugoslavia, the Federal Government has no longer any objections against the recognition of the German Democratic Republic by other states. . . . in the future Bonn will consider it a highly unfriendly action if a neutral country, without being forced to do so, sends an Ambassador to East Berlin." However, much of the European press comment noted the degree to which the federal government had relaxed its conditions and held that the removal of barriers confining policy would advance constructive relations with Eastern Europe.

Meanwhile from 1957 on, in the name of the doctrine Bonn's representatives held many conversations behind the scenes with statesmen of other countries, notably those of Africa and Asia. The success of the West German position is best exemplified by the reluctance of Arab countries to recognize the GDR. There could not be, it was then stated, in one capital two German ambassadors, one of whom represented the false Germany of the East. Halfway round the world a similar problem faced the Taiwan government, which also withheld ambassadors from capitals where Peking was represented. In both cases trade missions were considered acceptable and partial substitutes, although their members were not accorded diplomatic status. This lessened the possibility of confrontation. At the same time mission personnel were not plenipotentiaries. Thus during the decades when there were no peace treaties the divided nations devised practical measures that made possible temporary solutions for postwar problems.

Its Significance

Any formal statement renouncing or modifying the Hallstein Doctrine is unlikely. The doctrine exists as a pronouncement of the Foreign Office; it has not been embodied in a parliamentary resolution. The reason for it is well understood, but its application will be subject to increasing question as ambassadors of the Federal Republic carry on their duties in Bucharest, in Belgrade, in Moscow, and elsewhere, ignoring for the most part the presence of emissaries from Pankow. For some in the outside world, particularly in circles that have abandoned all thought of an eventually reunified Germany, the doctrine is now almost devoid of significance.

Admittedly, the question of recognition is one which irritates and confuses nonprofessional persons who are usually unaware of the legal aspects and fail to take seriously problems of protocol. Moreover from the standpoint of 1969, when new policies engage the attention of Bonn and other foreign capitals, there is a tendency to overlook the significance of the Hallstein Doctrine in the years from 1956 to 1966. But officials responsible for the conduct of foreign affairs consider that in certain cases during that decade the doctrine held the line and clarified consideration of the German situation, particularly by the newly emerging nations. Without some such statement and the explanatory efforts which backed it up, many African countries would have failed to appreciate the special nature of the German problem. It is worthy of note that Cairo, in spite of some connections with the GDR, long withheld recognition and that, with the exception of Cuba, no Latin American country has established relations with the GDR.

Now that the German question has come to be understood in all world capitals, the importance of the Hallstein Doctrine has declined. But the doctrine still has meaning, even though it cannot be applied to nations, such as the members of the Warsaw Pact, which are not free to choose their relations with East Germany.[7] No leading official has advocated the jettisoning of the Hallstein Doctrine. In the adaptable world of diplomacy account has been taken of the purpose of this policy, and the doctrine has been regarded as a deterrent to the recognition of the GDR by those countries which are free to choose. The agreements with Romania and Yugoslavia do not present the kind of situation which was envisaged in the doctrine and could not rationally be expected to be affected by it.

There has been no recent test of how the Federal Republic will apply the doctrine in the future. But any assumption that the whole concept has been nullified is premature. Bonn officials are or

[7] Dulles, *Berlin*, p. 221.

the alert for anything which might create the impression that, in spite of the Four-Power Agreement, the lack of self-determination, and the presence of Soviet garrison forces on her soil, East Germany possesses a representative and legitimate government. One troubling minor problem faced by the Federal Republic has been the proper treatment of the GDR teams during the Olympic Games. Questions arose concerning the flag, the songs, the parade, and the awards. Another problem has been the effort to prevent the use of maps showing a permanent line drawn at the borders as they now exist for operational purposes and so making it appear that these are national boundaries. There has also been the question of the representation of American businesses at the Leipzig Fair, decried in Washington for many years but now accepted. And of the GDR's visa on tourist passports, disturbing to Washington and other capitals but not prohibited except in special cases. Other smaller and larger issues have been and continue to be numerous.

In their diplomatic and other relations the Bonn authorities endeavor to keep alive the legal, political, and historic image of a unified Germany. In the course of years of frustration they have been forced to recognize the limited means at their disposal. They have put the Republic behind the efforts to gain passes for travelers. They have endeavored to start a dialogue in their 1966 proposals for East-West debates in the GDR and FRG on matters of mutual interest. They have taken a genuine interest in interzonal trade. They have maintained consistently that this trade is not foreign commerce but rather the continuation of the former trade within Germany. They had hoped that, by constantly maintaining this position and with the help of the Western Allies, they could achieve a new situation in which self-determination with free elections would be permitted in East Germany. Although their hopes have been dampened by the intensifying control exercised by Walter Ulbricht and by East Germany's raising of the Berlin Wall, they recognize that only by holding on to legal rights can they expect eventually, in the distant future, to gain their objective. Thus for twenty years they approached the East-West problem with mixed feelings of hope and despair. After 1965 however there was a new initiative.

THE CHANGE IN POLICY

The policy of the Federal Republic toward the countries of Eastern Europe has changed. Weary of the slogan "No Experiments," West Germany has become increasingly concerned with making approaches to neighboring countries and new contacts with the area under Ulbricht's control.

Policy Prior to 1965

With the termination of the occupation in 1955, Bonn felt that more direct contacts and meaningful conversations would tend to fortify its efforts to secure a peace treaty. It was also not unaware of the truth of the adage "Know your enemy." So relations with the Soviets were normalized, and Ambassador Wilhelm Haas went to Moscow in 1955. He was succeeded by Ambassador Hans Kroll who was there from 1956 until 1962.[8] Soviet Ambassador Valerin A. Zorin arrived in Bonn on November 24, 1955, and left in July 1956. He was followed by a little-known Russian, Andrei Andrevich Smirnov.

During the years between 1955 and 1965 West Germany experienced various shifts of opinion. The possibility of neutralizing the center of Europe was discussed. For a time the Social Democratic Party (SPD) leaned in the direction of pacifism, and some of its members demonstrated against "atom death." Later the Suez Crisis and the Far Eastern situation induced a realistic and somewhat disillusioned feeling among political leaders. The establishment of the NATO Council however and the consequent military planning presented issues which held the attention of government officials. Meanwhile the mood of the people shifted further away from the idea of a disarmed nation, and men were recruited for the new army.

From 1955 on it was increasingly clear that West Germany would be one of the most significant contributors to NATO.[9]

[8] Kroll was succeeded by Horst Groepper. The present ambassador is Gebhardt Walter.

[9] The Federal Republic now has more than 420,000 men under the NATO command.

Neutralization, which might have become a reality if there had been no harassment of Berlin and if the talk of coexistence had been more convincing, was not seriously considered. As West Germany developed her economic strength and as the horrors of the postwar period receded into the past, the idea of a strong West Germany gained ground and was promulgated by the small but relatively impotent National Party (DRP), elements of which were later absorbed by the new National Democratic Party (NPD).

Many of the younger politicians, both Right and Left, stressed the anomaly of an important nation maintaining diplomatic relations with Western nations while behaving as if there were a complete vacuum between itself and Moscow. There was a stir of restlessness in the air. Accepted policy was subjected to superficial criticisms which overlooked the fact that without the financial help and political support of the United States and its allies West Germany could have had no strong government or meaningful policy. These critics were quick to refer to the policy of stalemate and the lack of progress toward reunification.

On the Threshold of a New Policy

The main outlines of the new policy were discussed with me during my stay in Germany in the summer of 1965. The most vigorous in pressing their views were the students, but a few of the older politicians were at least looking in the same direction. Discussion focused on but was not confined to the question of contacts with East Germany. Those with whom I talked seemed to feel hemmed in. The sense of implicit involvement in the affairs of Poland, Czechoslovakia, Romania, and other Warsaw Pact countries colored their attitudes. They urged the importance of intellectual communication with the communists, particularly the German communists. They thought that, if a strong effort were made, they could get permission to travel to Eastern Europe, that the authorities had not pressed sufficiently hard to secure passes and did not really desire to open the channels of communication for students and others.

The development of this new attitude toward the countries

of Eastern Europe and toward the Soviet Union was evidence of the extent to which the events of the previous years had been overlooked or forgotten. For the younger politicians, the experiences of the early postwar years were remote, the Marshall Plan and the beginning of NATO almost irrelevant. Some of them had not even participated in the stormy crises of the first postwar years. The excesses of the Russian armies in 1945 and 1946 were no longer real; events in Czechoslovakia in 1948, Berlin in 1953, Hungary in 1956 were historical memories. As the young Germans had become accustomed to the continuing existence of the communist world and to the many East-West exchanges between the leaders of the two main power blocs, their desire for normal relations had increased. The conflict between the two major ideologies had ceased to hold any personal or immediate interest for them.

By the same token, to the average man the struggle of the democratic nations to protect West Germany from communist pressures and incursions had little significance. The impression of danger had been blunted and the importance of the NATO "sword and shield" was questioned. The hesitations of those who feared entrapment and the knowledge of those who had been exposed to communist aims over several decades were considered obstructive. The younger men did not feel it necessary to evaluate the sources of German strength or always to give credit to those who had built up the country in previous years with courage and insight. They stressed the failures as well as the successes of the past. Moreover conversations, negotiations, and trade with the East seemed reasonable and normal. No possible harm could come, they said, from cultural exchanges and the sale of commodities. Here, as elsewhere, the theory of beneficent contacts was spreading widely.

In spite of some illusions, the vigor behind the new aims undoubtedly has given a healthy impetus to foreign policy. But it cannot and has not overcome those political, administrative, economic, and psychological obstacles which can only be surmounted with time.[10] On the political side, for instance, it is evident that Ulbricht has recently hardened his policy. Propaganda chief Albert

[10] See chapter 2.

Norden, Erich Honecker, and others have refused on political grounds to facilitate cultural exchanges.

On the administrative side, those in the Federal Republic who are concerned with East-West dealings are fearful of changing the routine. They are not authorized to do this, and considerable time will be required to put relations on a freer basis.

On the economic side, the problems stem from the fact that there cannot be a balanced exchange in commerce or finance. The Eastern countries, including the GDR, are unable to export adequate amounts to pay their debts and now owe sizable credits. A substantial increase in trade can only be effected through longer term financing, which would increase the economic risk for West Germany and other creditors. The quantity of goods which can be sold in the West before the needs in the East are satisfied has dwindled to insignificant amounts.

On the psychological side, the restraints are the result of tradition and such hostile acts as the shooting of refugees, political imprisonment, and lack of good faith.

The keynote of much of the discussion was the emphasis on elementary restrictions by the Federal Republic that hampered the exploitation of opportunities for trade or other fruitful relations and so for the building of bridges.

Such were the lines along which talk ran in 1964 and 1965.

The New Course

In 1966 the new coalition government in Bonn put forward concrete proposals without any hint of a Rapallo-type treaty with the Soviets or suggestion of turning away from NATO. There was a desire for the normalization of relations in Europe, both East and West. Bankers, traders, and diplomats who traveled to the European countries behind the Iron Curtain made a serious attempt to lessen antagonisms and to foster easy relations. The new policy was set in the direction of constructive effort and more relaxed conditions, to the disregard of communist threats and pressures.

In this diplomatic offensive, Bonn was impelled by considerations of both prestige and economic advantage. Diplomatic relations tend to facilitate the expansion of commerce. By the end of

Table 2
Trade Between the FRG and Communist States, 1938–1967
(In Millions of DM)

	1938	*1963*	*1965*	*1966*	*% Change*	*1967*	*% Change*
Bulgaria							
Imports	84.3	116.7	165.3	171.0		177.6	
Exports	56.4	93.9	221.1	433.0		339.7	
Total	140.7	210.6	386.4	604.0	+56.4	517.3	−14.3
Poland							
Imports	95.5	321.1	435.6	481.7		439.6	
Exports	102.6	260.7	366.2	375.8		491.8	
Total	198.1	581.8	801.8	857.5	+ 6.9	931.4	+ 8.7
Romania							
Imports	140.4	224.5	289.5	297.9		350.7	
Exports	148.8	292.3	462.4	558.1		961.0	
Total	289.2	516.8	751.9	856.0	+13.8	1,311.7	+53.2
Czechoslovakia							
Imports	129.7	260.1	336.4	346.6		361.2	
Exports	135.6	234.3	402.4	503.1		525.4	
Total	265.3	494.4	738.8	849.7	+15.0	886.6	+ 4.3
Hungary							
Imports	109.8	231.0	287.5	321.2		275.9	
Exports	110.0	252.1	307.8	371.3		420.5	
Total	219.8	483.1	595.3	692.5	+16.3	696.4	+ 0.6
USSR							
Imports	47.4	834.7	1,101.1	1,153.0		1,099.5	
Exports	31.8	614.1	585.3	541.3		792.1	
Total	79.2	1,448.8	1,686.4	1,694.3	+ 0.4	1,891.6	+11.7
Yugoslavia							
Imports	107.9	359.2	473.4	541.3		483.8	
Exports	118.0	426.9	532.7	756.6		1,165.5	
Total	225.9	786.1	1,006.1	1,297.9	+26.0	1,649.3	+27.1
All communist countries (including China)							
Total	1,635.3	4,745.4	6,573.7	7,739.3	+17.7	9,016.7	+16.5

Source: Deutsche Bank, Frankfurt.

1967, total West German trade with the Warsaw Pact countries and Yugoslavia amounted to almost DM 8 billion (see table 2), or more than 5 percent of the total value (DM 150 billion) of her combined exports and imports, excluding interzonal trade. Yet because of the quality of West German goods and because of the credits she extended, this commerce was more important to her trading partners than to West Germany herself.

The new diplomatic initiative was increasingly favored by several high officials in Bonn, and the ideas underlying the new policy were eagerly espoused by the younger men and by bankers and businessmen in search of new fields to conquer. But the choice of targets was still in doubt. The Polish attitude was assumed to be rigidly forbidding. The Yugoslav situation was complicated by the 1957 break in relations. The other members of the Warsaw Pact were variously appraised according to the degree of Soviet control. There were signs of loosening cohesion among the members of the bloc. Bonn's approach to new engagements had to be made by trial and error; its emissaries went on their way to see where they could find an opening.

ROMANIA

The first steps taken by Bonn in pursuit of its new policy had not been wholly encouraging. It was therefore a matter of surprise to some and of gratification to many when in 1966 Bucharest showed signs of interest. Many West Germans had hoped for closer economic ties, but few had expected that by January 1967 there would be full-scale diplomatic relations. Here, as so often, change in relations between other countries had passed unnoticed until it was full-blown. There had, indeed, been early signs of polycentrism within the East European bloc, but they had been obscured by the stereotypes which had been formed. While it is not possible to appraise the degree of Romania's independence, her response to Bonn's overtures made clear her intention to stand fast against the Soviet Union on this point.

The steady increase in West German trade with Romania from 1963 sheds light on Bonn's motives in seeking diplomatic relations. By 1966 the total value of Romanian exports to and imports from

West Germany had reached DM 856 million. During the years 1963 to 1967, it had grown from DM 516.8 million to DM 1,311.7 million. The Federal Republic's exports to Romania had grown much more rapidly than its imports from that country. The total West German trade with Romania was now comparable in value to that with Poland or Czechoslovakia.

The coalition government of the Federal Republic hailed this diplomatic agreement as a notable success for its *Ostpolitik*. In fact, however, early approaches had been discreetly made before Kurt Georg Kiesinger became chancellor or Willy Brandt foreign minister. Nevertheless the agreement took the general public by surprise and stimulated a feeling that at last there was a policy of movement. This led to an exclamatory press, which hindered rather than helped further action and which may well have contributed to the curbs put on the Czechoslovakian response to Bonn's overtures in the months that followed.

The beginning of what has been termed the slow thaw was the subject of an article in *German International*, June 1965, which described the efforts made by the Federation of German Industries (BDI) and by representatives of individual firms to make a breakthrough in commercial relations with the Eastern bloc's "go-it-alone" Romania. One of the operations went back to 1964 when the Germans undertook the supervision and planning of the steelworks in which the head of the BDI was particularly interested.

The Quiet Revolt

As far as Romania's relations with the Soviet Union were concerned, the slow thaw had begun much earlier. The efforts of First Party Secretary Nikita Khrushchev in June 1962 to press for the complete integration of Eastern Europe, using Comecon as one instrument, ran counter to Romanian aims and plans.[11] At this point the struggle over both ideological and practical issues burst into the open. The Romanians, dissatisfied with the goods they were getting from East Germany and Czechoslovakia and easily able to dispose of their valuable raw materials on world markets, wanted to go elsewhere. Their economic skills were impressive, and

[11] David Floyd, *Rumania*, pp. 70–91.

the growth in their production was rapid. They were unwilling to be hampered by restrictions in Comecon. They won their battle in a meeting in Moscow in July 1963 and continued their efforts both secretly and in public in 1964 and later.

An important element in this dispute was the Galati Steel project, for which the Romanians won approval in the teeth of serious Russian objections; two years later they were receiving West German help in it. The bargaining about this took place at a time when the USSR was struggling with its differences with China and after it had had to turn its ships back in the face of U.S. demands in the Cuban missile crisis.

In the spring of 1963 the Romanians decided to adopt a policy of neutrality with regard to the differences between Moscow and Peking. In the autumn of that year they voted against the Russians in the General Assembly of the United Nations. Shortly afterward they established diplomatic relations with the British and French governments. Their economic and diplomatic moves have been characterized as a "quiet revolt" against Russian control.

In a speech on February 15, 1964, the late Gheorghe Gheorghiu-Dej, then head of the Romanian Communist Party, claimed that as a result of the new measures his country's production was 74 percent above its 1959 level.[12] He named major plants that had been established and told of success in agriculture. The Romanians attributed their success to their independence in Comecon. In the course of 1964 Russian and Romanian radio stations exchanged accusations concerning Bucharest's economic dealings with capitalist countries, and the Romanians let it be known that "the clumsier aspects of Soviet policy" were attributable to Khrushchev,[13] almost as though they were aware of his impending downfall. Their leaders were as confident of the new course they had mapped for Romania's future as they were of their past achievements.

Opening the Door

During 1965 the Romanian leaders were hard at work broadening their contacts and striving to break down the rigid barriers

[12] Ibid., p. 102.
[13] Ibid., p. 107.

between East and West. It was this situation which afforded the West Germans their opportunity, and it was because of this economic rapprochement between 1962 and 1965 that the Soviets apparently concluded that they could not interfere effectively when Romania and West Germany established diplomatic relations in January 1967. In these varied relations Nicolae Ceausescu, party chief for the past four years, has shown notable skill.

Romania's management of her problems, though less widely recognized than Yugoslavia's, has been no less interesting. The Romanians, however, have remained in the Warsaw Pact. They have not abandoned their communist methods or ideas, but they have gained a measure of independence which offers hope for further changes in the relationships between the two worlds. Alard von Schack, writing early in 1968, made the following observations on these developments:

> The significance of the establishment of diplomatic relations with Rumania has not, as many people in the East have suspected, lain in breaching the front of Warsaw Pact countries, trying to split this alliance or isolating the Soviet Zone. The possibility of any such suspicion should have been a pointer to the Federal government not to start the ball rolling with Rumania. Great as is the importance attached to cooperation with Rumania it cannot be overemphasised that this country would do the same with any Eastern European country provided no stipulations are made that are impossible of fulfilment. This country's sole concern is to prove by means of specific examples the benefits that can be derived on all sides from cooperation between itself and socialist countries. It is certainly not this country's fault that so far Rumania is virtually the only one of these countries to enjoy the economic advantages of full relations with the Federal Republic and the accompanying liberalisation of trade.[14]

CZECHOSLOVAKIA

Inspired by its first success with Romania, Bonn intensified the efforts of its emissaries in Prague. German economic interests in Czechoslovakia were traditional and considerable, while the

[14] Alard von Schack, "The Next Stage in Federal Republic Eastern Policy," *German Tribune*, May 4, 1968, pp. 1, 2.

Czechs on their side were anxious to benefit from West German imports and technical assistance. Their industrial plant was outmoded, and they were in clear need of help from abroad. The personal relations that the Bonn emissaries had established in Czechoslovakia were for the most part good, and it seemed probable that a momentum had been generated that would lead to an exchange of ambassadors. But difficulties arose, and the restraining hand of Moscow prevented a successful conclusion to the tentative negotiations.

All that the Bonn emissaries were able to achieve at this time was work of the type normally performed by an active trade mission. The disappointment in the Bonn Foreign Office was considerable in spite of the fact that, under the able direction of Otto Heipertz and Werner Rouget, former Bonn officials, its emissaries performed a number of useful functions in facilitating communication between the two governments. Egon Bahr, who had gone to Prague several times with the personal rank of ambassador in an eager attempt to establish diplomatic relations, had to lower his sights and be content with this lesser accomplishment.

Dr. von Schack has made the following comments on the problems of cementing relations with Czechoslovakia:

> It has already been pointed out that Czechoslovakia and the Federal Republic have a special interest in each other because they share frontiers. Cultural exchange and tourist traffic will be able to intensify without the slightest trouble in Czechoslovakia's case. Further consideration must be given as to how to expand trade links. Czechoslovakia recently concluded a comprehensive trade agreement with the Soviet Union. Its economic potential is already bespoke to a large extent. But as Czechoslovakia and the Federal Republic have roughly kept pace in technological development there will always be specific areas, gaps where one can help the other, for example by means of manufacture under licence and exchanging industrial production processes. Economic, technological and scientific cooperation can flourish.
>
> As there are no quarrels about frontiers the only issues that can be cleared up between now and a full-scale political settlement are the minor issues connected with the 1938 Munich Agreement. The Federal government has already stated that the agreement was morally indefensible as it involved the use of force and

"no longer valid." Czechoslovakia wants a declaration that the Munich Agreement was null and void "from the start." The Federal Republic's hesitation to comply is not the result of easygoing morals or legalistic ingenuity. The government is worried that the former inhabitants of Czechoslovakia now entrusted to this country, the Sudeten Germans, might thereby be put at a disadvantage as regards their individual legal rights. In order to reach a conclusion that is both straightforward and satisfies all it might not be a bad idea if the group of Czechoslovak and Federal Republic legal experts planned for some time were to meet and discuss the matter.[15]

The early months of 1968 brought significant changes to the Prague political scene—changes that disturbed Ulbricht and caused tremors in Moscow. Antonin Novotny, first secretary of the Central Committee, was overthrown, and Czech expressions of revolt against restraint surprised the outside world.

Movement Toward Liberalization

Visitors to Prague had commented on the freedom with which the Czechs discussed their political and economic conditions. Observers had been impressed by signs of creative impulse in the arts, particularly the movies and theater; some films produced in Czechoslovakia had won international recognition. Many spoke of the independence of spirit they found, without being able to forecast what new attitudes it might portend toward communist control from Moscow.

To understand the Czech moves toward liberalization, it is important to consider the history of restlessness and criticism of the Communist party that began in 1952 or perhaps even earlier. Certainly, in 1953 the Writers' Union showed signs of nonconformism, "but the Writers' Congress, scheduled for that year, had been quietly called off."[16] When this congress eventually met in 1956, it took as its motto "Writers should become the conscience of the nation." The excitement generated in this gathering dis-

[15] Ibid., p. 4.
[16] Zdenek Elias and Jaromir Netik, "Czechoslovakia," in *Communism in Europe*, ed. William E. Griffith, vol. 2, pp. 225, 226.

turbed the party leaders. Meanwhile the feeling of restlessness spread widely, and the Spring Festival, permitted for the first time in several years, followed the traditional gay national pattern. Students paraded in Prague and Bratislava, demonstrating against the regime and demanding more freedom of press and radio. But expressions of dissatisfaction with the bureaucracy were not confined to students; they came also from the party rank and file.[17] There was talk of de-Stalinization. The issue of the Slansky trial in 1952 was raised,[18] and it gradually became known that a number of political prisoners held under Slansky's Stalin-type security measures had been released. Some concessions had been made in the special session of the Communist Party of Czechoslovakia (KSC) Congress called earlier while Antonin Novotny was party chief.

The extent of de-Stalinization at this time was limited. Many citizens, confronted by the repressive measures adopted against the uprisings in Hungary and Poland and influenced by their own memories of both the Nazi occupation and the sudden communist coup of 1948, tempered their rebellious instincts in the hope of survival under difficult conditions. Moreover it was said that the cadres in the KSC were prepared to handle any crisis that might develop. As far as the outside world was concerned, the more spectacular events in Hungary and Poland caught the public imagination, and the Czech stirrings at that time were largely forgotten. Meantime the *Apparat* strengthened its control, and in foreign affairs Prague was completely under the dominance of Moscow. Although Novotny went to Peking in December 1959, yet at the 1960 meeting of the Romanian Communist Party he fully supported the Khrushchev line, and as the Sino-Soviet split widened Prague clearly leaned toward Moscow. Moreover the constitutional law of 1956 and changes in national institutions in 1960 precluded Slovak autonomy. The experts Elias and Netik state that the promulgation of the constitution in 1956 marked the culmination of

[17] Zdenek Elias and Jaromir Netik, "1956: Effects of the Twentieth CPSU Congress," in *Communism in Europe*, ed. William E. Griffith, vol. 2, p. 224.

[18] The trial revealed his brutal security measures which had not been widely known before.

the power and authority of the KSC. Subsequently its cadres were aware of the dissension in the communist ranks at home and abroad, and as the evidence of economic failure mounted, the party's decline began.[19]

Economic difficulties became severe in 1962. Various failures under the 1960–1965 Five-Year Plan indicated investment and balance of payment problems as well as difficulties in the collectivization of agriculture. Military expenses "related to the Berlin crisis of 1961" were higher than expected. In 1963 the Five-Year Plan was abandoned, to be followed in 1964 by a Seven-Year Plan.

In the political sphere, the years 1962 and 1963 marked the struggle of the party to maintain its authority in what was later to be called a losing battle.[20] For the first time in fifteen years the psychological development in the country was clearly out of communist control. The Sino-Soviet split and the theoretical results it entailed, together with the failure of the economic and agricultural measures inside Czechoslovakia, affected Czech attitudes. Pragmatism and materialism dominated the scene; mistrust of politicians was rife, and public morale declined. A new system of management, the so-called New Economic Model (NEM) which had been in preparation for some months, was about to be installed. The program contained some capitalist elements and lessened the extent of centralized planning.

It has been suggested that the object of Khrushchev's visit to Prague in 1964—his last foreign journey—was to slow down the timetable for the NEM or to change its nature. His overthrow in October of that year was a blow to the efforts by the KSC leaders to maintain control. Two days after his fall the first official draft of the NEM was published. At this time changes were brewing and the Prague leaders were beginning to shake off some of the Soviet influence.

The NEM was applied experimentally in 1965. Its leading spirit was Ota Sik, former economics professor and member of the Central Committee, who was one of those mainly responsible for changing attitudes and methods. The NEM made each factory

[19] Elias and Netik, "Czechoslovakia," p. 237.
[20] Ibid., p. 264.

manager responsible for the production and sale of factory products. It was designed to improve management, to introduce advanced technical methods, and to "create the conditions for sound competition."[21] It was described as a part of the progressive development of socialism, but it was recognized that its results would go far beyond the economic and would permeate the entire life of the country. Some complained that it favored management and was a retreat from socialism. Its defenders insisted that the interests of the workers and of the Communist party lay in the improvement of skills and the success of mass production. Meanwhile, the party strongly reaffirmed Leninism, party discipline, and the need for stricter ideological education. Novotny asserted that a responsible social democracy which would not tolerate bourgeois ideology or morality was essential. Concern over weakness in party allegiance among the intelligentsia mounted, and the Thirteenth Party Congress in 1966 banned two journals and expelled one editor from the party.

Also at the Thirteenth Congress, Novotny called for a stronger Warsaw Pact. The party line in foreign policy was identical with that of Moscow, and the Congress passed anti-United States, pro-Hanoi resolutions and decided to ship arms to Egyptian President Gamel Abdel Nasser. Relations with the communist parties in other lands, including the then illegal Communist Party of West Germany,[22] were close. In November 1966 a West German delegation visited Prague.

The intellectual ferment and the demonstrations by the young continued to grow. A student protest in October 1967 was of such severity that it led to intervention by the police. In December the government made some concessions in view of the "harsh actions" taken on that occasion.[23] The many evidences of disunity in the KSC led to a serious effort to "re-evaluate its organization and its role in Czechoslovak life."[24] The party did not wish to increase its

[21] Hoover Institution on War, Revolution, and Peace, *Yearbook on International Communist Affairs, 1966*, p. 51.
[22] Ibid., p. 53.
[23] Hoover Institution on War, Revolution, and Peace, *Yearbook on International Communist Affairs, 1968*, pp. 172–73.
[24] Ibid., pp. 173–75.

membership but rather to sustain it at a level which would assure penetration of all phases of life. In the early winter of 1967 rumors began to circulate of the possible resignation of Novotny from his post as head of the party, if not from the presidency, and also of the resignation of Jiri Hendrych, who was second in the party leadership. Slovak influence was on the rise. Ota Sik called for the right to form opposition groups within the KSC. But it was not until January 3, 1968, that the party's Central Committee finally decided on the removal of Novotny and named Alexander Dubcek first secretary.

Foreign Policy During 1967

Throughout 1967 the foreign policy of Prague continued to be identical with that of Moscow. Forty percent of its foreign trade was with Moscow, and the Soviet Union continued to supply essential raw materials to Czechoslovakia. With East Germany Czech military, political, and cultural relations were close, and there was considerable tourism between the two areas. With both East Germany and Poland Prague signed treaties of friendship, cooperation, and mutual assistance which supported existing boundaries, warned of revanchism from West Germany, and declared the Munich Agreement of 1938 invalid. In spite of the reference to West Germany, however, it was denied that these treaties were directed *against* any country. In addition, government officials made various visits to and affirmations of solidarity with the Warsaw Pact countries and attempted to develop new systems within Comecon.

As the *Yearbook on International Communist Affairs* states:

> A leading issue on the foreign policy agenda was the problem of European security, and in particular relations with Bonn. Following the announcement in December 1966, of German Chancellor Kiesinger's new *Ostpolitik,* Czechoslovakia indicated interest in the possibility for the future establishment of diplomatic relations (but drew a specific distinction between diplomatic relations and "normalization" of relations). However, following the Rumanian step to establish diplomatic relations with Bonn, the subsequent visit by Leonid Brezhnev to Prague (4–6 Feb-

ruary 1967), and the Warsaw Pact foreign ministers' meeting (8–10 February 1967), the earlier cautious interest seemed to disappear.[25]

A series of bilateral pacts precluded the undertaking of diplomatic relations with West Germany unless Bonn agreed to:

- Forego the possession of nuclear weapons in any way whatsoever
- Declare that the Munich Agreement was null and void from the day it was signed
- Recognize the Oder-Neisse line as the frontier
- Recognize the Soviet Zone as a second German state
- Recognize West Berlin as a special political unit

This went far to halt Bonn's *Ostpolitik.*

Yet throughout 1967, at various levels Czechoslovakia continued to express interest in closer relations with West Germany. On August 3, after long negotiations the two nations signed an agreement to exchange trade missions, and another for the exchange of "goods and payments" for the period 1967–1969. During 1968 the German mission performed a number of typical diplomatic functions. Its relations with Czech officials, though informal, were excellent.

Developments in 1968

In 1968, changes of far-reaching consequence seemed to be imminent. An article by David Binder in the *New York Times* referred to the press as a major force in the continued democratization which began with the election of Dubcek as party leader.[26] According to a Prague radio editor, Czech journalists who had kept silent for years suddenly became fighters for liberty. A liberal communist newsman was quoted as saying that, if the Russians put pressure on Czechoslovakia, "you can be sure we will expose them, not to worsen relations but to warn them that we are engaged in a peaceful democratic revolution and will brook no interference." Thus, twenty years after the communist takeover in 1948 new

[25] Ibid., p. 176.
[26] *New York Times,* May 6, 1968.

forces were stirring and change was shaking the foundations of the party structure. A reform program, summarized on April 10, 1968, included among other points a reaffirmation of the two-Germanys policy.[27] The program reiterated many of the familiar cliches, but this fact should not be allowed to conceal the important underlying conflicts, and the move toward liberalization which has taken place—a move that will not come to a permanent halt even though it will slow down in the next few months because, as was evident in July 1968, the Soviet Union cannot tolerate a complete break-away.

There is little reason to expect that the new leadership, occupied with many questions of critical importance, will turn its attention in the near future to improving relations with Bonn. Presumably however it will be possible for patient effort by members of trade missions and other representatives of the two nations to develop new and closer contacts, taking advantage of any liberalization which may take place. The ouster of Alexander Dubcek as first secretary in early 1969 has further complicated the prospects of relations between Czechoslovakia and the Federal Republic. Nevertheless officials in Bonn are still keenly interested in developments in Prague, and there is reason to think the Czechs have not lost their desire for improved contacts.

POLAND

The differences between Poland and West Germany are deep-seated and cannot easily be pushed aside. Even though sentiment in the Federal Republic has changed markedly with regard to Germany's former eastern territories, the Oder-Neisse line will continue to be an obstacle. The reaction to the support given by Foreign Minister Brandt, leader of the SPD, for renunciation of the former eastern territories and recognition of the line as a border was thought by some to suggest the existence of internal political barriers to acceptance of the existing situation. His statement, made shortly before the elections in Baden-Wuerttemberg, may have been a factor in the decline in SPD votes and the increase in the votes cast for the rightist NPD.

[27] Ibid., April 11, 1968.

Polish resentment over the German invasion of Poland in 1939, the lingering misinformation regarding the events of 1944 and the Katyn Woods massacres,[28] and the long-standing antagonism between the two nations cannot be lightly dismissed. There are therefore psychological barriers which will increase the difficulties in the path of West Germany's *Ostpolitik* and limit the desire to consummate diplomatic relations. So far Bonn has made few efforts in this direction although it has the matter under active consideration. Poland cannot be left out of its program for new relations with Eastern Europe.

One of the lessons of Polish history is that change, whether rapid or slow, is always to be expected. Divided, absorbed, reconstituted, and with different frontiers over the years, Poland has survived for many centuries as a real entity and as an issue of which the world's statesmen have had to take account. The responsibility of the Big Four for the present boundaries makes them also responsible for some, but not all, of the difficulties which make the stabilization of this part of Europe impossible at this time. As time goes on, the children of the people expelled from their country after World War II become increasingly indifferent to the idea of return to their ancestral farms and villages; many of the millions transferred to the West have become completely adapted to their new homes. Thus the pressure on the West German government to strive for the return of the former eastern territories lessens each year. In ten years or so this issue may well have vanished from practical politics; but because of its deep roots in the past the bitterness between Germans and Poles will continue.

The "Polish Road to Socialism"

The attitude of Poland to Russia similarly stems from brutal events which are hard to forget. The Poles still have vivid memories of their betrayal by the Russian generals when they made their vain struggle for freedom during the last weeks of the war. They have always manifested special attitudes toward communism. Wladyslaw Gomulka, Polish party chief, in particular supported

[28] See chapter 8, p. 200, fn.

the "Polish road to socialism" which differed in its methods and sequences from the orthodox Moscow line.[29] Stalin, in his drive against Titoism after 1948, was especially critical of Gomulka. In 1949 Gomulka and three close associates were put under arrest.[30] The uprisings in 1956, which brought him back to power in October, were the result of economic misery and a nationalist sentiment that was frustrated by politics. Gomulka however recognized that good relations with the Soviets were essential to the safety of his borders with East Germany and avoided actions that might have led to a bloody military intervention such as that which repressed the Hungarian revolt. He played a complicated political game, taking account of the disputes between the members of the Warsaw Pact and even their differences with China. He was vitally anxious for security from attack.

Thus it was his foreign minister, Adam Rapacki, who in 1957 proposed a partial demilitarization in Europe and the establishment of a nuclear-free zone in central Europe.[31] This attempt at detente and solution of the problems between Poland and Germany, East and West, was supported by Khrushchev. It was designed to modify the NATO position and to make definitive the existing borders of Poland and thus, by reducing the tensions both to the East and to the West, to strengthen the position of Gomulka's Communist party.

The situation changed with the speech Khrushchev delivered on November 10, 1958, in honor of Gomulka's visit to Moscow. The pressure on Berlin was accentuated by the November 27 ultimatum that followed. On the question of Berlin and West Germany the interests of Khrushchev and Gomulka largely coincided. Both feared the rising strength of the Federal Republic and the disturbing influence of Berlin on East Germany.[32] Gomulka was a consistent and strong communist in spite of the fact that he adhered to his own brand of communism and had shown independence in his

[29] Hansjakob Stehle, "Polish Communism," in *Communism in Europe*, ed. William E. Griffith, vol. 1, p. 97.

[30] Ibid., pp. 99–108.

[31] See chapter 5.

[32] Jean E. Smith, *The Defense of Berlin*, p. 183.

relations with the bloc nations. He maintained a close working relationship with Khrushchev, whom he backed on many issues, but questioned the feasibility of the Soviet proposals for "general and complete disarmament" and favored the more limited and, to him, more practical Rapacki Plan. Rapacki indicated at this time that defense expenditures depended primarily on the extent of West German armament. There was also evidence of uneasiness about East Germany and recurring concern over the western borders of Poland. There was constant trouble over the economic situation and particularly over the agricultural collectivization. The system was changed during the years after 1956. Farm policy became more flexible, and more liberal economic practices, with a high level of investment, were gradually developed; while there was considerable restlessness, the economic conditions improved. Meanwhile a generation which had not known the war was exerting increasing influence.

The little freedoms the Gomulka regime granted for travel and cultural activities and its accommodation to the religious influence that is still strong in Poland compared favorably with the situation in the other Warsaw Pact countries.[33] The contrast with the more restrictive policy in East Germany was particularly noteworthy. A meeting of the party's Union of Polish Writers early in 1964 reacted moderately in the face of sharp criticism of censorship. The significant concessions then made were an indication of official vulnerability.

The Outlook for Polish-German Rapprochement

The increasing flexibility was accompanied by instability and uncertainty in Poland's economic, cultural, and party relations. In view of this the nation is in fear of German aggression and of the growing capacity of the West and also to some extent of the GDR. All this is bound to make the next step difficult for Bonn. It is not easy to see what measures can be taken to encourage closer relations. While the progress made with Romania, Yugoslavia, and Czechoslovakia may make for new attitudes in Poland, the out-

[33] Stehle, "Polish Communism," pp. 169–70.

come will depend in the main on Moscow's decisions and programs. The gradual acceptance of the Oder-Neisse line in many capitals,[34] including Bonn, will make some difference but will not be enough to change the general climate. It may well be that Poland's improved economic conditions and feeling of enhanced security will improve the climate for her relations with West Germany. But a nation that for centuries has known so much uncertainty will not quickly change its attitude. It will not be easy for West Germany to alter her relations with Poland. Yet this is a matter that Bonn cannot afford to neglect, for it is only with a general improvement of atmosphere and with a change in communist intentions that this part of the picture can fall into place and normal contacts can be established between Poland and West Germany.

Eberhard Schulz, in his analysis of West Germany's relations with the states of Eastern Europe, declares that the most determined opponent of German reunification is Poland, that the Poles consider that the joining of the two parts of Germany would threaten their very existence.[35] For this reason Schulz stresses the importance of renewed efforts to solve the problems, though in fact in other sections of his book he offers little hope for real reunification or for anything beyond association. The trade mission in Warsaw he regards as ineffective; he states that since it has been there relations between the two states have worsened. He points out that Gerhard Schroeder (then foreign minister, later minister of defense) hoped for a semidiplomatic status that would serve as a channel for effective communication. This result has not been realized; the head of the trade mission has had almost no diplomatic, cultural, or general contacts and deals only with the commercial authorities. In sum, little progress has been made.

YUGOSLAVIA

A meeting of representatives of Yugoslavia and the Federal Republic in January 1968 brought quick and, to some people,

[34] President de Gaulle made his pronouncement earlier.
[35] Schulz, *An Ulbricht*, p. 97.

unexpected diplomatic agreement. Tito's independence, which has made him a symbol of the *separate road to socialism* and given evidence of polycentrism in what had earlier been considered a monolithic structure, has increased the importance of his relations with Bonn. Tito himself has pursued a maverick course in the Eastern complex of communist states. His nation is definitely communist but is not a member of the Warsaw Pact or of Comecon; it has accepted aid from the United States; it has on occasion broken with the Soviets, as in 1948, and at other times reconciled some of the policy differences that existed between itself and them, as in 1957; it has been attacked by the Chinese communists and courted by the Western capitals. Yugoslavia in fact has followed a varied and unpredictable policy in a situation which has become increasingly fluid.

The Renewal of Diplomatic Relations With Bonn

The renewal of diplomatic relations accomplished in January 1968 has been considered a milestone in the *Ostpolitik*. It attested to the existence of a new flexibility in Bonn as well as in Belgrade. It showed that the Federal Republic considered its position in the outside world sufficiently strong to allow it to stretch the Hallstein Doctrine and maintain its claim to represent the whole of Germany even though Belgrade had an ambassador in East Germany. It evidenced a degree of freedom from former restraints in West Germany and brought hopes of further progress in dealing with Eastern Europe. These hopes were rudely shaken in the summer of 1968.

The agreement also evidenced the degree to which Yugoslav memories of German aggression in 1941 had faded. The lapse of more than twenty years since the German occupation had blurred the sharpness of recollections which had for some years been deeply etched on Yugoslav consciousness. Some of this postwar resentment had been kept alive by the fact that the West Germans had broken the relations established in 1956. But the new situation, based on two decades of postwar experience, is likely to be on a more solid footing. There is some ground for concluding that skill in Bonn and a change in climate behind the Iron Curtain in the next few years may facilitate economic and diplomatic activity in Belgrade and other capitals.

In the case of Yugoslavia, a number of considerations of practical economics and labor relations operate in favor of closer diplomatic relations with West Germany. They include the problems of the many Yugoslavs working as guest laborers in the Federal Republic; the trade opportunities that could be favored by such relations; the question of indemnification for damage in the Second World War; and the problems connected with Yugoslav exiles in the Federal Republic.

The Separate Road to Socialism

Yugoslavia indicated in a number of ways her desire to remain in the socialist family, but in a family that had considerably changed its character, "that was no longer a prison but a commonwealth."[36] The Yugoslavs feared pressure from the Chinese and welcomed contacts with the Togliatti Communist party in Italy and with the progressive communists in Romania and elsewhere. Tito had always stressed the wider international aspects of communism. He leaned toward a Balkan communist federation and, though the creation of such a federation was impossible, thought of himself as pursuing an independent foreign policy. He did not wish to risk the loss of Russian support, but he intended to go as far toward an independent policy as was consistent with his need for cooperation and to proceed always on a basis of "equality."[37] A second break came in 1957 as the result partly of Tito's attitude in sheltering some Hungarians during the Hungarian revolt, partly of the growing split between China and Russia, and partly of such other matters as relations with the newly developing countries.

To some extent the contacts with Bonn represented a search for new opportunities, an improvement in economic conditions, and a better understanding of the changing shape of foreign relations in Europe. It is possible that the step taken in January 1968 may

[36] Viktor Meier, "Yugoslav Communism," in *Communism in Europe*, ed William E. Griffith, vol. 1, p. 80.

[37] Ibid., pp. 29, 33.

prove to be of considerable importance in the further development of diverse types of communism.

The shifting tactics of Belgrade and the changing attitude to Yugoslavia on the part of the more conventional members of the bloc are highly important in the politics of Central Europe. They show Tito's notable capacity to choose the special road to socialism, and how this road may at some points come close to the paths of uncommitted and even capitalist nations. No other member of the bloc has offered so outright a challenge to Soviet leadership. Even before 1948 Tito's Yugoslavia was not a satellite. In Dr. Meier's view she will not become one; geographic, historical, and ethnic characteristics have made her unique. In recent months the danger of a new domination by Moscow has led Tito to place greater reliance on his own popular support and to make some internal concessions. There has been a tendency toward liberal developments.[38]

Relations With the West

In recent years, in his pursuit of trade and credits Tito had reached out to the nations of the West, to members of the EEC and the signatories of the General Agreement on Tariffs and Trade (GATT).[39] Then he was forced to retreat in the face of Soviet anti-Yugoslav measures, including the refusal to allow Yugoslav observers to attend the meeting of Comecon in August 1960. There were other annoying and hostile moves. It was however natural for Yugoslavia to consider the benefits that could accrue from links with the West as long as these were compatible with communist planning and economic philosophy.

To those in Yugoslavia concerned with improvement of production, the remarkable economic recovery and the highly sophisticated techniques of West Germany had a natural appeal. There can be little doubt that the hope for assistance with industrial production and techniques has helped to convince Belgrade of the desirability of closer relations with Bonn. If West German diplo-

[38] Ibid., p. 83.
[39] Ibid., p. 24.

mats and economists can now play their cards with skill, they will be able to bring about a significant advance in their country's policy. The possibilities of working with Tito are especially interesting to Western Europe following his independent and significant visit to Prague when Czechoslovakia was attempting to defend new freedoms in July 1968.

OVERVIEW OF THE NEW POLICY

West Germany, more than any other Western European nation, is in a position to offer not only assistance in industrial modernization but also credits to facilitate trade expansion. Hungary and Bulgaria as well as the other nations already discussed have all been seeking special trade opportunities, talking with the bankers in Frankfurt and elsewhere, and looking to the gains they hope to reap from new business with Eastern Europe. In short, the economic progress of the Federal Republic, already impressive and perhaps due to accelerate over the next few years, may prove to be the magnet that will draw together in practical association nations which political differences had previously kept apart. While it is unlikely that diplomatic relations with Hungary or Bulgaria will be established in the near future, over the years, if there is no serious opposition from Moscow, consideration will undoubtedly be given to their possibility. Talk so far has been tentative, but the motive for further progress will be obvious from a glance at the steadily increasing trade of various communist countries with the Federal Republic (see table 2). The total annual value of exports and imports for the years 1964 through 1967 was:[40]

	Million DM
1964	5,613
1965	6,574
1966	7,739
1967	9,017

The Elements To Be Considered

Analysis of the *Ostpolitik* of the Federal Republic reveals thre main elements: (a) the Federal Republic's dealings with the S

[40] *Source:* Deutsche Bank, Frankfurt am Main.

viet Union; (b) its relations with the satellite countries; and (c) questions connected with contacts with East Germany, international attitudes toward reunification, and other issues such as the Oder-Neisse line, the Hallstein Doctrine, and West Germany's membership in NATO as this affects the Berlin situation and her *Ostpolitik* in general.

Ever since the exchange of diplomatic representatives in 1955 Bonn has endeavored to conduct business with the Soviet Union in a normal and unaggressive manner. Communications with Moscow concerning Berlin and other questions have followed the usual diplomatic tradition. They have been correct and restrained. Wherever appropriate, they have been coordinated with the policy of the three Western powers and the aims of the NATO capitals. They have appeared to have the unanimous support of all parties in the Federal Republic. Frustration over the lack of progress toward a peace treaty has been alleviated by recognition of the limits imposed by the Russian-American conflicts, of the European situation, and of the fact that Russia has not yet convincingly abandoned expansionism. Little change can be expected in this policy focus in the next few years, although in their desire for a detente some politicians may support policies bordering on acceptance of sweeping changes in security measures.

The second element in West Germany's *Ostpolitik* involves her efforts to extend and normalize relations (some of which have been considered in the foregoing pages) with Bulgaria, Czechoslovakia, Hungary, Romania, Poland, and Yugoslavia.[41] Here the degree of success she has achieved in the past few years varies considerably from one country to another. Overall however a better atmosphere has been created, and a noticeable enthusiasm for further action has developed in official quarters in Bonn. There is hope, vaguely felt, that West Germany's capacity to act in Eastern areas will increase and that as a result of her new contacts she will be in a position of greater authority in all her international relations.

The often technical and complex elements involved in the third field of action, which relates most closely to future association or

[41] Albania has allied itself with communist China.

union with East Germany, are considered in some detail in chapter 5. Meantime it is worthy of note that the fluctuating sentiments and political issues involved sometimes become the subject of interparty strife. The younger politicians, who are assuming more and more responsibility for the policies of the federal government, and the students will address themselves to such issues and press for greater flexibility and experimentation.

The Issues Involved

In general, West Germany's *Ostpolitik* attests to her full restoration to the community of nations as a member authorized to extend her diplomatic influence in all directions. The policy is considered of major importance by Foreign Minister Brandt. Chancellor Kiesinger is fully committed to it. Herbert Wehner, the outstanding intellectual in the Social Democratic party and minister of all-German affairs, stands behind it. The politicians in general support it. Subject to its aim of eventual German reunification, it seeks normal exchanges and relations with all nations, communist and noncommunist alike. These agreements and relations, while providing means to increase commerce and extend cultural exchanges, would of course have to be consistent with the long-range interests of the Federal Republic. They would be the beginning—not the end—of the new policy.

Within a dozen years, perhaps more, Bonn's present policy could result in a nation whose strength and key location would exert a balancing influence on the European situation. The word "bridge" is frequently used to describe the position of influence that Bonn seeks. Since the present chasm disturbs and limits progress, whether in the European Economic Community, in the European Free Trade Area, or in Comecon and Warsaw Pact countries, the change would be constructive. If it can be assumed that the Russian leaders will be willing to risk a larger degree of freedom and to give up any intention of aggressively pressing the dominance of international communism, then the intentions of the Bonn government are realistic and could be fruitful.

How far can Bonn go with its new program? This question is bound up with the question of German reunification, the future of

Berlin, and the place of Germany in Europe. If the Soviets are prepared to force West Germany into a resentful, frustrated, and rebellious mood, knowing the continuing strong commitment of the Western big powers and knowing her inherent capacity, they will of necessity take a Stalinist-type course. They might, by their invasion of Czechoslovakia and by their political threats and military presence, force a new submissiveness on their satellites. They could prohibit by various means the extension of contacts with the free democracies and support an iron rule in East Germany. If they did this, however, they would create forces endangering the peace of Europe and might turn emotional hostility into concrete plans for action.

The Soviets have been quick to accuse the Federal Republic of intervention in Czech affairs in 1968. This is no new approach. Dr. Schack noted this tactic early in 1968:

> On the basis of the unfounded imputation that the Federal Republic wants to split the Warsaw Pact, isolate the Soviet Zone from its allies or foster a rift between the countries of Eastern Europe and the Soviet Union Moscow, Warsaw and East Berlin in particular, immediately after the establishment of diplomatic relations between Rumania and this country, began to work out a plan of defence. The result of a large number of conferences, trips and talks is a system of bilateral pacts between the countries of Eastern Europe with the exception of Rumania, Albania and Yugoslavia in which every country concerned virtually undertakes to every other not to establish diplomatic relations with the Federal Republic before a number of demands have been fulfilled.[42]

Now, several years after Bonn embarked on the new policy, crucial issues will emerge which will, as time goes on, increasingly reveal the genuine nature of Soviet intentions. As the Federal Republic attempts to exploit the financial and political interests of the Warsaw Pact countries, and as these nations recognize the potential scope of their own development, either they will take a new line offering prospects of broader international relations or they will reluctantly and grudgingly submit to the limitations im-

[42] Schack, "Eastern Policy," p. 2.

posed by Moscow. Such a rebuff to expectations and hopes now clearly before their eyes would postpone but not eliminate their will for independence.

The new policy in Bonn carries with it the possibility of far-reaching eventual consequences for the United States and for all the Western democracies. An increase in traffic of all kinds between East and West Europe, if permitted, would change the atmosphere and alter the scope of economic and political relations. Even with the Iron Curtain between East and West Germany and the continued physical existence of the Berlin Wall, there would be an interchange of ideas, of goods, of persons, which would permeate and modify the nature of government, the behavior of people, and the expectation of people for freedom.

Two aspects of the East-West confrontation need to be examined briefly at this point. One is the significance of Berlin; the other is the position of Walter Ulbricht and his associates in power in the GDR.

The Significance of Berlin

The existence of a restored Berlin, determined, productive, and protected by the NATO shield, is a constant reminder to the Russians of the dangers that would face them if they returned to a policy of repression and increased their aggressive action in Europe. It is evidence of the fact that they cannot secure a detente if they insist on frustrating the persistent and natural interests of West Germany in Eastern Europe and the possibilities of association with East Germany. It indicates that, even though West Germany has renounced the use of force in her quest for reunification, there remain less tangible factors that will continue to keep the question alive. Can the currents of revolt and opposition to communist pressures be moderated and held in check? Without Berlin, the only limit on Russian capacity to seal off Eastern Europe would be the limit on the amount of force the Soviets would exert on the Warsaw Pact countries. With Berlin, they must consider also the sensitive elements in the West. This was the reason that Khrushchev tried to neutralize Berlin's spirit and crush its will for freedom. This is the reason that the Kremlin has since 1948 waged against Berlin a war of harassment, pressures, and seduction. And it is because of Berlin that the Kremlin has failed.

Ulbricht and the GDR

In an East Germany situated between a restless Poland and a disturbed and rebellious Czechoslovakia, and with West Germany hostile to his regime, Ulbricht has special problems. The crucial choice between Stalinist repression and permission for contacts with neighboring countries can be resolved negatively in the short run, as it has been so far. In the longer run the isolation of the area, because it is unnatural, can breed the seeds of revolt. A mistake in anticipating the psychological pressures could bring an upset to the uneasy equilibrium now prevailing from Moscow to the western boundaries of the GDR. Moreover neither the SED nor the Russians can count on a smooth transition once Ulbricht has given up his command to his successor, nor can they risk loss of control over the East Germans. Their fear of an East Germany freed from restraint would outweigh any concern they might feel over a West Germany absorbed into and sharing the responsibilities of NATO.

For these reasons, any decisions the Soviets may make with regard to Czechoslovakia, Poland, and other Eastern European nations must be consistent with their policy toward the GDR. In their response to Bonn's program of extending its relations eastward, they have currently little freedom of choice.

Context of the Reunification Problem

Bonn's *Ostpolitik* can only be considered in the context of conditions within the GDR, the position of Ulbricht, the attitudes toward reunification, particularly in Europe and the United States, the significance of Berlin, the strength of the Federal Republic, and the broad policies of both communist and noncommunist countries. In the chapters which follow, these matters will be explored in order to throw light on the future course of Bonn's policy. It will be found that the GDR possesses important potential and also latent problems; that the outlook for reunification has become more remote, but that reunification continues nonetheless to be a problem for West Germany and for Europe as a whole; that the Federal Republic, while facing political pitfalls, has grown in maturity and can face its problems openly and vigorously as a result of its prosperous economy and its will to become a strong democracy.

Meanwhile policy, both East and West, tends to give the Federal Republic more scope for action, and the men in Bonn can now to a considerable extent shape their own destiny. Although conditions cannot be normalized without a peace treaty, great progress in this direction has been made, with the concurrence of the West and with the reluctant acquiescence of the East.

The matters taken up in chapters 4 to 9 are all interwoven and interdependent. None of them can be usefully considered in isolation. For the "German problem," like most international problems, is complex and bears within it enormous possibilities for evil and for good. American action and understanding can affect the balance.

LESSONS OF THE CRISIS IN CZECHOSLOVAKIA

The events of the year 1968 in Czechoslovakia call for special comment because they bear directly on all the Federal Republic's dealings with Eastern Europe. During many weeks observers in Bonn and Germans in Prague watched with bated breath the increase in nationalism and independence in Czechoslovakia. The West Germans knew that the needs of the economy were great, but they refrained from extending credits or from assisting with goods or technical aid because they did not wish to disturb the Dubcek policy of moderate reform within the Warsaw Pact. They carefully avoided any act which might seem to be intervention.

When in June the seventy writers published their 2,000 words, an historic document manifesting great courage and an avid desire for party responsibility to the people and for genuine democracy, it was realized that the Czechs had gone further than their neighbors in their program of reform and had come close to challenging the authority of Moscow. Nevertheless, because of the firm communist stand of the Czech leaders and the absence of open revolt or inflammatory demonstrations, it seemed possible that they might hold the gains of the past six months without provoking Soviet aggression. This was the ardent hope of the men in Bonn toward the end of July when the Soviet leaders, party first secretary Leonid Brezhnev and Premier Alexei N. Kosygin, agreed to meet with Dubcek and Premier Oldrich Cernik on Czech soil.

West Germany, like the rest of the noncommunist world, was surprised and shocked when in August Russian troops and tanks, with the assistance of various other members of the Warsaw Pact, were sent into Prague and occupied the surrounding countryside in a sudden invasion. The act came as a tragic blow to a country which had a significant degree of popular sympathy with Moscow and confounded many of the experts. At one stroke the hopes of an early detente in Central Europe were destroyed. It was clear that the Soviets would not tolerate independence of thought or act in their sphere of influence. They reacted in panic to a modicum of freedom manifested by the dedicated communists of Czechoslovakia.

The Brezhnev doctrine, published in *Pravda* in September and expounded by Ambassador Gromyko in the United Nations in October, announced the intention of the Soviets to intervene with whatever force was necessary in any "socialist state" where the socialist system was threatened. Since it was their clear intention to assess nonsocialist tendencies according to their own fears and standards, the implications were far-reaching. No nation could substantially alter the party composition or the manner of controling cultural, educational, or economic matters without endangering its government's independence or facing the threat of invasion. This doctrine, combined with the physical presence of the invaders in Czechoslovakia, drove underground the feeling of creative democracy and brought back terror.

The crushing nature of the action and the doctrine were apparent from the protests of the Communist parties in the West and from the criticism in Moscow, in East Germany, and in many other countries where the violent nature of Soviet repression had destroyed many hopes. It was clear to the West Germans that their program of increasing contacts had to be relegated to the far-distant future.

In 1969 the fate of the brave men in Czechoslovakia is still precarious. Their peril is a loss not only for West Germany but for all the free world.

CHAPTER 4

The German Democratic Republic

AN UNEASY VASSAL

The German Democratic Republic (GDR), carved out of the remnants of the Third Reich, differs in many ways from other nations now under Russian influence and control.[1] Its people are not inclined to communist systems. Their productive economy is built on a capitalistic structure created in the free enterprise system, their work habits are German, their standards are West European.[2] They do not like the Russians. Their borders are unnatural, and their limited contacts with their neighbors are poisoned by present uncertainty and the memories of past hostility. They have been torn away from old traditions and customs. They do not fit in an acceptable way into the role they are asked to assume. They are not easy for the Soviet system to absorb, but at the same time they are too strong for Moscow to ignore.

The spirit of resistance which these contradictions might easily have engendered was sapped by the flight of the young and vigorous to the West during the dozen years before the raising of the Berlin Wall in 1961.[3] Among the millions of refugees went hundreds of potential leaders for freedom. The will which was crushed by the Nazis has had little chance to revive in the years of oppression by Soviet divisions and the harsh communist regime ruling from Pankow. West Berlin, which for more than a decade had stood as a shining example of life in the democratic West, is represented to the East Germans whom the Wall now shuts out as a neonlighted center of empty materialism, a minor stumbling

[1] For comment on the Yalta Agreements on zonal occupation, see chapter 8. For the division after the blockade of Berlin, see chapter 5.

[2] Even the nationalized industry is built on the past structure and techniques.

[3] Eleanor Lansing Dulles, *Berlin*, pp. 56, 103.

block on the road to socialization. Its meaning has ceased to inspire them.

ULBRICHT

The drama of the reviving economy and aggressive political system in the GDR is bound up with the story of Walter Ulbricht. The West Germans anxiously watching the development of the GDR have come to recognize the durability and effectiveness of the man now at its head. In some measure a tool of Moscow and occasionally pushed to the edge of dismissal—then reinstated, as conditions required a man of his ability to keep the Zone firmly in the communist camp—he has nonetheless created a striking, if hated, image in the minds of the leaders of West Germany.

Moscow's Initial Miscalculation and Later Attitude

When the Russians pushed westward in 1945, they misunderstood the character of the German and Austrian peoples and were slow to recognize the firm intention of the United States to give diplomatic and financial support to the recovery and rehabilitation of the Austrian and German states. The oppressive measures taken under Stalin—the kidnappings and property seizures—were largely failures: their effect was felt in only a limited area and was made possible only by the use of hundreds of thousands of occupation troops. In Austria the Soviets failed in both tactics and strategy. Through miscalculation, they permitted the existence and functioning of a central government with a veto in reverse: laws passed by the Austrians came into force after 31 days unless unanimously rejected by the four occupying powers. This permitted the West in 1945 and subsequent years to assist the government in its democratic endeavors.[4]

Meanwhile, the speech of Secretary of State James F. Byrnes in Stuttgart on September 6, 1946, had warned the Soviets that the United States would aid the prostrate economy of Germany, would reverse the decision to withdraw American troops from Europe,

[4] This experience, whose effect on Soviet policy in Germany has been underrated, merits further examination.

and would continue to maintain significant forces there.[5] This announcement paved the way for the Truman Doctrine in 1947 and Marshall Plan assistance in 1948–1951 and laid the basis for NATO in 1949. The reaction to the Russian attempt to blockade Berlin in 1948 was a further demonstration of American determination. Thus the situation which the Russians faced in 1952 was vastly different from the situation they faced in 1945 when they began the occupation of the eastern part of Germany and in effect gave Germany's former eastern territories to the Poles.

The combination of German industry and drive with communist techniques of planning has created a unique situation. To the rulers in the regime it has brought both problems and opportunities. Nowhere else has a basically anticommunist population that disliked Russia and Russian influence set to work to produce a productive, highly mechanized industrial plant. The test of strength between conflicting ideas and methods has so far been conducted under conditions which are highly artificial. Separated from neighboring economies, lacking a fully developed price system, but not completely subservient to Soviet all-pervasive controls, it has slowly gathered momentum and achieved high levels of production. The next phase, which can only be reached if there is a solution to the problems of distribution, is a challenge which is gradually coming to be recognized. It may bring a plateau of growth and prevent the attainment of goals which call for equalling and surpassing capitalist countries.

The characteristic German industry and drive in production and Ulbricht's increasing effectiveness became evident only after considerable changes in the Soviet attitude to East Germany. These changes accompanied modifications of attitude within the USSR itself, not excluding those resulting from the strains and conflicts within the world communist movement. The Soviets were also influenced by their experience in dealing with Austria, West Germany, and the NATO powers. Gradually they came to realize that the absorption of Germany and Austria was not the easy task they had at first assumed and that it would not be tolerated by their

[5] For excerpts from this speech, see pp. 287–88.

former allies in World War II. In 1947 and 1948 they changed their course. They were not flexible enough to avoid a split with Yugoslavia but they succeeded in winning control of Czechoslovakia and they held on to East Germany. Their oppression of individual East Germans, removals of equipment and produce, and isolation of the area from the *Bundesrepublik*, all tended to discourage the people and to hamper reconstruction.

It has been said that Lavrenti Beria was charged with developing the methods of occupation used in Germany. In the light of the manner in which the controls were carried out, this may well have been true. In any case, fear of the occupiers led to an outflow of refugees which became significant after the Berlin blockade of 1948–1949 and rose to unprecedented and alarming proportions in 1953 as news of the doctors' trials and the purges in the USSR and the Slansky trial in Czechoslovakia became general. The flight of thousands in dread of an intensification of oppressive measures in their towns and cities was a measure of the anxiety which prevailed before Stalin's death in March 1953.

Ulbricht's Early Postwar Activities

The position of Ulbricht fluctuated with the changing times.[6] He had been in the communist movement since the age of nineteen and had been trained in the Lenin School in Moscow in the early 1920s. On April 30, 1945, he and several colleagues were flown into the area between Frankfurt an der Oder and Kuestrin. A few days later the "Ulbricht Group" reached the neighborhood of Berlin. During the summer he was engaged largely in the reorganization of the German Communist Party (KPD) and in efforts to consolidate the communist elements of the population and gain control over the Berlin government. In this he was thwarted by the Allied Kommandatura and by the resistance of the Berliners themselves. In a March 31, 1946, plebiscite the Social Democratic Party (SPD) had expressed itself against immediate amalgamation with the KPD. Nevertheless Ulbricht vigorously pressed the work of amalgamation and at a conference of communist officials in Octo-

[6] Carola Stern, *Ulbricht*, pp. 27, 121, 133.

ber announced the unification of the two workers' parties into the Socialist Unity Party (SED). The speeches made on this occasion upheld the thesis of a separate German road to socialism.

Walter Ulbricht, Wilhelm Pieck, Otto Grotewohl, and the other members of the communist group suffered their first defeat when in the Berlin voting of October 20, 1946, the SED failed to get a majority and came out with only 19.8 percent of the votes as compared with 48.7 percent for the SPD, 22.1 percent for the CDU, and 9.4 percent for the Free Democratic Party (FDP).[7] To the man in the street the SED was known as the Russian party. Its defeat at the polls caused some of the advocates of a separate German road to socialism to question whether the Ulbricht program was acceptable to a nation which did not wish to be chained to Russia. Meanwhile the SED pursued an energetic program of education and training through the establishment of special schools and the communist youth organization, the Free German Youth (FDJ). In January 1947, in response to questions raised by dissenters within the SED, some further independence was seemingly granted and the termination of Russian dismantling of industrial plant was announced; but in fact the dismantling continued until 1954.

In 1946 and 1947 the communists made strong efforts to capture the women's organization, the Democratic Women's League (DFB). They brought together four women: Frau Vierkaut representing the Christian Democratic Union (CDU), Frau Schirmer-Proscher representing the FDP, Frau Elly Schmidt representing the SED, and Barbara Renthe Fink, representative at large. The communists took advantage of their chairmanship of the Kommandatura, when it rotated round to them, to bring these women together in an attempt to consolidate the *Bund* under their control. The four were convinced at first that such unification was in the interests of all Germany. At their meeting Ulrich Biel, then on the staff of the U.S. Military Government, fought against the communist plan and persuaded all but Elly Schmidt that there was serious danger of betraying German democracy. As a result of his efforts

[7] Wolfgang Leonhard, *Child of the Revolution*, pp. 359, 361, 364; Erich W. Gniffke, *Jahre mit Ulbricht*, pp. 211–19.

and their dawning understanding of the purpose of the meeting, most of the leaders walked out of the women's central control (*Zentralverwaltung*). They, together with others who were also keenly watchful of the sinister influences, helped defeat the communist attempt to capture the mayoralty. Their influence was particularly strong because of the preponderant number of women in a city that had lost hundreds of thousands of men in the war. The communists managed temporarily to block the top position from Ernst Reuter, a former communist who had turned away from the doctrine and who later became mayor of West Berlin. In the meantime Louise Schroeder, a gallant woman in fragile health who remained staunchly pro-Western under trying circumstances, held this post.

His Leadership From 1948 On

The SED's true character was finally revealed by the Berlin blockade in 1948. From that time on, Ulbricht's leadership in the East Zone became increasingly evident. Developments at this time are viewed by Carola Stern as connected with the Soviet-Yugoslav conflict in 1948.[8] Moscow demanded that the communist parties within the satellites be clearly aligned with itself. At a time when the Western Zones of Germany were re-establishing a sound basis for economic reconstruction following the monetary reform of 1948, the authorities in the Soviet Zone were pushing ahead with nationalization and with the planned economy with which Ulbricht had been concerned from 1945 on. The Bolshevization of the party organization also brought about political and social changes. In all these developments Ulbricht took a leading part. He overshadowed Pieck and Grotewohl and demonstrated, as Herbert Wehner[9] said, his major talent, of tireless industry ("*unermuedliche Geschaeftigkeit*"). In his position as general secretary of the SED he claimed that the energy and drive in the GDR would bring about an industrial development not possible in any capitalist system.

[8] Carola Stern, "East Germany," in *Communism in Europe*, ed. William E. Griffith, vol. 2, pp. 75, 135, 136.

[9] Herbert Wehner is now (September 1969) minister of all-German affairs.

Ulbricht's fortunes, as already suggested, changed with changing conditions in Germany and with Moscow's changing estimates of the extent to which it could keep the situation under control. It was not at first clear to the leaders in the Kremlin that the *Spitzbart*—the "one with the goatee"—was necessarily the one to hold the Germans in the East in line. There is reason to think that in 1952 Ulbricht was on his way out. In that year Stalin offered a draft treaty proposing reunification of Germany, conditional on the neutralization of middle Europe and middle Germany and the disarmament of German areas under NATO. At this moment Ulbricht's future was in the balance; the Russians as they strove to weaken the German state and hold it in a nonaligned position could well have thrown him overboard. But this Soviet approach to the German problem was rejected by the Allies and by Bonn as impractical in the long run and clearly at variance with the cold war strategy which had emerged after 1946.

About this time also the tide of refugees from the East Zone became a flood. Their number had not been noticeable until after the blockade and only became a serious issue toward the end of 1952 and the beginning of 1953. By February they were arriving in West Germany at the rate of a thousand a day over the weekends, and in a steady stream throughout the week. The East Germans had become alarmed by the Stalinist policy of oppression and political arrests, and Moscow, fearing that conditions would become unmanageable, had decided on a vigorous Sovietizing policy.

The 1953 Revolt

Production was at a low level; the number of men in the labor force was inadequate; the morale of the people was depressed. The peasants who refused collectivization suffered considerable persecution. Administrative reforms had already been announced in July 1952. The SED Politburo, aware of the catastrophic economic and political consequences of forced socialization, reached the conclusion that a "quick change in the situation was necessary yet impossible without foreign [Soviet] help. . . . Ulbricht especially expected that Stalin . . . would come to his aid with a powerful injection of rubles."[10] But no help was forthcoming, and the word after Stalin's death was that the hard socialization policy was to come to a halt. Ulbricht however refused to take this line and instead turned to hard Stalinist methods. The result was the revolt in Berlin and the revolutionary resistance that spread like wildfire throughout East Germany. The trigger had been the plasterers' demonstration in the Stalinallee on June 16–17, 1953. This in turn had been set off by the decision of May 28 to increase the norms or work requirements. For days the fate of the regime throughout East Germany was challenged. The norms were later lowered.[11]

Even before the revolt, however, Vladimir S. Semenov, the newly appointed high commissioner of the USSR in Germany, had come to Berlin to arrange the changes to be inaugurated as the New Course. This program would have lessened class warfare, halted the struggle against the church, and provided concessions in travel and other liberalizations. The fact that the uprising was a dramatic challenge to the system, that it was blamed on "fascist provocation"[12] and Allied incitement against the regime, may have saved Ulbricht from removal. His dismissal was said to have been planned in Moscow together with a comprehensive purge and many concessions to the middle classes in an effort to improve the economy. The effort came too late. Ulbricht's determination to avoid concessions to the mutinous workers played a part in re-establishing him. For the next two years he worked under the resolutions of the Fifteenth Party Congress, held in July, and instituted a program of tough measures that, he claimed, were raising the standard of living and increasing the availability of consumer goods. In fact in the course of the next few years he did succeed, in spite of many crises, in effecting a few minor improvements in production. Thus the policy of socialization stagnated, and in East Germany the post-Stalinist policy was put into effect by a "notorious Stalinist."[13]

[10] Stern, "East Germany," pp. 69, 70.
[11] Stefan Brant, *The East German Rising*, passim.
[12] Stern, "East Germany," p. 71.
[13] Ibid., p. 72.

Ulbricht and Khrushchev

Meantime Ulbricht managed to keep in the good graces of Nikita Khrushchev, insisted on the importance of separation from the western part of Germany, denounced NATO, rejected free elections, and pressed for a tough Russian policy toward the Federal Republic, as did the Kremlin fifteen years later in the case of Czechoslovakia. Thus he could count as a success the fact that Khrushchev tried in November 1958 to force the Western Allies out of Berlin and to end the occupation. This aggressive aim was followed by a period of maneuver in Geneva and Washington, during which Khrushchev secured from the meeting of the foreign ministers in Geneva in 1959 the promise of a summit conference and an invitation to Washington.[14] There was talk of coexistence, and the word "detente" was heard in many quarters. There was no apparent desire in Russia or in Washington to bring matters in Germany to a critical stage. This left Ulbricht unsatisfied but still able to pursue his aims in the GDR itself. There was no substantial change in his position until 1961.

The Vienna meeting of Kennedy and Khrushchev in that year and the note demanding the withdrawal of the Allied occupying forces from Berlin marked the next major development that worked to Ulbricht's advantage. Anxiety in the GDR over what the United States President might do and the signs of a possible change in U.S. policy, suggested in speeches by various Senators in Washington during the period between the presentation of the note in June and its rejection in July, led to a strong upsurge in the number of refugees fleeing the Zone. This exodus convinced Ulbricht that the stability of his regime was shaken. He went to Moscow for help.[15]

The Berlin Wall

Subsequent events indicate that Ulbricht was assured of the support he requested and that from this time until the Cuban

[14] The summit meeting which was to have taken place in Paris in May 1960 was cancelled when Khrushchev used the pretext of the U-2 flights to leave in anger.

[15] Kurt L. Shell, *Bedrohung und Bewaehrung*, pp. 27–53, 353–78.

missile crisis in 1962 the Kremlin left GDR policy and programs largely in his control. The result was the Wall, built in 1961 on the assumption that the Western powers would not intervene and that they and the Soviets were more concerned with events elsewhere—in Cuba, in Africa, in the Middle East, and in Southeast Asia.

The Wall led to a major change in the eastern part of Germany as for the first time its inhabitants saw their escape route cut off.[16] Factory managers could now rely on their labor force being the same on Monday morning as it had been at the close of the preceding week. Those who could not leave had to consider how they could best live under a political system which seemed firmly entrenched and destined to set the boundaries for their activities for long years to come. They examined the local opportunities for training, promotion, and the pursuit of power. They heard the communists in Pankow speak with a new confidence, they learned that production in the GDR was climbing, and they found that the food and clothing available were sufficient to provide a standard of decency, though little beyond. Cynically they accepted conditions which they were powerless to change as they adapted themselves to the system against which they had formerly wished to revolt.

The Wall was the inevitable result of the Soviet leaders' decision to limit the policy of detente[17] and to maintain a separate socialist state between the Federal Republic and Poland and Czechoslovakia. Except for Berlin, the previous separation of the area had been nearly complete; along the "green border" stretching from the Baltic to Bavaria the "death strip," the electric fences, the watch towers and patrols were a threat to life and limb. But until 1961 no threats or partial measures had sufficed to stem the outpouring of men that denuded the factories and farms of considerable portions of the labor force. The more the harsh methods of Stalinist Ulbricht were used to consolidate socialism, the greater the problem became. For years the question had been whether in the long run restrictions within East Germany coupled with strong measures

[16] Dulles, *Berlin*, p. 50. For a detailed study of this period, see the chapter entitled "The Wall," pp. 47–78 and the references cited on pp. 48, 50, 52.
[17] Eleanor Lansing Dulles and Robert Dickson Crane, eds., *Détente*, pp. 121–37.

against external travel might suffice. In the end Ulbricht risked the adverse propaganda and took the ugly measures needed to divide the City of Berlin. They proved simple and effective. The Western Allies countered bricks and concrete with familiar words of protest and condemnation—and beyond that, almost nothing.[18]

Ulbricht's Character and Achievement

The verdict on Ulbricht varies, though all admit his extraordinary organizing ability. He has, on the one hand, failed to win a peace treaty or to prevail on the Soviets to grant the independence of action which he seemed to desire. Russian troops have not been withdrawn. The expansion of the economy, on the other hand, has been impressive. He effected a certain amount of de-Stalinization, and his emphasis on a new youth policy made him seem more attractive in some quarters. It is difficult to judge the state of opinion among people who have no free press, limited discussion, and no institutions for self-expression. Certainly Ulbricht held almost unquestioned and dictatorial power during these years. Some have used the word "charisma" in describing him, and as the unchallenged head of the party apparatus, he is accepted by a few as a father image.[19]

In the absence of more evidence, one can only speculate as to how many within the GDR would describe him in the words used by James F. Brown:

> Personally he has never had much to recommend him; unfriendly, unsympathetic, and cowardly, he is a thoroughly dislikable man. As far as ability is concerned, however, he should not be underestimated. He has great intelligence, a rare memory, notable political skill, talents of the highest order as an administrator and organizer. These qualities are undermined however by an almost complete lack of imagination and flexibility, and a rigid devotion to dogmatic communism. As a Comintern organizer, he must have been superb.

[18] In cooperation with the other NATO allies temporary travel documents were denied to East German officials and business travelers, slowing down trade for some months.

[19] Ernst Richert, *Macht ohne Mandat*, pp. 78, 258.

> As leader of the GDR he made an already impossible situation more impossible.[20]

This assessment of his ability is supported by the following description by Wolfgang Leonhard:

> His strong points were his talents as an organizer, his phenomenal memory for names, his skill in foreseeing each successive change in the Party line, and his tireless industry. He never seemed to be exhausted even after the longest day's work. I seldom saw him laugh, and I do not remember ever having detected any signs of personal emotion. Being entirely innocent of theoretical ideas or personal feelings, to the best of my knowledge he never failed to carry out the directives transmitted to him by the Soviet authorities with ruthlessness and skill.[21]

ECONOMIC DEVELOPMENT

About the substantial increase in production in the GDR there has been no serious debate for the last three years. The history of this economic development has been marked by occasional drama; it has been throughout closely tied to the fortunes of Walter Ulbricht; and while in theory the economy has been planned, in fact it has been affected in large measure by political events which threatened the very foundations of Germany, both East and West.

The war had destroyed the monetary, transport, and industrial systems throughout Germany. The Soviet authorities, taking full advantage of the leeway allowed them for reparation removals, took from their Zone industrial capital and enormous amounts of machinery and equipment valued by them at approximately 25 billion DM, in addition to uncompensated deliveries out of current production.[22] Western estimates are quoted as between DM 45 and 60 billion. During this chaotic period, the Russian soldiers lived off the land, and their looting and disorderly behavior prevented the

[20] James F. Brown, *The New Eastern Europe*, p. 263.
[21] Leonhard, *Child of the Revolution*, p. 288.
[22] Joachim Hoffman, *Zentralverwaltungswirtschaft am Beispiel der SPD*, pp. 31, 40.

re-establishment of economic activities. Total losses to the economy through equipment dismantling, deliveries out of current production, and goods taken out at artificially low prices have been estimated at DM 66,440 billion. An accurate accounting is not available. Recovery did not begin for some years.[23]

In spite of these difficulties, Ulbricht attempted to spur on the industrial workers by increasing the demands for higher norms of output. The revolt in Berlin and the uprising throughout the Zone in June 1953 came at the time when the New Course had been ordered from Moscow. But neither Stalin's death in March nor the new policy in the Kremlin had any appreciable influence on Ulbricht.

Economic Plans and Progress

The course of the economic planning in the GDR is somewhat puzzling since plans were announced and then altered in mid-course. The schedule was as follows:

1949–1950 two-year plan
1950–1955 first five-year plan
1956–1959 second five-year plan
1959–1961 seven-year plan, broken off in 1961
1964–1970 "perspective" plan[24]

In appraising the actual development, the difference between these various plans is not of major importance. The plans are mentioned here mainly to assist the reader who will find varying statements in various sources, some of which are neither consistent nor clear. Each plan changed the emphasis as between the different categories of production and was thus of great importance to those who allocated resources and set standards for output. The planners however failed to realize how slowly the forced collectivization of the farms would take effect. The result was that agricultural shortages were a continuous burden on the economy.

[23] Bundesministerium fuer Gesamtdeutsche Fragen, *SBZ von A-Z*, p. 400; Joachim Nawrocki, *Das geplante Wunder*, pp. 19–21. Walter Ulbricht and others in the GDR have estimated the total loss, including that associated with the flight of refugees, at DM 120 billion.

[24] Bundesministerium fuer Gesamtdeutsche Fragen, *SBZ von A-Z*, pp. 534–37.

To the outsider, the early planning appears to have been relatively ineffective. In spite of Ulbricht's urgent and strongly enforced efforts to get the factories going, production continued at a low level until 1953. In that year the major reparation removals stopped; and from then on the demands for occupation costs and deliveries at discount prices were reduced from billions to hundreds of millions.[25]

During these years the rigid system of economic control aroused resistance among the workers, millions of whom fled to the West. Industry made little progress, and there were clear signs of retrogression in agriculture. Ulbricht's independence was limited, and the presence of Soviet soldiers was visual proof of the area's subservient state. The Zone's inhabitants were isolated between a forbidden West and a tightly ruled bloc of satellites. After the 1953 revolt the Iron Curtain—stretching from the Baltic to Bavaria—was more closely watched than ever, and travel from the Zone's outlying provinces to Berlin grew increasingly dangerous. But many young men in the GDR still thought that they could win freedom by resistance. It was only gradually that Ulbricht consolidated his power and improved his standing in Moscow. As time passed, he began to take more account of the German mentality and habits of work and to appeal to the material instincts of the wage earner.

Dr. Erich Apel, a major planner, committed suicide in East Berlin on December 3, 1965. This made a profound impression in East and West Germany. His death was considered to be a protest against Soviet economic methods and in particular Moscow's uncompensated trade demands that made reconstruction of the GDR more difficult and thwarted the new economic system. Although his death was unique in its dramatic impact, he had not been alone in his efforts to achieve greater independence for his countrymen.

In summarizing the state of the economy, if the whole decade between 1945 and 1955 is considered separately as a time of struggle and confusion, the years after 1955 seem to fall roughly into four periods: (1) the postreparation period; (2) the beginning of marked recovery (1955 to 1961); (3) the major upswing after the

[25] Jean E. Smith, "The German Democratic Republic and the West," *International Journal*, Spring 1967, pp. 231–52.

Wall, when forced collectivization produced a more efficient agriculture, and stabilization of the labor force permitted an increase in production; (4) the years following Apel's death when attempts were made to follow the course of development in other lands and attention was given to electrification, automation, and more advanced methods of production. Increases in wages and other financial incentives followed, and the goal of the 5-day 44-hour week was announced.

The "Planned Miracle"

Two main conclusions may be drawn from consideration of the many facts and figures available from both official and unofficial sources. The first is that in spite of various obstacles and setbacks Ulbricht and his associates have achieved a kind of "geplante Wunder."[26] In comparison with the Federal Republic, the GDR started with an initial handicap: during the earlier years after 1950 the difference in living standards, per capita production, and other significant indices was approximately 40 percent. In the early 1960s the GDR began to close the gap. In 1968 it has, according to most observers, reduced it to 25 or 30 percent. Since the improvement during those years in both consumer and producer goods in the Federal Republic continued to be substantial, it can be estimated that the living standards of the GDR in 1968 approximated those of the FRG in the mid-fifties. The pace of further progress is open to question.

The second general conclusion is that Ulbricht and his administrators must expect difficulties in the path ahead. These have been foreshadowed to some extent in statements made on November 23 and 24, 1967, in the third plenary meeting of the SED Central Committee. In this meeting Guenther Mittag, secretary of economic affairs, openly discussed the "acute economic problems"[27] facing the economy. He stated that the products of the GDR were competitive neither in quality nor in price with those in other countries. It would not be possible, he said, to abolish the export subsidies unless improvements were made, since the plan under

[26] Nawrocki, *Wunder*, passim.

[27] See Carola Stern summary (processed), Bonn, November 1967.

which the economy was operating was inadequate both because of insufficient nationalization and because of unsatisfactory progress in automation. Ulbricht asserted that the goals the plan set forth would be reached but added that the export industries could not be considered the best part of the economy.

Table 3
Foreign Trade of the GDR, 1950–1967
(In Millions of Valuta Marks)

	Exports	*Imports*
1950	1,705.3	1,972.5
1955	5,368.2	4,925.4
1960	9,200.4	9,112.9
1965	12,732.2	11,568.4
1966	13,354.0	13,219.1
1967	14,398.5	13,454.3

Source: Staatliche Zentralverwaltung fuer Statistik, *Statistisches Jahrbuch der DDR, 1968*, p. 32.

The growth of foreign trade from 1950 to 1967 (see table 3) has been steady but not as rapid as the reported growth in production. There appears to have been some recent dissatisfaction with the situation. In 1967 the trade—sometimes forced rather than free—with socialist countries accounted for 20,786.8 million marks out of a total of 27,852.8 million marks for all exports and imports. The more competitive trade with "capitalist industry countries" accounted for 5,800.5 million marks and that with developing countries for 1,265.5.

Some believe that the development of industry may be stalled by the inadequacy of transport, the lack of modern techniques, the failure to innovate, and the absence of a price-market system to guide production in a more flexible manner than is possible under centralized planning. The perennial and growing indebtedness of the GDR in its trade with West Germany is a sign of unmastered difficulties. Manfred von Arden, a leading member of the *Volkskammer*, told the writer in July 1967 that the economic disparity between East and West Germany was still too great to permit freedom of travel. The Wall would have to be kept, he said, to obviate the risk of further labor losses to the West.

Thus, in spite of the substantial accomplishments in the past ten years, the future of the economy remains uncertain. Russia is said to have required a larger share of the production in 1968 than in 1967.[28] Agricultural problems are still not completely solved. The attempt to introduce incentives may have reached limits which will not easily be surpassed.

Gross National Product

The tables in the official *Statistisches Jahrbuch der DDR* are revealing, but they do not tell the whole story. A detailed study of the interaction of many sectors of the economy would be needed to throw light on future prospects. One of the best overall indicators is the measurement of the increases in the Gross National Product (see table 4). Between 1950 and 1955 production increased each year as organization improved and the country gradually recovered

Table 4
Economic Growth of the GDR, 1950–1967
(In Millions of Valuta Marks)

	Gross National Product	*Industry*	*National Income*[a] *(net)*
1950	53,894	34,150	29,109
1951	64,592	41,391	35,252
1952	74,962	47,468	40,130
1953	81,836	52,218	42,443
1954	89,040	59,953	46,063
1955	96,432	64,471	50,037
1960	142,885	98,348	70,520
1965	198,640	137,433	82,802
1966	201,562	144,227	87,167
1967	226,980	154,390	92,210

Source: Statistisches Jahrbuch der DDR, 1968, p. 17.

Note: The categories are not directly comparable to those for the Federal Republic, but the general significance is the same.

[a] Equivalent to net social product but according to the Ministry of All-German Affairs does not include such special services as civil services, housing, banks, insurance.

[28] Ibid.

from the effects of the war, political interference, and the various losses it had sustained through Soviet occupation.[29]

While it is impossible to demonstrate the accuracy of these figures, most economists in West Germany accept them as valid indications of the changes which have been taking place. There were also plausible figures showing an increase in exports and improvement in living conditions for some years. The rate of change is impressive and was not at first fully appreciated outside the GDR. The main drag on the economy was a deficiency in services, transport, and agriculture.

Heavy Industry

In considering particular branches of industrial production, steel is of primary interest.[30] It was not until 1953 that the production of crude steel equalled and surpassed the 1936 production. By 1960 it was three times the prewar figure, rising again by approximately 20 percent in the output for 1966 (see table 5). The increases in steel production in the Federal Republic were substantial, but the major

Table 5
Coal, Iron, and Steel Production in the GDR, 1950–1967
(In Thousands of Tons)

	Crude Brown Coal	*Brown Coal Briquettes*	*Pig Iron*	*Crude Steel*	*Rolled Steel*
1950	137,050	37,697	337.2	998.7	780.7
1955	200,612	50,967	1,516.6	2,507.5	1,884.1
1960	225,465	56,047	1,994.7	3,337.0	2,613.3
1965	250,839	60,380	2,338.0	3,890.0	2,986.3
1966	249,040	59,426	2,447.7	4,084.5	3,051.0
1967	242,027	56,087	2,525.0	4,243.2	3,075.2

Source: Statistisches Jahrbuch der DDR, 1968, p. 22.

Note: The figures seem to show that although brown coal production declined in 1966, iron and steel production continued to rise. This probably indicates that (1) the GDR increased its import of brown coal; or (2) different types of fuel are now being used; or (3) production methods have been improved.

[29] Staatliche Zentralverwaltung fuer Statistik, *Statistisches Jahrbuch der Deutschen Demokratischen Republik*, (hereafter cited as *Statistisches Jahrbuch der DDR*) gives totals required by USSR as MDN 11,121.9 million in 1967 and MDN 11,777.1 million in 1968.

[30] See also *Statistisches Jahrbuch der DDR*, 1968, p. 25.

Table 6
Industrial Production in the GDR, 1950–1967: Selected Areas
(In Units)

	Turbines	*Electric locomotives*	*Tractors*[a]	*Automobiles*	*Motorcycles and Scooters*
1950	4,422	71	5,170	7,165	9,607
1955	4,851	212	7,792	22,247	61,141
1960	5,778	420	9,076	64,071	90,319
1965	3,546	283	12,923	102,877	63,800
1966	3,332	247	12,210	106,460	67,464
1967	2,959	123	11,120	111,516	62,769

	Household Refrigerators	*Electric Washing Machines*	*Radios*[b]	*Televisions*
1950	658	769	277,258	—
1955	17,329	18,409	724,659	38,610
1960	138,569	132,461	809,582	416,490
1965	364,805	288,908	808,008	536,744
1966	359,625	314,324	900,751	561,564
1967	402,984	323,913	932,009	474,657

Source: Statistisches Jahrbuch der DDR, 1968, pp. 23, 24.

[a] In 1948, tractor production stood at 45 units produced. The 1955 to 1960 increase is also somewhat misleading as, between those years, production reached a low of 3,881 units.

[b] In 1962, production was over 1 million, while in 1964 it dropped to approximately 625,000 units.

postwar rise in production came earlier. Production in all major categories of heavy goods in East Germany exhibited a similar upward trend (see table 6).

Transport

Although the figures for internal transport show steady growth in the tonnage transported by rail and by truck, there is reason to think that efficiency is low and facilities inadequate. Certainly the conditions for road traffic and the state of the flow of goods appear primitive by comparison with those obtaining in West Germany and comparable to those prevailing in other European countries immediately after the war. Some annual transport totals since 1950 have been:[31]

[31] Ibid., p. 29.

	Thousand Tons
1950	225,794
1955	389,667
1960	522,148
1965	624,634
1966	640,814
1967	646,623

In these totals, the increase in truck transport has been more substantial than that in rail transport. The use of air freight is not indicated in the statistical reports. The general conclusion to be drawn both from comments in the press and from the appearance of the equipment is that this aspect of the economy has lagged behind the others. The number of persons transported, as might be expected in view of the desire to limit mobility, has scarcely increased at all over the last sixteen years. Goods transport by rail and by road is still far below the requirements of industry. This branch of the economy suffered particularly heavy losses through war destruction and removals. Moreover the competition for steel with the growing industry planned with USSR interests in mind has been a retarding factor. The result is seen in the notorious lack of new trucks and cars and in the lack of modernization of railroad equipment.

Agriculture

The weakest area of production has been agriculture (see table 7). Here the attack on tradition and custom has been violent but

Table 7
Agricultural Production in the GDR, 1950–1967
(In Thousands)

	Head of Cattle	*Tons of Grain*	*Tons of Potatoes*	*Tons of Sugar Beets*
1950	3,614.7	2,724.0	4,804.0	5,429.7
1955	3,759.5	2,041.7	3,429.9	4,914.4
1960	4,675.3	1,881.8	3,441.1	6,516.7
1965	4,762.3	2,220.5	3,820.3	5,389.6
1966	4,918.3	2,161.4	3,800.0	6,119.5
1967	5,018.5	2,166.3	3,938.2	6,113.7

Source: Statistisches Jahrbuch der DDR, 1968, pp. 27, 28.

only partially successful. The proportion of small farms abolished in the process of forced collectivization reached more than 93 percent by the end of 1967. This program had met with resistance and was not pressed aggressively until after the building of the Berlin Wall. Before that time there had been a continuous exodus of farmers from the Zone. In spite of resistance, the number of large cooperative farms[32] rose rapidly from 10,132 in 1959 to 19,261 in 1960. By 1963, 5,981 thousand hectares had been socialized while 413 thousand remained unsocialized.[33] Slight increases are reported for pigs, poultry, and some other categories of products. But it is clear that agriculture suffered from inadequate organization, disruption consequent on the shift to collective farms and loss of motivation. The situation, as reported by the communist government, has been far from satisfactory. Staple foods are in considerably better supply than a few years ago, and food rationing was abolished in 1958. But commodities still lack quality and variety, and the supply of reasonably priced foods is inadequate. Thousands with low earning power are close to the poverty line.

Trade with the Federal Republic

The continuing exchange of goods in interzonal trade is still—as it has been for the past ten years—an important element in the relations between the Federal Republic and the GDR (see table 8). Its advocates urge that the Federal Republic should increase deliveries to East Germany and enlarge the "swing" or credit available to the GDR for unbalanced deliveries. Some have even asked: "Why don't we in the Federal Republic have a Marshall Plan for the East?" They urge the advantage of trade contacts, the desirability of improving living standards in the GDR, and the influence that a prosperous economy would have in making East Germany more independent and liberal in her politics. Its opponents, on the other hand, urge that unbalanced deliveries to those who cannot pay for them are not good either for those who send the goods or for those who incur the debts. They even suggest that industrial exports of this type only serve to boost Ulbricht's

[32] *Landwirtschaftliche Produktionsgenossenschaften* (LPGs).

[33] Bundesministerium fuer Gesamtdeutsche Fragen, *Vierter Taetigkeitsbericht 1961/1965*, 1965, p. 92.

Table 8
Exchange of Goods and Services Between the FRG and the GDR, 1950–1967
(In Millions of DM)

	Received by the FRG[a]	*Delivered by the FRG*[a]	*Totals*
1950	450.8	359.0	809.8
1955	583.5	576.4	1,159.9
1960	1,007.3	1,030.3	2,037.6
1965	1,249.0	1,224.9	2,473.9
1966	1,323.7	1,680.8	3,004.5
1967	1,255.0	1,491.0	2,746.0

Source: Mimeographed tables prepared by Federal Ministry for Economics, FRG.
[a] Including West Berlin.

trength. Or they state that a more liberal attitude toward the GDR would be viewed by the West as subsidizing communism. They remember the time when Washington inquired: "Why hould we support Berlin with aid if you are supplying goods on avorable terms to those who harass and threaten the freedom of he city?" That was some years ago, and since then the situation in Europe and in Germany has become more complex. Moreover the ttitude toward East-West trade has altered in many quarters. No ecent objection to interzonal trade has been voiced either in Germany or outside. The total value has increased every year since 962, except in 1967. In that year there was an almost 9 percent decline. The increase in the uncompensated deliveries by the FRG was approximately DM 236 million in 1967—an increase in the debt of the GDR.

THE GDR TODAY

Torn as it is between conflicting ideologies and between gravitaional pulls toward capitalism and toward socialism, toward the East and toward the West, toward the past and toward an uncharted future, the GDR cannot continue indefinitely in its present situation. Under existing conditions the problem cannot be esolved. Its future solution will depend on developments within he GDR itself and in the states that border it. Meanwhile the gulf between the two parts of Germany widens, while within the GD the disagreements and variations of opinion are suppressed but no unrecognized.[34]

The GDR cannot be a nation until it has undergone majo changes. The Soviets must have ceased to be its main source o security, and its people must have achieved the freedom of choic now enjoyed, even in many nations part-free and part-slave unde dictatorship. The many educational opportunities now open in th GDR will eventually increase the desire for more political freedom Pressures to conform will not be able to continue to repress th minds of oncoming generations in a country that is surrounded b nations where stirrings of unrest have already broken out into th open. The legal basis for more freedom is said to be well develope An intricate structure of useful councils, assemblies, chambers, an courts is already in existence.[35]

As stated at the beginning of this chapter, the GDR differs fro other Soviet satellites. It is at one and the same time more of colony and more Western in its background and methods. As it is member of the Warsaw Pact, its troops are completely integrate in Warsaw Pact forces. Its territory is still occupied by the Sovie army, and Ulbricht has on numerous occasions been to Moscow fo orders and for help. Ernst Richert analyzes the major politica military, and economic differences that distinguish the GDR fron the other satellites and emphasizes its peculiar legal status.[36] Thes differences afford an explanation, though not a justification, for th isolation of an area that could in some circumstances be unsettle by contacts with neighboring states.

It may be that the present phase is a temporary pause betwee the past period of vocal protest and flight to the West and a futur

[34] Only passing reference can be made here to the problems of adjustin East German law to Marxism, which constitutes a major element in the po litical life. The changes developed constitute another barrier between th two parts of Germany. They are explored in *Die Lage des Rechts in Mitte deutschland* (ed. Fritz Rittner et al.), and Siegfried Mampel, *The Politic Structure of the Soviet Sector and Its Relationship to the Soviet Zone*, p. 2

[35] David Childs, "The East German Elite: The Red Jesuits and Others, *The World Today* (January 1966) 22:32–41; Richert, *Macht ohne Manda* pp. 24–53.

[36] Richert, *Macht ohne Mandat*, pp. 1–23.

time of restlessness and struggle for a freer system, with freedom for travel, access to information from abroad, and freedom of cultural expression. If such a trend emerges in the next five or ten years, it will present the Federal Republic with new problems and questions that could not be answered in Washington or Moscow, or easily in Bonn.

The Shackles on Religious Freedom

Professor Jean Smith asserts that "the political and social institutions created in the GDR seem to have taken root." He adds that "the church policy of the GDR has been consistently the most liberal and enlightened of any state in East Europe,"[37] but his view is not borne out by other commentators. My visit to East Germany and my discussions with churchmen and others in Bonn and Berlin left me with a different impression. The power of the state over the church and the difficulties of communication between East and West were manifest in one instance in the sudden reversal of plans for the October 1967 celebration in Wittenberg of Martin Luther's *Stand* 450 years earlier. Many who had expected to participate were not allowed to attend the meeting. It is reported that the situation is becoming steadily worse. Both Welles Hangen[38] and Markus Barth[39] place considerable blame on the church in West Germany for the lack of communication. In his analysis of the problem of the church in the GDR, Barth discusses how far and in what fashion religious leaders there must accommodate to conditions and Marxist doctrines in order to survive. Some of the Christians, he said, consider themselves as Christians in exile; but the church lives.

Intellectual and Academic Freedom

In the intellectual world, the dismissal from the East German Academy of Science on April 10, 1966, of Robert Havemann,[40]

[37] Jean Edward Smith, "Red Prussianism," *Bulletin of the Atomic Scientists*, May 1967, pp. 25, 28, 30.
[38] Welles Hangen, *The Muted Revolution*, pp. 181, 182.
[39] Markus Barth, "Church and Communism in East Germany," *Christian Century*, November 23–30, 1966, pp. 1440–43.
[40] In 1968 Havemann's two sons were on trial in East Berlin for expressing views on Czechoslovakia.

distinguished professor of physical chemistry, did not go unnoticed. In mid-1965 the SED Central Committee had turned against "many artists, editors, and cultural functionaries who had allegedly fallen victims to subversive tendencies, nihilistic and anarchistic attitudes, or revisionist trends,"[41] and further criticism of writers and artists in September of the same year indicated that all was not well in this area.

The authorities in East Germany are not unaware of the restlessness in East Europe and of the possibility that the firm control they seem to exercise may yield to new and uncontrollable elements. They were said in March 1968 to be planning university reforms.[42] According to the news story, the students were to be given larger influence in planning courses. A study, to be conducted by economic and public authorities, was to examine the conditions which motivated young students to become "socialist personalities," and to analyze their patterns of behavior in school, at home, and in their leisure time. The same news item stated: "In a further step of cautious restraint, the East German regime was reported to have barred marches in East Berlin and at other major centers in protest against the war in Vietnam."

There is no doubt that the leaders in Pankow are anxious to expand the capacity of their educational system and that they are providing training to as many young people as possible. The total numbers of students enrolled in the *Hochschule* (advanced schools and colleges) and universities in various years between 1951 and 1965 are given as: [43]

1951	31,512
1955	74,742
1960	101,773
1961	112,929
1962	114,002
1963	115,673
1964	110,664
1965	108,313[44]

[41] Hoover Institution on War, Revolution, and Peace, *Yearbook on International Communist Affairs, 1966*, p. 58.

[42] *New York Times*, March 16, 1968.

[43] See *Statistisches Jahrbuch der DDR, 1966*, p. 474.

[44] 63.6 per 10,000 inhabitants.

Certain fundamental educational questions however remain so far unanswered.[45] What conception, for instance, do the men in Pankow have of education? Do they understand the process of widening horizons and broadening the mind? Can they risk encouraging true research and the questioning of dogma? Is it possible to permit freedom of thought and new ideas in their schools and universities? The predominance among a growing number of university students of education in the physical sciences is an indication of the emphasis of the present system and the rewards and pressures which guide the choices of youth. The number of university students enrolled in the liberal arts curriculum amounts to only about 4 percent of the total student body. Analysis of the 108,313 students in *Hochschule* and universities in 1965 gave the following statistics for enrollment in various fields:[46]

Mathematics	8,632
Technical studies	27,451
Agricultural, veterinary and forestry	8,208
Medicine	13,630
Economics and Law	13,249
Philosophy, languages and music	2,618
Art	1,604
Physical education	1,117
Theology	642
Pedagogy	31,162

Speculation as to future psychological developments and independence is hazardous. The reason for questioning the content of education in the GDR lies in the silence of students whose counterparts elsewhere question and object. There are few reasons to believe that the men at the top realize the potential for change that lies under the surface in East Germany.

Debate will continue as to the durability of a system which lacks revolutionary fervor, the inspiration of individualism, or the vigor of representative democracy. The fact that there is no immediate

[45] For general discussion of these problems see *Dokumente zur Jugendpolitik der SED* (ed. Siegfried Duebel), and Joachim H. Knoll and Horst Siebert, *Erwachsenenbildung, Erwachsenenqualifizierung.*

[46] See *Statistisches Jahrbuch der DDR, 1966,* pp. 475, 476.

intention to allow free contacts with the outside world and the fact that there are still more than 200,000 Soviet soldiers garrisoned in the GDR,[47] indicate that those who are in command in Pankow and in Moscow do not consider the regime to be secure. The progress made so far has been in material production—in pounds and in bushels. Administration has been tightened, techniques have been sharpened, wages have risen, enterprises have been socialized. It is impossible to deny these and other substantial changes over the last decade. How long this drive will continue and what levels of prosperity will be reached cannot now be forecast. Sooner or later efforts will be made to modernize the economy further by wider contacts with the outside world. This trend and the predictable restlessness of the younger generation, now impressed by the recovery from dire want to a reasonable standard of living, will in this later phase stir new impulses in the people in the GDR. It is hard to imagine that a state of affairs can continue with East Germany the most oppressed and the most controlled of the states within the Russian sphere of influence. The day of reckoning for the rulers may be distant, but it will come. The GDR cannot in years ahead stand alone: it does not lean to the East, it cannot align with the West. This is the current paradox which puzzles impartial observers, both East and West.

Ulbricht himself has modified his position slightly over the last twenty years. He cannot be blind and deaf to what has happened in Czechoslovakia, to the students' agitation in Poland and elsewhere; he and his associates must realize that it is increasingly difficult to isolate a nation. The infection of ideas surmounts the Wall and penetrates beyond the barrier of the Iron Curtain.[48] Over the world the young are storming the barriers of tradition and system. The Germans of the oncoming generation cannot be expected to stand

[47] The Institute for Strategic Studies, *The Military Balance, 1968–69,* p. 6, states that there are twenty divisions in East Germany, two in Poland and four in Hungary. Ten tank divisions are in East Germany. The total size of the army is estimated at 2,000,000 men in 140 divisions.

[48] Ossip K. Flechtheim, *Weltkommunismus im Wandel,* pp. 236–41. There is still a fortified, electrified barbed wire area, mined, enclosed, and with closely spaced watch towers dividing German territory—the Iron Curtain.

apart and accept without protest what is being imposed on them by men in their sixties and seventies. It is too early yet for Ulbricht to think of himself as King Canute. But it seems safe to forecast that at some time, he will see the tide of independent thought and emotion rolling in irresistibly—relentlessly. For this he and his fellows in Pankow are ill prepared. They are entrenched in a rigid system. It may be that the men in the Kremlin, with their experience of changing relations with Yugoslavia, Czechoslovakia, and China, fear the possibility of revisionism or revolt more than Ulbricht fears it.

Strength and Weakness

The strength of the GDR is political, economic, and military. The total of its regular armed forces at present is 127,000 men in the army, navy, and air force. There are in addition 70,000 security and border troops and 250,000 armed workers in the *Betriebskampfgruppen* organization. This not inconsiderable number of men is supplemented and supported for many purposes by the 200,000 or more Soviet soldiers garrisoned in the country. Meanwhile the training of the young men in paramilitary units goes on.[49]

The economic strength is obvious. It may however have reached a plateau as more complex types of production and more varied consumption make the process of planning more difficult. Questions of quality and standards of output are destined to come to the fore. Demands for better and cheaper goods are inevitable. As already stated, the future of exports depends on considerable improvement in quality to meet foreign competition.

The political stability and control so long associated with Ulbricht are no longer so assured, now that prospective changes in leadership are impending. Although none of the experts now writing forecasts serious trouble in the next few years, it should be remembered that many unpredicted changes have taken place in Europe and elsewhere. The GDR cannot escape the stirrings of unrest among young people which have been so widely manifest.

[49] Institute for Strategic Studies, *Military Balance*, p. 3.

When such challenges to the established order will emerge cannot be forecast. The main complaints at present are against travel restrictions and party control in the field of the arts.

In 1968 the authorities in Pankow showed considerable concern. On January 30 the Politburo's Ideological Commission issued a report that "the enemy" was "making special efforts to halt the building of Socialism by psychological warfare." Kurt Hager, the well-known communist journalist, warned of "so-called cultural exchanges" of publishers, writers, professors, and artists. This report also attacked the "dangerous convergence theory" which was designed "to destroy" the socialist system. The fact that it also gave considerable attention to "subversive" Western theories suggests that the break with capitalist West Germany was not as complete as the SED leaders wished.

As the 1968 reforms in Czechoslovakia progressed, the fear of contamination in the GDR mounted. Ulbricht expressed his anger at the Czechoslovak developments in the six-nation communist summit meeting in Dresden in the spring and later in Warsaw in July. He tried to use his influence to slow down the pace of change. His sensitivity to change in nearby countries increased.

The most visible sign of weakness is the Wall. The manifestation of fear of defection and revolt is the Iron Curtain and the well-named death strip along the western frontier. Those who rule the GDR cannot risk the influence of and comparison with life in the free democratic world. They cannot offer the same quality of living. They must therefore isolate their workers and keep their young men from traveling. Only after the Wall has been dismantled and the barbed wire has been torn from the frontier will it be possible to make a different assessment.

Significance to Other Nations

The significance of the GDR for the Russians, for the Germans in the West, and for the United States calls for continuing examination. Russia's hopes of ruling most of central Europe after the war were dashed when Austria escaped communist domination, West Germany joined NATO, and resistance to Soviet expansion led to a revision of the Moscow timetable.[50] The Soviet Zone, however, has served as a richly productive workshop and a bulwark protecting the western flank of the Soviet empire. The gains from this situation are not necessarily without cost in their relations to other countries. As time goes on, neither the economic situation nor the security aspects will be the same as they have been in the past decades.

In the present fluid situation the leaders in Moscow cannot stand still: they must either adjust to the increasing pressures of their former satellites for wider contacts and greater independence or return to the more brutal methods of the Lenin-Stalin past. Either course would influence the attitudes and drives of the East Germans and modify—perhaps limit—the economic and political forces within the GDR which now seem to be working in favor of the Soviets. The conditions under which the Kremlin would change whatever price it may set for freeing the East Germans can only dimly be discerned. The concessions it would require in return for permitting the GDR's association with the community of Western Europe would change with changing conditions both inside and outside the area.

For Bonn too the situation is affected by its internal capacities and the external situation.[51] In the early postwar period Konrad Adenauer and his associates deliberately decided that NATO membership and close alliance with the West must take priority.[52] This choice was made specific on many occasions, notably in the response to the Soviet proposal of March 10, 1952, for the neutralization of Germany.[53] Fifteen years later, when the Federal Republic had significantly increased its strength and the security issues in Europe had changed, Bonn began to show a different emphasis in its attitude to future relations with the GDR. In face of the

[50] The Soviets in exploiting their zone of occupation deprived the area of equipment worth billions of DM. See p. 69 above and Ferenc A. Vali, *The Quest for a United Germany*, pp. 139, 140.

[51] For a discussion of current West German policy, see chapter 3.

[52] Konrad Adenauer, *Erinnerungen 1953–1955*, pp. 66–82.

[53] U.S. Department of State, *Documents on Germany, 1944–1959*, pp. 85–88.

increasing stability of the Pankow regime and the improvement in the East German economy, the question of future possibilities took on a different form. To the older generation the significance of East-West association with the cooperation of 70 million people has remained a vital element in long-run foreign policy but has become a distant goal—a goal to be reached only in the context of a new Europe, a comprehensive cooperative system, and at the cost of abandoned illusions[54] and of adjustment between different types of institutions now strongly entrenched in the two societies.

To the United States the division of Germany has been disturbing on two counts. There has been concern over possible revanchism in Germany and anxiety over the unstable situation in Europe because of Germany. Some Americans have considered that the existence of two German states meant a diminished threat to world peace, but the majority of statesmen and experts have not shared this view. They have held to the policy, often reiterated in connection with their position on Berlin and on the German question generally, that the United States support the policy of reunification. But they recognize that conditions change and that the terms of bargaining and methods of achieving progress must also change.

The United Kingdom, France,[55] and the other nations of Europe have the GDR under constant observation. Sometimes interest in reunification declines to a low point, but the major powers weigh the accomplishments of the GDR and estimate its attitudes as they seek to measure the degree of its subordination and the seriousness of its claims to independence.

In the light of the many swift and unpredictable developments that may take place in Europe, prophecy of future trends is unwise. The best service that can be rendered in this connection consists of

[54] One of these illusions was abandoned with the widespread acceptance in the late 1960s of the loss of the territories east of the Oder-Neisse line.

[55] The statements made by government officials in France and the United Kingdom are interesting and various, but their concurrence in the position of the United States makes an inclusion of these pronouncements unnecessary at this point. British and French policy is considered in more detail in chapter 9.

examination of the evident facts and study of the different possible directions in which events may move. One can note the reasons why complete communization is unlikely and yet understand why early reunification is impossible. In the evolving situation economic conditions and political personalities all play a part. The existence of Ulbricht has been a major factor in making possible Soviet control of the Zone. After his time is over, new elements will emerge. No sharp and immediate change in direction is predictable, but readjustments are to be expected both in the GDR and in its neighboring states.[56]

A TRIP TO EAST GERMANY

In July 1967 I made an eight-day trip to the southeast part of the GDR. My objective was to gather firsthand impressions of political and economic conditions in East Germany. I recognized that I could not explore conditions and opinions in depth, but I considered it essential to have certain bench marks—personal contacts and visual impressions—which would give more meaning to future studies in some instances and correct past impressions.

Personal impressions of this type are often superficial and misleading, but without such impressions it is difficult to weigh and judge the categorical, often dogmatic, statements in the voluminous recent literature in this controversial area. Writers and critics differ in their interpretation of the extent and meaning of the economic progress made so far, the position of Ulbricht, the attitude of the seventeen million East Germans toward their government and toward the outside world, and their thoughts about the future of Germany and the Germans. A number of newsmen and others, seeking to compensate for misjudgments in earlier appraisals of conditions in the GDR, now tend to exaggerate the progress and emphasize the achievements of this communist administration and planned economy.[57] This shift is useful since it can serve as a warning to those who took it for granted that the early postwar attitudes and policies could be continued unchanged. Moreover miscalculation on the part of a few in the West has led to a

[56] See discussion of Czechoslovakia and other states in chapter 3.
[57] See "East Germany," *Time*, April 7, 1967, pp. 24–26.

complacency in Bonn and elsewhere which may have slowed down constructive action and new policies.

From 1959 on, a more imaginative and adventurous policy might conceivably have been attempted, but it is difficult even in hindsight to say what such a program could in fact have been. Khrushchev was talking of coexistence, but few people knew what his words meant or what his intentions really were. The result was a slowing down of policy decisions and a lack of aggressive policy in the West, which left its mark on the East Germans. It was clear from my conversations in the GDR that its residents could not understand the lack of clarity in past policy and the failure to take action.[58]

My trip took me from Berlin to Leipzig, Halle, Weimar, Eisenach, Jena, Dresden, Karl Marx Stadt (Chemnitz), Meissen, and back to Berlin. The conditions were favorable. I had a young American companion, Marc Catudal, to drive the small rented Volkswagen in which we traveled some 1,200 or 1,300 kilometers in good weather over small roads and major highways. I was free to talk to a considerable number of people in conditions of relative privacy. Although I was followed throughout the trip by one or more officials assigned to this job, they did not interfere with my doings. The managers of the hotels and some of the servants kept track of my comings and goings. The pressure was there, but occasionally I was alone in a Gaststaette, in a hotel, on a streetcar, or on the street and could exchange unmonitored views with an average German. On one occasion a workman drew up beside the car and said, "You are American, you are lucky." The persons I met seemed free to say what they wished, but usually they spoke in low voices and with a look over the shoulder. In general their views ranged from complacency to sharp criticism. But on some points they were unanimous: they were cynical about reunification; they thought economic progress had been substantial in the past ten years; with the exception of a few officials, they felt and said that the political and cultural conditions were unsatisfactory; they found life dull.

[58] The later development of government positions is discussed in chapter 3 (FRG), chapter 8 (USSR), and chapter 9 (United States).

There was little that I saw and heard that differed from Welles Hangen's story in *The Muted Revolution.* But the emphasis I found differed from that reported in Hans Apel's interviews.[59] As stated earlier, I cannot concur in Jean Smith's general conclusions as to "better living," the acceptance of the treatment of the church by the communist government, or with some of his economic conclusions.[60] But a number of statements in his article in the *International Journal* are valid if taken with a degree of reserve. I concur in his stress on the persistence of "Germanness." No new man has been created in East Germany.

There were many points at which my experiences were similar to those recounted by Countess Doenhoff, Dr. Rudolf Walter Leonhardt, and Theo Sommer, in their book about their journey in March 1964.[61] Many of their observations are still valid: there is a spirit of doubt in the GDR; there are pressures toward a market economy; there will be little prospect of holes in the Wall until the standard of living is higher; while the hate promulgated by the communist authorities finds little echo among the people, there is no likelihood of a counterrevolution against the system; contacts between the two Germanys, where possible, can be useful and can in any case do little harm. It is nearly three years since my conclusions were drawn, and some progress may have been made since then. But the road ahead is long—"*Wir sitzen am laengeren Hebel. Was uns Not tut ist mehr Selbstvertrauen.*" Patience and steadfastness are essential.

Only the more general impressions gained from my trip are noted here. These include attitudes of mind, the appearance of the countryside, the activity in industry, evidence of living standards, and the drabness of the cities. Some of the evident weaknesses of the system are trivial in comparison with the major increases in production, but others indicate the vulnerability, in human terms, of the dictatorial system over the decades. Moreover the improve-

[59] Hans Apel, *Ohne Begleiter.*

[60] Smith, "Red Prussianism," p. 29; idem, "The German Democratic Republic and the West," passim.

[61] Marion Countess Doenhoff, Rudolf Walter Leonhardt, and Theo Sommer, *Reise in ein fernes Land,* pp. 142–43.

ments in the standard of living have stopped short of quality, variety, and style. Some of the shops that I saw had many items such as cheese, butter, chocolate, cigarettes on their shelves, but few people were buying—some said it was only the elite who had the necessary money or privileges to secure luxury goods. Meat still appeared to be scarce. Fruit was almost unobtainable. Clothing was limited in variety and high priced.

Opinions and Attitudes

Conversations with people in the GDR could provide only a sampling of the attitudes to be found, but this sampling led to doubts concerning the repetitive rosy, facile statements to be found not only in the propaganda of the communists but also in books by some recent Western visitors.

Casual meetings without a monitor and the longer conversations that were occasionally possible revealed acceptance, cynicism, and sometimes a sense of recent economic accomplishment. Comments on cultural life were few. Education was praised in terms of its availability but not of its quality.[62] In these unscheduled interviews, only three or four out of some fifty or sixty persons scattered here and there were pro-communist. On the other hand, no one spoke in terms of an uprising or showed any sign of expecting resistance against the regime—there was obviously no place for the dissatisfied to go. The psychological and political walls were as all-encompassing as the physical barriers. Some of the younger men reflected the attitude of the skilled worker who said, "When I was a boy, all was *kaput*. Now things are better." The wife of a high GDR official insisted in argumentative tones: "We were robbed by the Russians; we were helped by no Marshall Plan; but we see what great things we have done in our economy." A junior official in the school system spoke of the dependable advancement and the security offered under the communist regime.

Older workers and intellectuals had a different attitude. They shrugged and said: "There is nothing we can do. We are forgotten

[62] Hangen, *Muted Revolution*, p. 119, quotes from one of his conversations: "Our artists are discouraged by narrow-minded conceptions imposed on them."

by the West, we are oppressed by the government, but we have to live." One worker spoke so bitterly against the administration of his factory and of his locality that I warned him he might be overheard by an official seated a few tables away. He continued in the same vein in spite of my warning. Even those who felt the regime had done an unexpectedly good job in restoring the economy did not speak with enthusiasm. Most of those with whom I talked had a divided view on the United States. They were envious and admiring of luxury and economic accomplishments which they were sure they would never equal. They wished they could go to the United States but felt shut off from all the Western world and resented the fact that in most cases they could not even travel in Eastern Europe. Conscious of their own helplessness, they were bewildered about what went on in other lands. A few spoke of Vietnam but not so vigorously as had the young men in West Germany. Perhaps they were satiated with a propaganda which invariably referred to the United States as the land of murderers and warmongers. No one in the Zone found any appeal in the reiterated slogans, the large red banners, the repetitive messages of hate spread abroad in the cities. One man, talking in a small group of four or five friends, said: "I don't like the war in Vietnam, but if you don't hold there who will stand against communism here or there?"

Political dissatisfaction appeared to have been effectively silenced by the struggle for material survival, the suppression of debate, the presence of informers, and the fear of penalties. The comments showed that there was no hope and little interest in the question of reunification with West Germany. A few spoke of the social benefits and protection available in the GDR, not realizing how far the Western world had moved in the direction of assuring public welfare. Others assumed that the West Germans were indifferent to the fate of those in the East. The restraint which seemed to characterize the life of all who were not officially part of the apparatus was evident in the lack of expressions of their obvious anti-Russian feelings, sense of oppression, and dislike of the communist methods. They were willing to settle for today's bread and butter and hoped that the bread would improve and the butter become cheaper. They were not concerned with such questions as the balance of terror or nuclear extinction. They do not expect the Soviets to fight the Atlantic powers, but they are not convinced that the Western nations have a constructive policy to hold the center of Europe from communism. Their disillusion over the failure of the 1953 uprising has been dimmed by time, but the sense of betrayal remains even as they recognize the capacity for repression possessed by a communist regime that works with the support of more than twenty Russian divisions still in barracks near the large cities.

Living Conditions

Personal ambition—for example, the ownership of a motor scooter or a small car—is still a major goal, to be achieved by hard work, promotion on the job, and saving over a period of several years. Although the recent statistics of car ownership show gains, it is still possible to park at the curb anywhere at any time in the more populated cities. The roads are in fair condition. The scarcity of gas stations is more telling than the official figures in regard to car ownership and use.[63]

Amusement places are few. In the bright July weather and the long summer evenings, one looked in vain for parks with bands, for gay beer terraces and dance halls. There were few cinemas; and the theaters, operas, and concert halls were in their annual closing period of approximately eight weeks.

Some of the museums were frequented by the Germans and also by Russian soldiers. There, as elsewhere, there was a dull and dusty appearance which suggested that the diligence and standards of the workers were declining, except in those pursuits where strict regimentation brought the natural inclination to be industrious into a thoroughly disciplined procedure. There was talk of education and

[63] The number of licensed passenger vehicles is reported in the East German statistics—in thousands—as follows: 1955, 117; 1960, 299; 1964, 581; 1965, 662; 1966, 721; 1967, 827. Except for privileged individuals, the price is extraordinarily high and the waiting time for delivery two or three years. The ratio is less than 5 per 100. See Staatliche Zentralverwaltung fuer Statistik, *Statistical Pocketbook of the German Democratic Republic* (Berlin: Deutscher Zentralverlag, 1966), p. 81.

of the fact that it was free and universally available. But there were no visible signs that intellectual stimulus spread from the classroom to more casual pursuits. Although the volume of publication is considerable, the bookstores were few and far between, and not many persons were buying books. The scattered kiosks had few newspapers or magazines. Reading material was confined to a large extent to repetitious propaganda. Even in the hotel there were few newspapers. Only one or two copies of the communist journals were on the racks, and no Western papers could be found.

The hotels were clearly for party officials, businessmen, and foreigners. The local people were not supposed to eat in the dining rooms. The meals were pretentious in the Astoria in Leipzig, in the Elephant in Weimar, in the Interhotel in Halle. In Jena, Dresden, and Karl Marx Stadt (Chemnitz) the menus were fourteen or sixteen inches long, with many delicacies listed[64]—but the dishes named were frequently not to be had, and the wines and beers were expensive and inferior. Many said that Leipzig was different at fairtime—but clearly at other seasons the effort to impress foreigners leaves much to be desired. Some ninety special services were advertised in the hotels, but in Halle the purchase of a postage stamp was a major project.

The Cities

There was considerable building in the larger cities, but planning was not evident. The impression one got in the cities I visited was not the impression that the visitor gets in East Berlin. In East Berlin, even at night there is some activity. The buildings concentrated in the center, near Alexander Platz, give an effect of newness, while some of the restoration of Unter den Linden pleases the eye. Visitors who do not see the outlying districts and find the lack of traffic congestion agreeable have said they like this quarter better than the *Kurfuerstendamm.* Many foreigners jump to conclusions about the rest of the GDR. They forget the political pressure on the communists to polish the area close to the bright stores and luxury restaurants of West Berlin. In Weimar and Dresden the

[64] This may be a surprise to some thinking of a simpler communist approach.

incentive and the funds available are not the same. "Why is not Dresden restored?" asks Leonhardt.[65] Neither the new nor the old buildings in the city give any reflection of its past glory. The geometrical style of the new apartments and of the model cities seem to me to serve emergency needs in a tasteless manner, scarcely above the standards of wartime building.

Welles Hangen, the American reporter, writes perceptively of his travels in the GDR.[66] He speaks of the "tonnage ideology." He describes the fate of the farmers as they were driven to despair by collectivization. The small farm is doomed, he says, but the figures he gives for production on the large farms give ground for far less optimism than that suggested by a casual reading of the official tables. He discusses the problems of fertilizers in some detail. He writes of the plight of the old cities that used to be centers of European culture. Weimar he describes as fading like an old lithograph and "sinking into the moist Thueringian earth." Of Dresden he says: "For a city of half a million souls, Dresden must be more poorly equipped with hotel space than any other comparable town in the world."[67] He speaks of the grotesque, unrepaired ruins and the monotonous new buildings going up in several quarters, while the old districts are falling into decay. These I saw and placed in my memory beside the shining city with its cafes and museums that I had seen in 1922. The only restored building reminiscent of the past was the world-renowned Zwinger gallery which had been rebuilt from the shattered ruins according to the original plans. It housed more than 3,000 pictures, retrieved from the salt mines or freight cars in which they had been hidden during the war and most of them returned by way of Moscow. Hangen's impression of the general aspect of the city, like mine, was one of empty and dingy streets with "acres of rubble and ghostly facades." The destruction in February 1945 and the communist rule today give

[65] "Aber Dresden war andererseits auch nicht soviel staerker zerstoert als etwa Koeln. Warum ist dann heute Koeln wieder Koeln, aber Dresden nicht wieder Dresden?" (Rudolf W. Leonhardt, "Kultur nach Plan," in Doenhoff, Leonhardt, and Sommer, *Reise*, p. 79).

[66] Hangen, *Muted Revolution*, p. 87.

[67] Ibid., p. 131.

tragic testimony to the folly of those who wage war and create dictatorships to crush the spirit and the works of the spirit.

The Church

The churches are interesting, whether on a Sunday or on a weekday. Many are badly in need of repair. The condition of buildings and cemeteries is much better in the small towns than in the large cities. This difference helps to confirm other signs that party activities are not as prevalent in the villages as they are in the urban centers. The pastors and priests are very conscious of the heavy burdens which they carry and of the importance of ministering to the people who accept some measure of risk in remaining faithful. "The authorities do not wish trouble with us," several said. "They count on the erosion of time and the shortage of funds to lessen our influence and reduce the church membership." The party tries to wean away the youth by holding marches and meetings on Sunday. Now that the church no longer denies the sacrament to those who conform to party demands, the *Jugendweihe*[68] poses less of a problem than it did. But it still means that the allegiance of the young is divided and to that extent the church has of necessity lost ground. The churchmen with whom I talked showed courage and clear thinking. Dr. Markus Barth of Pittsburgh attributes some of the troubles of the Christians in East Germany to their attitude toward socialism.[69] His conclusions are interesting, but they differ from the impressions which I gained in my conversations in the East and in the West as to the dangers the church leaders face and the careful course they have to pursue under the hostile scrutiny of local officials.

[68] Bundesministerium fuer Gesamtdeutsche Fragen, *SBZ von A-Z*, p. 228. "Jugend verpflichte sich ihre ganze Kraft fuer die grosse und edle Sache des Sozialismus einzusetzen." The *Jugendweihe*, which is a formulation of a philosophy which the SED asks all young people to accept, sounds relatively harmless to the casual reader, but it signifies for the Germans an acceptance of atheism, and a rejection of religious beliefs. It reads approximately as follows: "that I accept the obligation to devote my entire strength and will for the great and noble purposes of the Socialist system." See also Friedrich-Georg Hermann, *Der Kampf gegen Religion und Kirche in der Sowjetischen Besatzungszone Deutschlands*, pp. 61–67.

[69] Barth, "Church and Communism in East Germany."

The Pall of Drabness

The cause of the pall which spreads over much of southeast Germany goes deeper than the smoke and sulphur that permeate the air with their heavy fumes. It is to be found in the attitude of the people. This intangible element—which may be disputed by a few—cannot be measured and weighed, but it is still the most significant indication that the people will not remain forever under a system so alien to their character and traditions. As one travels over the countryside, one notices the absence of gaiety and misses the many bright little stores and beer terraces of West Germany. One looks in vain for the multicolored tents which in the summer are found by every river in the Federal Republic. There are few flowers, few happy young people, no singing in the streets. The marching of the youthful "Pioneers" is not gay. The women in the stores do not gossip and chatter. The hotels are gloomy, and long before dark the streets are empty. In the smaller towns, I looked for the neat vegetable gardens and flower borders to which I was accustomed in West Germany—and found only a few. Some of the churchyards were well tended, others were rank with weeds. The park outside the Schiller-Goethe tomb in Weimar was neglected and overgrown. The communist guide talked to me with pride and solemnity of the greatness of these two men, but the scene itself gave little evidence of care and attention. The churchgoers seemed intent and devoted, as did those in two of the "working churches" in the Soviet Union which I attended in July 1968.

The GDR is gaining materially, though spiritually it seems to the visitor to be a wasteland. It is an important workshop in the Soviet system. In return for material output and political conformity, it offers promise to some millions of workers of continued physical existence within firmly established limits and behind barriers of wire and concrete—with a visa for travel a much-coveted and sometimes realized reward. A vacation in resorts on the Baltic Sea or perhaps a trip to Czechoslovakia are special treats offered to brighten controlled and monotonous lives.

My impressions, gained by eye and ear and supplemented by analysis of written material, do not constitute proof of either progress or decline. The validity of personal opinions is limited by the time span and the extent of the observations on which they are based. My observations did not go beyond a few score conversations and experiences in a particular month and in a handful of cities. I was convinced, however, that my impressions were valid.

In the GDR, as I found it, the people had little or no sense of nationhood. They felt deprived of traditions; they had no inspiration to take the place of religion, free speech, amusements, free travel, free choice, and a sense of personal independence. This suggests that the choice of the future will be between a return to the police state or an expansion of freedom. These, as it seemed to me, are the elements and decisions which the West must watch and which the East must fear.

Return to Freedom

It was a hot, dusty ride back to Berlin on July 11, 1967. We tried to pass some of the large superannuated smoke-breathing trucks on some of the smaller roads but had to draw off to the side to gain a respite from the fumes. The small car of our official companion that had followed us on the road from Karl Marx Stadt through Meissen northward, left us at Juterbog near Berlin. We were back in the city at dusk. There was a two-hour delay at "Checkpoint Charlie." Why had we spent so much money, they asked. We showed our hotel bills, we had bought nothing but postal cards. Where was the engine on the Volkswagen? We said it was in the back. (Since the official had already examined the front of the car, we thought he could have known.) I had a moment of panic when he insisted that he did not have my passport and then found it under the counter where he had put it. This episode seemed like playing games. We could have flown to London in less time than it took us to clear the checkpoint. The officials did not look at our notebooks or make an exhaustive search; they simply used their petty authority to make us feel uncomfortable.

Our visa, good until midnight, had almost run out by the time we went through the barrier and checked with the American military police. We drove on to the center of the city, glad to feel our independence and regain the freedom of choice which had not been ours during the week of our journey.

CHAPTER 5

Reunification

WHY REUNIFICATION?

A visitor to the GDR who knew nothing of German history, postwar Allied commitments, or the nature of the Cold War might well wonder what the quest for reunification meant. If he did not look below the surface, he would imagine that the East German government was as stable and as firmly based as many a government elsewhere. He would find an economy which was expanding at a reassuring rate and a people who seemed to accept their condition with only a normal amount of complaint. Divided Berlin would present a puzzle which he could not easily dismiss. But many of the slogans of the past would sound unreal and unconvincing. He might ask why neither the GDR nor the FRG was in the United Nations and whether there were any signs of a closer relation between the two Germanys. Many of the younger men in East Germany—and even some in West Germany—who have not lived with history think in these terms. This attitude is one of the reasons why the political slogans which were applicable during the past twenty years no longer serve a useful purpose. The methods, timing, and tone of the approach to reunification must be altered, but the causes of the quest for reunification still hold true.

It is still of importance to Germans everywhere that the people in the GDR should have self-determination (*Selbstbestimmung*). It is still of great moment that they should be free of Russian soldiers and Moscow's demands. It is still crucial to the peace of Europe that a workable economic and political relation between East and West Germany be developed. It is still significant for the security of Europe that the Western orientation of the people now living under Ulbricht be recognized.

In an interview with the author a leading German expressed a view held by many when he said:

> If reunification is ever considered to be a dead issue, then the friendship between Germany and the Western powers is impossible. Many will think that they must negotiate with the East on their own. This would bring a very dangerous situation. While this statement might be denied by some, it is clear that a new issue would be introduced into internal German politics and the Western Alliance would suffer.
>
> The danger is sufficient to require very careful treatment of this issue by the Western Allies. If any nation, particularly the United States, were to abandon the reunification of Germany the entire blame for disappointment and frustration would fall on that nation and not on the Communists. There would be a profound sense that the United States had not used its power to aid Germany. Some would attach blame to decisions in 1945, some to inadequate action in 1948. Others would think of lost opportunities in 1953. Still others would find errors in United States policy at a later date. The revulsion of feeling which would come with such a denouement would serve as a breeding ground for anti-Americanism.

This statement, made in 1966, indicates underground currents which still emerge from time to time in German political life.

Inter-German relations are, as suggested in chapter 4, crucial for U.S. policy toward Europe, NATO, and the EEC. Washington regards the present unstable equilibrium as a threat to peace. Writers on this subject sometimes disregard this official view. They see the obstacles to early action, they expect the present situation to continue for years, and in some cases they question whether unification is desirable at any time. For Washington, the question goes beyond the fear of German neutralization; it embraces the future nature of Europe and the extension of communism in the free world. In other capitals attitudes are less clear cut. Paris, immersed in complex dealings with Russia and China, has not changed her policy from the official Allied position, but President de Gaulle had made some statements which led many to say that France does not favor reunification. Clearly sentiment there is divided and perhaps confused. Later, when specific issues revolving around German allegiance to the East or to the West come to the fore, the seriousness of the situation will evoke more impressive pronouncements. M. Pompidou, the new president, indicated continuity in policy during his visit to Bonn.

The Basis for Reunification

The basis for reunification has been stated many times in the past two decades but has never been formally revised.[1] Some in Germany and elsewhere would misunderstand any statement which would seem to discuss free elections in the GDR as prerequisite to reunification, even though most realists recognize that the absence of such elections should not preclude all other measures for bringing the two Germanys together.

The evolution of U.S. policy between Yalta in 1945 and the Geneva Conference of 1959 is outlined in chapter 9. The best statement of the classic principles for reunification is to be found in the Declaration by the Western Foreign Ministers on Free Elections on May 13, 1950. This called for a "freely elected all-German government," assurance of German economic unity through action by a German government, free movement of individuals, and other judicial and political guarantees to be carried out in the united territory then under four-power supervision. The policy depended on continuing the maintenance of the legal authority under the surrender terms and on holding the Soviets to a peace treaty to be worked out along lines laid down under those agreements. Until the 1959 Geneva Conference there was no change in the accepted formula—and then the modifications were not in fundamental principle but in detail.

The events of 1949 introduced a new dimension into the problem. The governmental institutions of the FRG, after the elections of August of that year, were designed to include the former eastern territories. Meanwhile East Germany was granted a degree of sovereignty by the Soviets on October 12, 1949, and received formal recognition three days later.[2] The legal basis remained unchanged by these developments, but as more and more people came to think in terms of two Germanys the psychology and practical politics of those concerned with the problem became drastically different.

[1] See chapter 9.

[2] Walther Hubatsch et al., eds., *The German Question*, pp. 152, 176.

EARLY POLICY AND MANEUVERS

During the twenty-years since the blockade various proposals for reunification have been made by the West and by the East. The seriousness of the proposals put forward by the Soviets, however, is open to question. Their central theme, notably in the case of the treaty proposals of 1952 and 1954 and the Rapacki Plan in 1957, was the neutralization of Central Europe. Washington and Berlin on their side made continuing efforts to seek some basis for an agreement with Moscow which would facilitate constructive action. At first the prostrate condition of the former Third Reich seemed to some to dispel any fear of a resurgent Germany. Those who did fear the emergence of German power welcomed German economic weakness and gave little thought to the dangers of a power vacuum in a geographic area of such strategic importance. Later both the Russians and the Western powers began to imagine the course that the future development of Germany might take, and policy statements were colored by fears of a strong army and an aggressive population. This was the stage the situation had reached by 1954 when the Berlin Conference seriously tackled the problem.

Although from 1945 to 1954 the Soviets had been adamant in respect to Austria and Germany and had resorted to blockade to threaten the Allied position in Berlin, there was still hope that some kind of agreement could be reached in Berlin.[3] The United States, Britain, and France had shown a firmness and unity which had led to close working relations with Bonn, and which might have proved a basis for eventual accommodation with Russia as fear of war diminished.

Much of the story of the German efforts from 1945 to 1966 to secure German unity is recounted in a "White Book" published by the German Foreign Office in April 1966.[4] This book is not easy to find and for some reason is considered by the government as out of circulation. It presents documents, discussions of abuses and offenses against human rights, the significance of the flight of 3,500,000

[3] See chapter 8.

[4] *Die Bemuehungen der deutschen Regierung und ihrer Verbuendeten um die Einheit Deutschlands*. See especially pages 29, 255, 268, 562.

refugees from the GDR, and reports the German initiative in September 1958 in proposing a four-power commission to prepare a peace treaty and to settle German borders.

The last item included in this volume is the German note on Disarmament and Security of March 3, 1966. In this Bonn affirms that a step-by-step reduction of causes of tension in the world is essential and that Germany would do all in her power to this end, with the knowledge that it was essential to the achievement of her freedom and control over her destiny.

The East-West Split

During the years 1946 to 1950 the Western Allies strove continuously for an Austrian State Treaty and a German peace treaty. They held many meetings—in London, Moscow, Paris, and New York—in an unremitting effort to resolve these unsettled problems that were so important to the future of Europe. Discouragement over the lack of success, the takeover of Czechoslovakia by the communists, the withdrawal of the Soviet Union from the Allied Control Council, the Berlin blockade, mounting troubles in the Far East, and signs of Soviet aggressive intent led Western Europe and the United States to band together in NATO. These considerations also determined the West to consolidate its zones into a single unit, which later became the nucleus of the future German nation with the inauguration of the Federal Republic after elections held in August and the election of Adenauer as chancellor in September. The Soviets countered these moves by official recognition of the GDR in October of that year and by the treaty which granted "sovereignty" to the area and Ulbricht's regime in 1954, and by the Warsaw Pact of May 14, 1955. Thus the governments emerged, one by elections and one by party action.

Meantime the communist attack on South Korea had upset many calculations as to the future. The many signs of Soviet expansionism in the Far East and elsewhere led the United States to adopt a bipartisan defense policy, to give vigorous support to the cooperation of Europe with the FRG, and increasingly to participate in and contribute to the NATO security system. After the end of the Berlin blockade, Washington increased its assistance to that city, building it into a strong industrial member of the democratic community, while production in West Germany mounted. Meanwhile, in the early 1950s the economy of the East German regime was still suffering from the large-scale Russian removals and predatory commercial policy. It was not yet clear whether Moscow would permit the Zone to develop a balanced economic system and improve the living conditions of its people. This change in policy came slowly, after the death of Stalin.

In Washington a Republican Administration took over from the Democrats in 1953. President Eisenhower and Secretary Dulles had supported the established American policy toward Germany and concurred in the official statements regarding the "security and welfare" of Berlin. On this score Bonn had nothing to fear. But among those who knew the iron grip that police states exert there was some puzzlement over U.S. pronouncements on the "rollback" of tyranny in Eastern Europe. It has been said that the campaigners in the 1952 election had been carried away by temporary enthusiasm for the prospect of freedom. There are also signs that John Foster Dulles, the new U.S. secretary of state, was so firmly convinced of the individual's inherent will for liberty that he overestimated the ability of subject peoples to overthrow a police state. The death of Stalin in March 1953 led to new uncertainties and reassessments. The timetable had to be reviewed and methods reconsidered.

The Berlin Conference, 1954

In July 1953 the three Western powers invited the USSR to a four-power conference to be held in Berlin to discuss German reunification through free elections. Such a meeting seemed particularly appropriate because of the change of rule in Russia and the new Administration in Washington. Interzonal restrictions were causing hardship, and echoes of the June uprising were still heard. New efforts were needed.

The conference lasted from January 25 to February 18, 1954. With the full concurrence of Secretary Dulles and French Foreign Minister Georges Bidault, Anthony Eden, British foreign secretary, on January 29 introduced a plan which called for the—

- Holding of free elections throughout Germany
- Convocation of the duly elected National Assembly
- Drafting of a constitution and the preparation of negotiations for a peace treaty
- Adoption of the constitution and the formation of an all-German government which would be responsible for the negotiation of the peace treaty
- Signature and entry into force of the peace treaty

The proposed electoral law was to provide for free movement, free association, freedom of the press, and other elementary rights. The elections were to be supervised by the four occupying powers. The preparations for these steps were to be agreed by the four foreign ministers. In recognition of the Soviet fear of too close an association of Germany with the West the plan provided that the new government should choose its future allies. This partial concession could not obscure the fact that the voting on this question would be swayed by the predominance of the Federal Republic.

On February 10 the Soviets introduced a "Proposal for a General European Treaty on Collective Security." The treaty was to last for fifty years. It called for the liquidation of NATO, but it did not provide for the withdrawal of Russian troops from East Germany or of course for the rearmament of the "united peace-loving German State." While not depriving the parties to the treaty of the right of individual or collective self-defense, it appeared to throw responsibility on the UN Security Council. This was the first in a series of proposals which had no practical feasibility in view of the threats to peace posed by communist expansionism.

Except insofar as it influenced the future course of the Western powers, the Berlin Conference was without result. The NATO powers pushed on with their integration of Germany into NATO; the Soviets continued to try to prevent her participation in Western organizations.

The Geneva Conference, 1955

The Geneva Summit Conference of 1955 reopened the German question in a new atmosphere following the Russian agreement to permit an Austrian State Treaty. But, as Ferenc A. Vali has commented, "The events of 1955 produced no evidence of any serious Soviet willingness to trade German unity for neutralization."[5] The communique issued at the end of the conference however reiterated the earlier declarations in the following terms:

> The heads of government, recognizing their common responsibility for the settlement of the German question and the reunification of Germany have agreed that the settlement of the German question and the reunification of Germany by means of free elections shall be carried out in conformity with the national interests of the German people and the interests of European security. The Foreign Ministers should by means of experts study measures, which could bring . . . elimination of barriers . . . freer contacts and exchanges . . . to the mutual advantage.[6]

Adenauer's Moscow Visit

During the years after the Geneva Summit Conference of 1955 it became apparent that, although the policy of firmness had built up a strong German nation in the West, it had not brought progress in uniting the two parts of Germany. Chancellor Adenauer's priority and Washington's choice were clear. But the need of action to avoid new dangers was imperative. Adenauer decided to go to Moscow.[7] He wished to keep his delegation relatively small, but he took with him Foreign Minister Heinrich von Brentano, Kurt Georg Kiesinger, Carlo Schmid, Karl Arnold, and several others as representatives of appropriate *Bundestag* committees.

Adenauer went to Moscow "without illusions." He said he was not convinced that Dulles' "optimistic point of view" was right and did not think the time was ripe for an East-West agreement. (Dulles was not as optimistic at this time as this statement implies.) Nothing must be done, he said, to weaken the position of the Western powers as expressed at Geneva or to insist unilaterally on reunification; thus the "question of reunification could only be mentioned. The solution was the responsibility of the four victor

[5] Ferenc A. Vali, *The Quest for a United Germany*, pp. 38, 39.

[6] U.S. Department of State, *Documents on Germany, 1944–1959*, pp. 153, 154.

[7] Konrad Adenauer, *Erinnerungen 1953–1955*, pp. 487, 491, 492, 495.

nations." The leaders in Washington, Paris, and London were keenly interested in these proposed conversations. Dulles in particular, according to Adenauer, expressed the view that there were changes coming in Russia, both because of the military strength of the West and because of the Russian desire for an improved standard of living. (Perhaps he was too quick to anticipate changes that were not to come until ten years later.) He thought, Adenauer added, that reunification might come in two to four years. Antoine Pinay in France was more pessimistic.

The results of the week's conversations that started on September 8 included an agreement to return German prisoners of war, to exchange diplomatic representatives, and to increase commerce between the Federal Republic and Russia. Bulganin stated that the prisoners of war were already free and that the only persons then held in the Soviet Union were 9,628 war criminals.[8] When Adenauer brought up the subject of reunification, Bulganin said that he recognized the importance of this to the Germans and shared their concern, that the Soviet Union "setzt und setzt sich weiter unermuedlich dafuer ein, dass Deutschland als einheitlicher und demokratischer Staat wiederhergestellt wird."[9] He added that Germany had been warned against military alliances such as NATO. A way must be found to overcome these obstacles, he said, so that Germany could gain unification within the context of collective European security. Khrushchev then took up the refrain and said the inclusion of Germany in NATO blocked the road to a solution of the German question for the near future.

The Soviet leaders apparently set great store by the exchange of diplomats but at the same time were reluctant to give precise assurances as to the return of war prisoners. In his review of these long and difficult negotiations, Adenauer wrote: "I could not get a written assurance of the return of war prisoners."[10] Khrushchev stated on his word of honor that the people on the list, if found to be really German citizens, would be returned. He said that he

[8] Ibid., p. 506.
[9] Ibid., p. 507.
[10] Ibid., p. 550.

doubted if the number were nearly as high as 130,000. (In fact, the number returned was 9,626.[11] The fate of the rest is still unknown.)

As he flew back to Germany in mid-September, Adenauer concluded that the restoration of diplomatic relations was not of great significance and did not in any way suggest a new Rapallo. Moreover the representation terms were so stated as to confirm neither the zonal boundaries nor the future of the territories within the FRG or the GDR. All such questions were left for the conclusion of a peace treaty. As regards reunification, the conclusion seemed to be that no acceptable grounds could be found for progress in 1955. The conversations had been direct and often heated; at one point the chancellor said he must insist that either he would drink water with the Russians or they would drink wine with him—their device of pretending their glasses were full of wine was obvious and unacceptable. Yet during these talks he came to the conclusion that at some distant day agreement would be reached with the men in the Kremlin. For the moment, the price set for reunification—withdrawal from NATO and more—was too high.

Meanwhile the gap between the eastern and western parts of Germany remained as wide as the split which affected all European policies. The harassment of Berlin continued. The communist pressures from 1954 to 1958 were evident in Latin America, in the Middle East, in Africa, in Southeast Asia, and elsewhere. They came to a head in the demand contained in Khrushchev's note of November 27, 1958, that the Western powers leave Berlin.

A DECADE OF ABORTIVE PROPOSALS

From September 1955 until the present time communist circles have shown little change in their treatment of the question of reunification. The Soviet proposals have all stressed the security question and NATO. Ulbricht's suggestions have differed in tone but not in substance. The difference has consisted mainly in the degree of emphasis given to the preservation of communist institutions in the GDR and the degree of insistence shown from time to time on the imposition of communism on West Germany.

[11] As reported to the writer by the German Embassy in Washington.

When the new constitution (scheduled to come into force April 9, 1968) was adopted on March 26, 1968, Ulbricht stated that the "constitution does not rule out rapprochement and eventual unification, but it stipulates that West Germany must first be transformed into a communist country."[12]

The Rapacki Plan

Between 1955 and 1957 the only proposal that attracted general interest was the well-known Rapacki Plan, presented in October 1957 by Polish Foreign Minister Adam Rapacki. This plan proposed an atom-free and neutralized zone in the middle of Europe.[13] It was in line with earlier Russian suggestions and was not new. As stated by Vali, the proposal was for a "zone of relaxation [which] would gradually be evacuated by all foreign forces and denuclearized; the four great powers and other participants in these agreements were to enter into a collective security convention."[14] The Rapacki Plan aroused no active interest in the West and was rarely discussed in Germany except in leftist circles.

The Deutschlandplan

Between the Khrushchev demands in late 1958 and the Geneva meeting of the four foreign ministers in the following year, the leaders (*Vorstand*) of the Social Democratic Party issued on March 18, 1959, a proposal called the *Deutschlandplan*.[15] It stated the obvious fact that the security of Europe and reunification were interdependent. It embodied elements drawn from various disengagement plans, including proposals by Hugh Gaitskell, George Kennan, Paul van Zeeland, Adam Rapacki, and others. It called for a meeting of the four great powers with advisers from the FRG and the GDR to provide for regional and controlled reduction of arma-

[12] *New York Times*, March 27, 1968.

[13] Hans Hartl and Werner Marx, *Fuenfzig Jahre sowjetische Deutschlandpolitik*, p. 44.

[14] Vali, *The Quest*, p. 71.

[15] Sozialistische Einheitspartei Deutschlands, Zentralkomittee, *Deutschlandplan der SPD*. This plan is rarely discussed and was kept out of active consideration after the first few weeks.

ments in Central Europe as essential to the eventual solution of military and political problems.

The reunification of Germany was to follow. This was to be effected in three stages. The first step—and the central idea—was to be the convening of an all-German conference. This step would provide for human rights and for the bringing together of the two economies, with enlarged interzonal trade, a bank for the entire region to provide investment funds, and a legal basis for the payment of pensions and other maintenance payments. The second phase was to be the establishment of an all-German parliamentary council which would arrange for elections and chart appropriate legislation to take care of rail, road, and canal traffic. A common market would then be developed as soon as possible, with monetary measures to facilitate internal trade. The third step was to be the securing of uniform tax and finance laws and other financial and social policies. The new council was to be empowered at any time when it had a two-thirds majority to call together a constitutional assembly. All these institutions were to have their seat in Berlin. In the final stage there were to be free secret elections, leading to an all-German government. The entire plan for reunification depended on a relaxation of tensions in Europe and a slowing down of moves toward rearmament.

Although some of these ideas had already been put forward and the idea of an all-German conference was to reappear in various forms in many later proposals, there was little response to the *Deutschlandplan.* The leading socialists Carlo Schmid and Fritz Erler, who had just returned from a Moscow visit and had been key figures in the plan's preparation, admitted that it did not meet all Moscow's demands.[16]

In view of the lack of response and the widespread view that the socialists should drop their neutralist policy, the plan was allowed to die. It was followed by a change in SPD policy that resulted in the Godesberg Plan, so named from the place of the November 15, 1959, party meeting that decided on the change. Vali describes this development as follows:

[16] Ibid., p. 46.

The practical implementation of this *volte face* took place on March 18, 1960, when SPD Deputy Chairman, Herbert Wehner declared in the name of his Party that the Deutschlandplan had become "outdated by developments." And on March 24, 1960, he submitted to the *Bundestag* a new, four-point program which contained proposals for relaxation in Central Europe "with the view of promoting the rapprochement of Germany's two parts"; for demonstrations by the people of Germany to induce the four powers to open the road toward reunification; for the strengthening of economic, social, and cultural ties between the divided parts of Germany; and for a combination of moves which would lead toward German unity or would, at least, relieve Berlin from Soviet pressures and prevent any final international recognition of Germany's partition.[17]

The Herter Plan

A Western peace plan was presented at Geneva on May 14, 1959. It was further amplified and completed by U.S. Secretary of State Christian Herter on May 26.[18] This plan was designed to combine European security measures and German reunification in one agreement and to provide for several stages of readjustment and reorganization. There were to be free elections for a Berlin constitutional council of 100 members who would draft a constitution for Greater Berlin and an election law. The four powers would establish suitable arrangements for the settlement of disputes prior to a German peace settlement with a reunified Germany. The Berlin part of the proposal was amplified on June 16.

One part of this package proposal by the Western Allies, handed to Gromyko in Geneva on June 16, 1959, and often called the Herter Plan, was directed more to the Berlin problem than to the question of reunification, but its overtones are of interest in connection with the larger question. It proposed that—

[17] Vali, *The Quest*, p. 74; Heinrich, Freiherr von Siegler, ed., *Wiedervereinigung und Sicherheit Deutschlands*, p. 307. Siegler gives a useful and extensive reprinting of documents relating to reunification and security.

[18] Otto Martin von der Gablentz, *Documents on Berlin, 1943–1963*, pp. 248, 249, 251; U.S. Department of State, *American Foreign Policy: Current Documents, 1959*, pp. 706–7.

- The Western forces in Berlin should be limited to the number at that time (11,000).
- The procedures in force in April 1959 should continue but might be carried out by German instead of Allied military personnel. There should be a four-power commission to settle any resulting disputes.
- Measures should be taken in both parts of Berlin to avoid activities which would disturb public order.
- These arrangements should continue until the reunification of Germany.[19]

It is fortunate for the West, many have concluded, that this proposal with its unbalanced concessions was turned down by Gromyko.

The Kroll-Khrushchev Talks

In 1962 Ambassador Hans Kroll engaged in private conversations in Moscow with the Russians about German problems. These talks had not been sponsored by Bonn and were regarded by the government there as unwise. They constituted one of the rare occasions on which a German official acted in this field of four-power jurisdiction without coordination with any of the four powers. Although in his official reports Ambassador Kroll claimed that his plan had been submitted with the knowledge of the Western Allies, no facts have been given in support of this. In fact, no significant conferences had preceded his talks in the Kremlin. There were four points in the Kroll "little solution": (1) the assurance of Berlin against communist attack; (2) the improvement of human rights in East Germany; (3) a change in conditions at the Wall, or the elimination of the Wall; and (4) the recognition of the right of East Germany to self-determination and reunification.[20]

There was no indication of any quid pro quo for these concessions on the part of the Soviets. Kroll is said to have concluded that Khrushchev thought reunification the "best possible result of a

[19] Gablentz, *Documents on Berlin, 1943–1963*, pp. 261, 262.
[20] Vali, *The Quest*, p. 120.

long-drawn-out historic process after the two German states had achieved a rapprochement and 'a reciprocal assimilation of their conditions.' "[21] One can guess that in his eagerness to act, the German ambassador ignored the fact that Khrushchev expected the reciprocal assimilation to confirm the onward march of communism. Kroll was recalled from Moscow as he failed to satisfy Adenauer over this episode.

BONN'S NEW COURSE

Peter Bender in a book published in 1964 presented the view that cooperation with the GDR was desirable and would help to bring about eventual close association or reunification.[22] He referred to breaks in the monolithic situation in the East and to a new generation in Russia. He considered the improvement in the standard of living in the GDR to be to the advantage of a more liberal policy. He did not think it constructive to weaken an opponent and suggested that help from the West would make the GDR less dependent on the Russians. He concluded that economic help was desirable.

There was a new attitude in West German circles; this was exemplified in the policy of "little steps." The *Passierschein* agreement for the issuance of passes to West Berliners to visit relatives in East Berlin was a successful "little step." Such agreements should be sought whenever possible in order to establish contacts. Soon after the Wall cut Berlin in half in 1961, the Berlin Council (*Senat*) endeavored to find ways of mitigating the resulting hardship. An agreement was concluded in December 1963 after much discussion of the terms on which the passes should be granted and the manner in which the agreement should be signed.[23] This was followed by a second agreement in September 1964. Several million people are estimated to have used the passes. In spite of further efforts, after the fourth agreement (in 1966) no further agreement was signed. Difficulties of protocol and unacceptable

[21] Ibid., pp. 118–21.
[22] Peter Bender, *Offensive Entspannung*, pp. 33, 52, 59, 73, 105, 109, 128, 130, 135, 138.
[23] Eleanor Lansing Dulles, *Berlin*, pp. 82–91.

demands prevented progress in 1965. Additional evidence of the stiffening of the East German attitude was given by Pankow's rejection in February 1966, after exchanges lasting some months, of the proposals for debates between leaders from the East and the West. These rebuffs greatly diminished Bonn's hopes for productive little steps.

Few advocates of further initiative and experimentation have proposed unconditional recognition of the GDR, but there has been considerable speculation as to what harm such a move might do. The knowledge that reunification will not be achieved for years to come has led some to conclude that the FRG must establish closer relations with the GDR to prevent wider and deeper alienation between the East and West Germans. They advocate the liberalization of credits in interzonal trade and the arrangement of interzonal dialogues.

These contacts and exchanges were among the proposals discussed in 1965 and 1966, but little could be done at that time; and since 1966 the Ulbricht regime has been even less receptive.

The policy of "little steps," which was actively discussed in the summer of 1965, had a certain allure. But it was motivated by the desire to do *something* when no big steps were possible.[24] In spite of the setbacks it experienced, its proponents continued to advocate it. Some urged changes in the telephone connections so as to permit direct talks between the two parts of Berlin instead of the roundabout routing by way of Frankfurt; others spoke of increased interzonal trade; still others suggested intellectual exchanges. But the GDR's attitude precluded the possibility of the conversations and debates which many wished to initiate. Pankow refused to sign *Passierschein* agreements again in 1967. Thus progress was infinitesimal.

Internal Differences of Opinion

Some feared that the evident West German desire for more contacts might lead to increased East German demands. Little steps, little cuts (*kleine Schritte, kleine Schnitte*) was their slogan.

[24] Ibid., pp. 82–91, contains a discussion of attitudes in Berlin on contacts between East and West.

Ernst Lemmer, former minister of all-German affairs, in discussing this urgent wish for a "policy of movement," argued that since the status quo plus was impossible at that time, any change would mean a status quo minus. The years from 1965 to 1967 however were years in which the restlessness of youth was beginning to tell and the willingness to experiment was leading to concrete proposals which showed a questioning of the accepted formulae and well-tried policies that had served the West German Republic well through more than a decade.

A dissonant note was struck by the late Professor Karl Jaspers in his writings about the future of Germany, East and West. He raised the issue of German guilt and the unworthiness of and lack of justification for the restoration of Bismarck's Reich. Freedom, he urged, was a right; self-determination should be won; but the geographic area, with its rivers, mountains, forests, and cities, need not be restored to a reunited national entity. Germany, by reason of aggression and wrong-doing, could not claim a return of what had been lost. Jaspers' thesis has been followed by a few others, including the sociologist Alexander Rustow. These views have not won wide acceptance. They contradict the policy of the four Allies in 1945, the communique issued at the end of the Summit Conference in Geneva in 1955, the continued stand of the three Western powers, the principles and goals of the Federal Republic, and the thinking of those who support the accepted policy on West Berlin. They are not widely discussed in the Federal Republic, though one is occasionally reminded of this line of reasoning when one hears some say, as I did in January 1968, that the only essential of future policy was self-determination for East Germany.

A very different approach has recently been put forward by a writer who believes that German unity is no less important and no less desired now than earlier. Wilhelm Wolfgang Schuetz takes an optimistic line.[25] He recognizes that reunification can come only with the consent of the Soviet Union but recommends an immediate strategy for the eventual achievement of this objective. He would call for a comprehensive move toward European security

[25] Wilhelm W. Schuetz, *Rethinking German Policy*, pp. 126–37.

through a peace conference which would handle the major problems still remaining from World War II. The heart of his proposal is a new security system which, he says somewhat optimistically, "would put an end to the present confrontation of the powers in Europe."[26] He recognizes that, without political rapprochement, neither side would accept the new military system he outlines which would override both NATO and the Warsaw Pact.

He refers to the many complicated steps which would be involved: the question of the nuclear deterrent; the withdrawal of troops from foreign soil; the guarantees that would be required; the reduction of armaments; and the use of economic aid as a tool to reinforce the entire operation. He indicates that several years would be required to implement such a program. He states clearly the fear of Germany felt in many quarters and notes that it is Berlin—and not the German people—that has captured the imagination and sympathy of the outside world.

The Germans, he writes, have lost their relationship to power and are now in search of a new relationship. This is an observation which bears on the policy of the West with regard to German reunification and membership in the European Community where economic power is already evident. Power which includes moral and spiritual values held without naïveté, he suggests, must come with the establishment of a dependable equilibrium in Europe as a whole. West Germany's objective in her quest for readjustment and change in the existing division must be not hegemony but self-determination. While his thought that a comprehensive conference working for years would achieve practical results is belied by recent esperience in the United Nations and elsewhere, many of his observations are useful and interesting. He would be the first to admit that his proposal can be within the reach of statecraft only if the Soviets change their attitude and want a new Europe. There is perhaps little in this proposal to suggest a practical change in policy, but there is a strong recommendation that plans be prepared and a strategy be developed to move as soon as possible beyond the present stalemate.

[26] Ibid., p. 132.

THE PROSPECTS FOR REUNIFICATION

The possibilities of reunification are confined within a rigid four-square framework. To the East, they are limited by Soviet intentions; to the West, by Allied policy, particularly Allied security measures. The remaining limits are set by Bonn's aims and requirements on the one side, and on the other side by the conditions and attitudes which have developed in East Germany. From 1947 to 1969, no substantial progress was made in the thinking or in the atmosphere surrounding the problem. Contacts of various kinds continue to facilitate economic relations and an increase in interzonal trade; there is support for a policy of movement and little steps in Bonn and in Berlin; and there is talk of a detente in Europe. In spite of all this neither Ulbricht nor the Soviet leaders have brought forward any serious proposal. Nor has the West promulgated any major plan. The future prospect is darkened by pessimism and in some quarters by indifference. And yet both parts of Germany are stronger, more prosperous, and more stable than they were ten or twenty years ago.

The stubborn resistance of the problem to the many different approaches advocated over the years in various quarters has been due, not to any lack of ingenuity and imagination, but to considerations of basic power. The Soviet desire to control all Germany and the American determination to stop the onward progress of international communism have been the two major blocks in the path of reunification.

The unwillingness of the NATO powers to accept a neutral Central Europe, that is, to allow the sway of Soviet communism in that area, set limits which the Russians represented as warmongering and imperialistic. But historically this policy was a recognition of the repression in Czechoslovakia, Hungary, Poland, and elsewhere, of the doctrine that communism had declared the capitalist world a threat to its existence, and of the fact that the party goal was world domination. Ulbricht took advantage of the opportunities offered him by this deadlock to consolidate his position and eventually demanded and received Moscow's permission to build the Berlin Wall. His control over the SED and over the economy was unquestioned. Neither Washington nor Bonn made attempts to intervene to preserve in East Germany essential human rights and free elections or to moderate the drive of international communism. The minimum requirements of the Western powers in their policy regarding East Germany were unacceptable to the Soviets and the GDR.

Any review of the situation in 1969 that took into account the obstacles that still prevented early solution of the German question would lead to a pessimistic conclusion for the near future. But the prospect is not all dark.

A number of recent developments have affected the Soviet position and influenced Soviet attitudes. These include the Sino-Soviet split, the Russian sense of accomplishment in space and armaments, the changing policy of de Gaulle, the stirrings in the satellite nations, and the evolving capacities and experience of both the GDR and the FRG.

Some of the obstacles to contacts are minor and could be surmounted if the Soviets were to conclude that a major change in European policy was desirable. The German attitude toward the former eastern territories has changed vastly in the last few years.[27] There is no question that the possibility of acceptance of the present Oder-Neisse line can be anticipated in West Germany. In East Germany it has already been recognized. The Munich Agreement of 1938, which had disturbed relations with Czechoslovakia, is no longer a genuine problem. West Germany's fear that a reunified Germany with a preponderantly socialist population would change her internal political balance is a real but not decisive factor. The religious differences between the church groups—Protestant and Catholic, with Lutherans predominating in the East—are sometimes discussed but can hardly be urged as a serious obstacle.

The task of integrating the two economies would be complex but is not regarded as a major hindrance to the adjustment of Central European relations. Similarly the differences between the two social systems, including such elements as social insurance

[27] See chapter 3 and Foreign Minister Brandt's statement on the Oder-Neisse line in March 1968.

measures, are not irreconcilable. Definite and concrete steps would of course have to be taken, but they could be of a kind that would not prove unduly disturbing. Given the concurrence and support of the Western Allies, reunification could be effected after a conference of leaders in the East and the West.

Possible Preliminary Steps

There is little latitude in the West for aggressive action to effect reunification. For the Germans in the Federal Republic, revanchism as usually understood is dead. There is no thought, except in extreme rightwing circles—comprising perhaps 2 or 3 percent of the voters—of attempting to restore a Germany patterned on the concept of power which existed thirty and forty years ago. There is no inclination to reject the commitment that bars the use of force. There is no likelihood of a war to end the present division. No policy of active intervention is contemplated by the United States. The U.S. position is well established and is based on adherence to accepted principles while keeping the door to future adjustments open. The significance of this stand is well understood in Bonn and in Berlin; the criticism that is sometimes heard had little political meaning.

Much thought has however been given to the question of preliminary steps that would be most likely to lead to reunification. Speculation centers on starting with some new type of association that would be easier to achieve. This might take the form of a close working relationship between the two governmental entities in a post-Ulbricht period with many special commissions to handle all-German affairs. Problems similar to those that would be encountered in taxation, transportation, social insurance and investment have been handled in the European Economic Community with notable success. Such an arrangement would initially retain the more important institutions in both parts of Germany but permit the free circulation of persons and a later gradual modification of institutions, as each area exerted an influence on the other. It would provide for increasing freedom of speech and self-determination in East Germany and, as time passed, for interzonal trade tending to free trade.

Some, going further, have even suggested that Berlin, East and West—perhaps excluding an enclave for the Pankow government —might then be given the status of a free port, with permission for free travel in and out and with special economic protection by both sides. Presumably a token international force could then give protection for a period of ten or twenty years as a symbol of its special status. Such arrangements could not be achieved in one year or two; they would require many months of hard technical work. They would necessitate some type of recognition for GDR officials. They could only come after Ulbricht had ceased to rule and after new leaders had come to power on both sides—leaders who would be willing to ignore signs of hatred and to work for practical and moral gains.

The East German economy would need to be linked to the European Common Market, perhaps on the basis of associate status. The military establishments on both sides would be reduced but not eliminated. Such a condition would be possible only if the Soviet leaders genuinely wished a relaxation of tensions in Europe, and if they set a higher value on economic progress than on political infiltration. It could come about only if the organizations for European economic cooperation continued and expanded on a liberal basis, and if the importance of NATO as the main protector of security decreased. This is a pattern of development which is not entirely unreasonable nor beyond the limits of accepted policy.

Would this mean two Germanys or one? It would be compromise between conditions in both East and West Germany. It would disappoint many conservatives and many progressives. If it were successful, however, it would be a step toward the stabilization of forces in Central Europe and would help assure peace.

Will Reunification Ever Be Effected?

To the question whether reunification will ever be effected, only a qualified answer can be given. Questions of when and how must be left open and re-examined from time to time in the light of changing world circumstances. Russia is changing; Europe, both East and West, is changing. Attitudes in the United States and elsewhere are not the same as they were in 1945—or in 1965.

Consideration of history, with its divisions, reunifications, and breakdowns of empires, and with its decay and resurgence of national power, brings a degree of humility to those who would otherwise make hard and fast judgments. Poland, a striking example of the unpredictable, has been from time to time destroyed, divided, suppressed, and re-established.

There are strong reasons, it seems to this writer, for believing that the eastern part of Germany (now the GDR) will eventually be closely associated and in some sense united with the FRG. These reasons are geopolitical and psychological. The Germans in the East Zone are, for the reasons stated in an earlier chapter, at present uneasy vassals in the communist world. In addition, their geographic location is such that they could not remain neutral over a long period of time. Thus, if East Germany were to become a truly sovereign state, a separate entity denying its Germanic history and held apart from the FRG by artificial restraints, it would be a constant menace and source of unrest. The present separate state, precariously maintained by the Berlin Wall and the Iron Curtain, is not compatible with assured and lasting peace. It is even, one must admit, ridiculous.

The search for positive ways to accelerate the slow-moving—even stalled—progress toward reunification must also take into account the outer limits which cannot be crossed, the elements of Western power which cannot be given away or bartered for a gain that, though real, is not beyond price. First, considerations of security, whether under NATO or in some other modified but dependable form, are paramount. Second, real freedom and self-determination must be assured for those who live in the GDR as well as for those in the FRG. Third, Berlin must not be sacrificed in any bargain which seems to offer hope of a united Germany. This requirement means that, if the self-determination should be even partially along communist lines, the institutions of West Berlin must be safeguarded. There are in fact principles and considerations whose value surpasses that of reunification. It is for this reason that the time will be long.

Factors which would advance reunification include—

- The further development of European cooperation in the EEC and elsewhere
- Changes in Russia—lessening of the fear of Germany, confidence in her own strength, and desire for further economic cooperation with the West
- Relaxation of tensions in the Cold War with a decreasing fear of war and increasing hopes for world and local peace
- Continued development of democratic institutions and reasonable interparty relations in West Germany to the point where she would have strength to absorb some of the new institutions in the Zone.

Bonn has renounced the use of force to gain reunification and there is reason to expect it will keep this pledge. If reunification is to be achieved, West Germany will have to accept adjustment and sacrifice, both political and economic, but not the surrender of her security. The two parts of Germany can only be reunited at the price of West German acceptance of and accommodation to some of the changes which have taken place in East Germany and at the cost of some internal modification. These adjustments are not impossible; they are only difficult.

CHAPTER 6

Berlin

THE IMPORTANCE OF THE CITY

The question of Berlin puzzles the historian and bewilders the politician. Some consider the U.S. position in Berlin to be one of the great blunders of the century. Others have found in the situation of the isolated city a unique barometer indicating the state of the cold war and a significant demonstration of West Germany's will to oppose the westward progress of communism.[1]

The international commitments entered into by the four powers at Potsdam in 1945, reiterated at Geneva in 1955, and repeated on numerous occasions by the three Western powers and the NATO countries are links in a continuous chain of legal provisions. All are clearly set forth and matters of public record. Fragile though they have appeared to some, they have served as a system of restraints against the aggressive attacks of the Soviets from the time of the blockade to the present day. Now, as earlier, weakening of these links would bring to Europe distrust, uncertainty, and fear which would open the doors to subversion, disunity, and disaster. Berlin today is a cornerstone of the structure of American deterrence and security.

Cuba, Formosa, Vietnam, and Suez are all key points that have been made significant by the confrontation of opposing political forces; but not one of them has the combination of geographic, political, and symbolic meaning which West Berlin in its present

[1] The problems of Berlin and its significance have not changed substantially since *Berlin: The Wall Is Not Forever* was written. Some of the material there can supplement the discussion here. There is also more recent material which gives other facts or points of view. There is a large number of books on the question of Berlin, many of which appear either in the bibliography accompanying the present text or in the ample bibliographies to be found in the sources there listed. Some aspects of the Berlin question are discussed in chapter 7 and elsewhere.

status possesses as an outpost of Western Europe. Many could wish it otherwise, but the facts are clear. The West cannot abandon Berlin; and a solution can be achieved only in the context of a broad and inclusive European settlement. The problem of Berlin will therefore endure for years, some say for decades.

Looking at the situation more narrowly, one can affirm that, without the Western presence in Berlin, the question of reunification would have been reduced to the vanishing point shortly after the Geneva Summit Conference more than a decade ago. Only the most belligerent communists however dare to challenge—and only the least imaginative Western leaders can ignore—a Berlin that votes for freedom, lives in a democratic political community with Western Europe, and enjoys the liberties (except that of contact with the surrounding country) enjoyed in the United States. In many ways West Berlin proclaims the pro-Western intentions of the Germans. Thus the question of the relation of the two parts of Germany continues to be a vital and controversial issue, hotly debated in the Federal Republic and much discussed in the outside world.

To the Germans in the East, West Berlin has brought an understanding of the difference between the dictatorship under which they live and the democracy of which they have had so little experience. It has offered them the spectacle of a city treated, not as a military outpost, but with extraordinary solicitude, and rebuilt with the help of more than a billion dollars in American aid. Until the building of the Wall, it provided them with an escape hatch and gave them the realization that they were not condemned to remain forever enclosed. Contact with it has given them courage when they suffered from physical and mental deprivation. To keep them from breaking loose in the course of the past twenty years has required a strict and oppressive set of controls, backed by hundreds of thousands of Soviet troops, many in actual occupation, others stationed nearby.

For the Soviets, as for the NATO powers, Berlin has been a testing ground, and they have used it as such. Their capacity to harass has been almost unlimited, but when they showed the intention of taking drastic steps to eject the occupying powers from the city, the resistance they encountered was impressive. Only in the case of minor annoyances (the flight of helicopters, delays to trucks entering the city, inflammatory propaganda) has the Western reaction sometimes been confused. Throughout the entire period since the blockade, however, Moscow has understood the West's determination to maintain its position.

In this connection, it is interesting to note Khrushchev's opinion as to the legal situation—after the somewhat erroneous appraisal in his 1958 ultimatum. An article by M. E. Bathurst quoted Khrushchev as replying on March 19, 1959, to a question by Sanakoyev, correspondent of Moscow's *International Affairs*, as to whether the Western Powers had rights and duties in Berlin:

> Yes, I believe that the United States, Britain and France do have lawful rights for their stay in Berlin. These rights ensue from the fact of the German surrender as the result of our joint struggle against Nazi Germany. Yet fourteen years have gone by since the end of the war, and there is no need for further occupation of West Berlin. That is why we have proposed that, at long last, a peace treaty be concluded with both German States. When a peace treaty is signed with the German Democratic Republic and the Federal Republic of Germany, the right to occupation becomes invalid.[2]

On August 28, 1961, Khrushchev said to Drew Pearson in Moscow:

> . . . in proposing conclusion of a German peace treaty we emphasize that freedom of West Berlin's communications must be guaranteed.
>
> The West Berlin government as any sovereign government, must have the right to maintain diplomatic, economic, and cultural ties with any country.[3]

[2] M. E. Bathurst, "The Legal Aspects of the Berlin Problem," in *British Yearbook of International Law*, ed. Sir Humphrey Waldock and R. Y. Jennings (London: Oxford University Press, 1962) p. 291. Attributed to *Soviet Booklet No. 53* (London, October 1959), p. 38.

[3] Otto Martin von der Gablentz, *Documents on Berlin, 1943–1963*, p. 300.

Berlin has been described as a bone in Khrushchev's throat, a nest of spies, an arrow pointed at the heart of the GDR, a provocation and a threat to the peace of the world. Soviet reassurances that the people and institutions of the Western half of the city would be protected are frequently rendered meaningless by harsh words and harassment. Some of the attacks on the city are a part of the tactics to strengthen Ulbricht; some are apparently the result of genuine hostility as well as confusion over what could constitute a feasible solution of the problem.

Since in spite of flourishes and declamations in the East no peace treaty has been signed, it is presumably the Soviet view that the rights of occupation remain. The Soviets have been strengthened in that view by the statement by the Department of State on December 20, 1958, *The Legal Basis for Holding Berlin.*[4] The men in the Kremlin are not yet ready to renounce their rights; their East German neighbor has a strength which they recognize and could in some circumstances fear.

The Soviets have come to depend on Ulbricht's administrative skill, but it is unlikely that they have counted on the communization of the inhabitants of the Zone. The exodus of refugees, the revolt of 1953, and the general character of the Germans have cast doubt on East German allegiance to communism. The Kremlin policy therefore has oscillated between exploitation and support, between conspicuous military occupation and an attitude of permissiveness. Meanwhile Moscow keeps cautious watch on the strength developing in the Zone and the assertiveness of the authorities in Pankow.

In a series of crises the Soviets have tested the firmness of the Western powers. They have found the road blocked by the words and the will which declared ". . . the security and welfare of Berlin, and the maintenance of the position of the three Powers there, are regarded by the three Powers as essential elements of the free world in the present international situation."[5] Neither the

[4] Statement by the Department of State on Legal Aspects of the Berlin Situation, December 20, 1958 (U.S. Senate, Committee on Foreign Relations, *Documents on Germany, 1944–1961,* December 1961, pp. 367–78).
[5] U.S. Department of State, *Documents on Germany, 1944–1959,* May 27, 1952, p. 103.

phrases nor the intentions have changed, and, in spite of what a few have occasionally held to be signs of weakness, the Soviets have looked on the commitment and found it significant.

The Paradox of Berlin

Strange as it may seem, a mistake in the mid-forties—one of the most serious miscalculations of this century—has become an instrument for the protection of Europe. Those who regard the hazards involved as too great and the risk of error as too grave may question the validity of this paradox. To make their position convincing, however, they would need to demonstrate how the Atlantic nations could otherwise have established a line of demarcation, and where and how such a line would have been manned. The United States has become involved in the fate of Berlin in a manner which no statesman at the end of the war could have planned or foreseen. To the isolationists such an involvement is of course a disaster. But those who consider the preservation of a democratic Europe essential to U.S. survival in liberty must examine the strange outcome in all its aspects.

At the cost of bold statesmanship, of a small contingent of troops, and of something over a billion dollars in aid the United States has an enclave in the middle of communist Europe. It has a listening post and a point of contact. It has gained an understanding of Soviet policy and a sympathy for endangered peoples that it would normally never have possessed. Neither the funds nor the men nor the engagement could have been secured from a war-weary nation, an often parsimonious Congress, and a prosperous and complacent population if the United States had not been drawn into the strange position of defender of Berlin. Much of the NATO "sword and shield," the concern for economic cooperation in Europe, and the structure of commercial and financial agreements was stimulated after the blockade had increased support for NATO in consequence of U.S. responsibility for the German situation. If the men responsible for the conduct of U.S. affairs had not seen what was threatening there, the defense programs now underway would have been slower to develop. What has been accomplished is imperfect, but it far exceeds what was thought possible in

1945. It is necessary to recognize the mistakes that were made; but it would be foolish to overlook byproducts that have bolstered the security of the free world.

MISCALCULATIONS

The errors made in 1945 were serious and costly. In misjudging the postwar problems, time, men, and money were squandered, and the world's progress toward freedom was set back by generations. In the writer's opinion, Berlin may prove to have been one of the less costly errors of that time and may in fact have helped to limit the losses incurred in other instances.

The errors in judgment were the result not so much of the failure to capture Berlin or of the drawing of the zonal line, as of other flaws in basic strategy and of changing relations with the USSR. The errors in planning the administration of the occupation were important, but they were not central. Washington's cardinal mistake was the failure to see the threat of aggressive communism in a USSR that was ruled by ruthless and ambitious men intent on expanding their control. In looking back after more than twenty years, it is hard now to recall the sense of peril in the 1940s that turned revolutionary Russia into an ally and the widespread expectation that the major nations would seek peace and prosperity through collaboration in the United Nations.

All the well-known leaders had a part in the mistakes made at that time. They were anxious to create a new world with means as yet untried and with partners who were little acquainted with each others' intentions. They knew little of the development of nuclear energy and could have only a faint picture of guided missiles, the use of outer space, the new tools of industry, new speeds, new communications, and new psychologies. Above all they were unprepared for the problems and relations that emerged in the postwar decade. Their strategic concepts fell short of what was needed. The errors made at that time are hard to condone, and the German people were later to scrutinize and to wonder about the treatment of Germany and how the division came to pass.

That Franklin D. Roosevelt was to a considerable degree responsible can scarcely be denied, but the blame must be shared among many others, not excluding Sir Winston Churchill. There was in 1944 and 1945 no clear realization of the aims and methods of the Soviet leaders. There was also no expectation that the treaty with Germany would be postponed for ten, twenty, or thirty years. If the Western leaders had ever envisaged such a contingency, they would have made very different provisions for the occupation of the country; their consideration of the balance of power in Europe would have been earlier and their consideration of spheres of influence more realistic.

Access to Berlin

The 1944 and 1945 plans were drawn for an occupation of six months or, as Roosevelt said at Yalta, of two years at the most.[6] The situation in Berlin during that period would obviously be one of great distress, but the problem would be not so much an East-West struggle as economic misery and the almost total lack of all supplies and institutions needed to make a city viable. Since it was assumed that the occupation forces would soon be withdrawn, access to and reconstruction of the city seemed of minor importance and were little considered. The fact that this major miscalculation was a part of the overall postwar planning does not excuse the particular decisions made, nor does it mean that other more favorable decisions could not have been made. It does however go far to explain why men of reasonable intentions and long experience neglected several important elements in their arrangements and did not give more careful consideration to the problem of corridors to Berlin. The weakness in planning is more obvious in the light of the conditions for the occupation of Austria which, though similar, were somewhat better.

Soviet Control of Central Europe

If a larger part of Central Europe had been taken and held by the Western Allies, it would have been more advantageous for the West. General Omar Bradley estimated in April 1944 that to take Berlin would mean the loss of 100,000 U.S. troops.[7] But even if this

[6] Winston S. Churchill, *Triumph and Tragedy*, p. 353.
[7] Omar N. Bradley, *A Soldier's Story*, p. 535.

course had been pursued, under the agreements made at Yalta the troops would have been withdrawn later, just as they were withdrawn from positions securely held in Austria and in Czechoslovakia. The military were subordinate to the civilian authorities in this matter. The civilian decision was to leave Central Europe to Soviet control pending sweeping worldwide settlements that were to be supervised by the United Nations. The USSR was thus given a sphere of influence which extended from the Baltic to the mid-Danube basin. These are decisions that can be understood only by those who lived through the anxious days of the Second World War and view the decisions then made in a broad perspective. They are unintelligible to those who did not come on to the international scene until after the war in Korea. They were made under the influence of hope for an effective supervision of the peace by the United Nations and of fear of the aggressive tendencies of former Nazi party members—and those who made them were still affected by the heroic and costly struggle of the Russians at Stalingrad. These circumstances of the mid-forties are already dim and for the most part forgotten. Those who view history from the standpoint of the late sixties find the Berlin situation difficult to explain.

From a purely military point of view, there is no dispute that the Western Allies could have taken and controlled more territory. What is less clear is the extent to which such an action would have minimized the chances of Soviet partnership in the war in the Pacific. Hiroshima still lay in the future. It is fruitless to base evaluations of foreign policy on tenuous and uncertain guesses; a glance at the many factors involved in the problem can help toward a more accurate analysis.

Conflicts and Consequences of Early Planning

The timetable of major decisions dates from 1943 and the preparations for Secretary Cordell Hull's trip to Moscow to discuss postwar settlements. Administration of the occupied territory did not start until after the Potsdam meeting in the summer of 1945. During these years those of us who worked on position papers for the European Advisory Commission and in similar capacities, saw the conflict of opinion and the shifts of view that were to characterize the treatment of the European problem. There was a continuing struggle between those who wanted a harsh peace and those who inclined to a more lenient approach. The compromises that were reached limited reparation payments, conceded some forced labor for reconstruction, gave high priority to de-Nazification and disarmament, and called for the trial of war criminals.

The economic policy that was incorporated in the postwar planning was especially important. President Roosevelt, dissatisfied with some of the position papers put before him, asked Henry Morgenthau, Jr., secretary of the treasury, to propose a plan for Germany. The resulting document was taken to Quebec in August 1943. It called for the dismantling of the Ruhr industries, the partition of Germany, twenty years of control over her economy by the United Nations, and the policing of Germany by military forces supplied by her neighbors. Responsibility for sustaining the German people was to rest on the Germans, who were to use such facilities as might be available to them. The Russians were to participate in military and civilian controls, and the plan contained no indication of separate treatment by the Soviets in their zone of occupation. This plan was provisionally approved by Roosevelt and Churchill but was never adopted as the official policy of the United States.

Even under the Morgenthau Plan, it was assumed that all parts of Germany, including Berlin, would be treated alike.[8] But neither in political nor in economic planning was any considerable attention given to the future of Berlin. It was puzzling that the Soviets were reluctant to have the Americans and British come to Berlin in June and had, it would seem, established their pre-eminence in the area from the beginning. Communist efforts to bring the labor groups under the control of their stooges caused difficulties in the troubled weeks of 1946 and 1947. It was not, however, until the beginning of the blockade in 1948 that the extent to which they were prepared to go in order to take over the city became evident.

[8] U.S. Senate, Committee on Foreign Relations, *A Decade of American Foreign Policy, 1941–1949*, October 18, 1949, pp. 502–505.

In the meantime the results of earlier miscalculations had become steadily more obvious, and the Berliners themselves were alert to the dangers. When the blockade came, they were quick to make their choice and to reject the threats and enticements of the Soviet commanders.

A Symbol Between Two Power Blocs

Later it became apparent that conditions as they developed in the decade after the war had given rise to three major consequences: (1) The Berliners, faced with a choice between communism and democracy, decided overwhelmingly and at great risk to throw in their lot with the Western powers. (2) The Soviets, checked in their efforts to take over all Germany, had to revise their policy for Europe. From 1946 on, their probes and hostile actions and their retreats from forward political positions were an index to their changing estimates of how and how far they could exert pressure on the free world. Western policymakers were thus afforded a useful barometer of tension.[9] (3) As the city of Berlin developed its democratic institutions and expanded its economy with capitalist help, the seventeen million East Germans living under communist rule had in their midst an outpost of the free world such as they had not witnessed since the beginning of Hitlerism. From this spectacle they gained ideas of freedom which prevented their absorption into the Soviet bloc and kept alive hope which would otherwise have been crushed before the mid-fifties. During the two decades of suppression by Stalin and Khrushchev in the East and rearmament and development of the Atlantic Alliance in the West, Berlin was significant evidence of how oppression could be and was deterred.

What would have happened to Berlin if either the USSR or the free world had achieved their goals? The first hypothesis predicates Western recognition of the GDR as a sovereign and separate German state. Such a move would have been inconsistent with the continued occupation of Berlin. The industry, administration, welfare, and lives of the people of West Berlin would have been

[9] Eleanor Lansing Dulles, "Berlin: Barometer of Tension," in *Détente*, ed. Eleanor Lansing Dulles and Robert Dickson Crane, pp. 121–137.

subject to an alien system and forced to accept controls and a government which they had fought for two decades to reject. As for the suggestion of making Berlin an international city, few would consider this a practical and workable solution. The city would be lost in the sea of communism. Only if there were notable changes in the GDR and in the Soviet Union, could the Western Allies allow such a situation. Perhaps at some distant date new relations may obtain, and the two parts of Germany may be brought into an association that will preserve the values and the ideals of the city as it is today. Berlin could then survive in freedom. But such contingencies can have no part in current decisions.

The other hypothesis supposes the acceptance of the earlier four-power formula—the reunification of Germany through free elections and the establishment of a single, free, and independent nation. These were the conditions prescribed for a postwar settlement and the conclusion of a peace treaty—the basis for the German policy enunciated at Yalta in 1945, Potsdam later in the same year, and Geneva in 1955. But after the blockade, the Warsaw Pact, and the recurrent harassment of Berlin the sincerity of the Soviets in subscribing to this formula was in doubt. If this formula were followed, however, the situation in Berlin would have to be changed: the government would have to be reorganized; provision would have to be made for compromises between some institutions and systems and for the abandonment of those not compatible with the effective cooperation of the two parts of Germany. The Berlin that has been created by the joint efforts of many people and nations would remain, but its horizons would have been enlarged and its responsibilities vastly increased.

In either case the treatment of Berlin is assumed to follow from the solution adopted. Of course, if substantial progress were to be made in European cooperation that reached far to the East, the Berlin problem would disappear entirely. In the meantime consideration of the contingencies just reviewed underscores the fact that the city, important though it is as an economic and social entity, derives its present meaning mainly from its position between two power blocs.

All the descriptions currently applied to Berlin—bulwark of freedom, tripwire for NATO, symbol, show window, or bridge between East and West—draw their special significance from the context of Soviet expansionist tendencies. As long as these tendencies persist, Berlin must be held by whatever means are necessary to effect it. This would remain true even if the city's industry should decline, its active cultural life should dim, and its morale should falter. The stakes at issue transcend all local considerations. Even if the more ominous prophecies should be fulfilled, the Allied garrisons are bound by commitment to remain. Conditions of distress for the citizens, such as those that were endured in the early postwar years, would not release the Western Allies from their promises but would rather accentuate the need for special support. Washington is not the only capital that recognizes this requirement; Bonn is increasingly alert to the dangers that might have to be faced if there were any diminution of interest in the city.

THE PHOENIX RISES FROM THE ASHES

A well-balanced recovery was essential to any solution of the problem of West Berlin. In the years immediately after 1945 the work of clearing the streets, building bridges, and restoring the public utilities, though not easy, had proceeded with encouraging speed. Then, with the end of the blockade in 1949, the emphasis for action shifted to the basic industries. In the decade which followed, many economists and government officials were involved in the reconstruction of Berlin. It was apparent that the city needed comprehensive plans, German and American financial help, and the cooperation of German business. Paul Hertz, a leading socialist and distinguished economist who had emigrated to the United States, returned to Berlin at the request of his friend Governing Mayor Reuter.[10] He became the outstanding planner for the reconstruction of Berlin, but he was helped by many others.

At this time the lack of capital equipment and a total of more than 300,000 unemployed workers were undermining the stability of the city and threatening an exodus which would have left it an empty shell. First assistance was given to metal foundries such as

[10] See the Paul Hertz Collection at the Hoover Institution, Stanford.

Borsig, the heavy electrical industry including the *Allgemeine Elektrizitaets Gesellschaft*, *Siemens und Halske* AG, and *Telefunken* AG, all of which employed large numbers of workers. Following this the consumer goods and the lighter industries received special help. A comprehensive report by Richardson Wood, member of a New York management firm, set the target of increasing the number of employed workers by 50,000 a year. Many Berliners said that this was impossible or that, if the plan was moderately successful, it would still leave 100,000 workers unemployed. Nevertheless, the target was retained, and in approximately six years most of the 300,000 had jobs. The increase in the Gross National Product was steady. By the early 1960s construction workers were in such demand that many projects were slowed by a labor shortage. Public buildings and—even more encouraging—unsubsidized private houses were going up, and the city was regaining some of its peacetime aspect. The result of this activity and of the rising standard of living was to be seen in the hotels, bars, restaurants, and centers of amusement. Berlin had become an exciting place in which to live.

As conditions improved, the United States cut down its financial aid but encouraged the Bonn government to take over an increasing share of the economic support which continued to be necessary. By 1965 the annual subsidy reached DM 2,500 million.[11] For a decade the workers had for patriotic reasons refrained from demands for higher wages, and strikes had been few and sporadic. The competitive position of the city was favorable, wages were below those in the Federal Republic, and the quality of production was high. To offset the frequent harassment of the access routes and the consequent risk of delay in shipment or of actual nondelivery of products ordered in the Federal Republic, special tax advantages cut the cost of production, and insurance covered part of the risk.

During the years 1949–1961 close to 100,000 workers daily crossed the sector border both ways to work in the other part of the city. This commuting back and forth was good for the economy

[11] Total assistance given by the Federal Republic in 1968 was approximately DM 3 billion.

and established useful contacts between the communist and the capitalist worlds. Workers in the GDR were well aware of the prosperity in West Berlin and many considered going to the Federal Republic where conditions were even more promising. This led to a basic unrest and a fear of being trapped in the Zone. In this period West Berlin was indeed a show window, and many East Germans fled to the West. There they were easily absorbed into the work force to help with the rapid reconstruction then in progress and to play an important part in the so-called economic miracle that was in truth no miracle but a marvel of hard work.

The Recurrent Crises

The political and geographic vulnerability of the city to recurrent communist pressure and the accompanying crises brought brief moments of panic. From time to time funds would be withdrawn from banks and families would move. On the whole however the times of trouble made little impression on the people and the economy of the city. On the political side, their effect was to strengthen the anticommunist vote and build up a vigorous democratic society with strong pro-American feeling. The people knew that without U.S. support they could not have a productive economy and that, without the presence of Allied troops as a symbol of NATO, they could not restrain the communists from more aggressive moves. The reason for holding off the communists and welcoming Allied troops went unquestioned in Berlin. Here was a political situation which even the most apolitical person could understand and appreciate. Berliners had seen the communists at their worst in the postwar years, whereas the Americans had come in as protectors.

The many communist probes, particularly Khrushchev's ultimatum in 1958, demonstrated to the Soviet leaders the facts that the determination of Berlin and the Allies toughened under pressure and that nothing could be gained by the kind of demand that directly attacked established Allied policy and legal rights. The effort to thrust the Western occupiers out appeared to be halted, at least for a time. After 1958 there was no major demand until the June 1961 ultimatum. In the years between 1959 and 1961 Soviet actions and words were such as to lead some to conclude that a genuine detente had begun. Others however were puzzled and skeptical; the city was still harassed, and there was no sign that Soviet long-range goals had changed. The people in West Germany and Berlin lost a little of the heroism of the past, however, and became more complacent in their economic success.

During these years there was relatively little talk of reunification; it was assumed that the Allies, in their attempts to improve security in free Europe, would somehow negotiate from a policy of strength agreements favorable to the Germans. Few realized that Germany had become one of the strong economic powers in the world and one of the largest contributors of men and arms to NATO. Without seeming to have addressed himself to this aspect of Germany's problems, Chancellor Adenauer had achieved his two main goals: the rehabilitation of the Federal Republic in the eyes of free-world statesmen and the restoration of the nation to the first rank of free-world powers.

The Legal Status of Berlin

While the Federal Republic was still preoccupied with its own restoration, Berlin had sometimes felt neglected by Bonn. Its status was peculiar in law as well as in practice. West German legislators were however careful to keep in mind the vulnerability of the city, its special relations to the Federal Republic, and the fact that it was not a *Land* incorporated in the Federation.

Professor Elmer Plischke has explained the situation in an article in the *Journal of Politics* in which he described the city and mentioned some of its legal characteristics. In some respects, he wrote, it resembles a national capital. It is a major metropolis with a complete municipal system of governance that comprises all the normal legislative, executive, and judicial organs, de jure for the whole city, de facto for the three Western sectors or West Berlin. Moreover, under the West German Constitution the metropolis is a *Land* or state. It has, however, a unique international status, manifest in the commitments of the three Western powers. He concluded:

> In summary, Berlin possesses characteristics of a national capital, a populous metropolitan city, an associated quasi-integrated element in a federal union, and a political community of considerable international significance. Yet, in each of these respects, and in all of them conjointly, Berlin is unusual, if not unique.[12]

Berlin was, as he stated, distinguished from the rest of Germany in the Allied protocol of September 12, 1944. It was to be dealt with separately from the rest of Germany in the administration of the occupation and to be governed by the prospective Kommandatura. When at a later date the Western powers terminated the occupation of West Germany in the Conventions of May 1952 and October 1954, they specifically reserved their rights and responsibilities with respect to Berlin.[13] In a letter to the chancellor the three Western high commissioners stated that they had decided to exercise their rights "in such a way as to facilitate the carrying out by the Federal Republic of its Declaration of Aid to Berlin." This declaration pledged the Federal Republic "to continue its aid to the political, cultural, economic and financial reconstruction."[14]

Meantime, in October 1951 the Berlin House of Representatives had passed the Cover Law (*Mantelgesetz*) to assure that "provisions of implementing ordinances or regulations under the Federal Law may be valid in Berlin by issuance or reference or otherwise." The Allied Kommandatura supported this arrangement. Similarly the "Berlin Clause" was outlined in a communication from the Allied Kommandatura on May 21, 1952, to assure that the name Berlin would be included in international treaties of the Federal Republic and that the terms of such treaties would be extended to Berlin. The *Mantelgesetz* and the "Berlin Clause" were needed to

[12] Elmer Plischke, "Integrating Berlin and the Federal Republic of Germany," *Journal of Politics* February 1965, p. 37. See also Charles B. Robson and Werner Zohlnhoefer, "Berlinproblem und 'Deutsche Frage,'" in *Jahrbuch fuer die Geschichte Mittel- und Ostdeutschlands Politik*, pp. 297–323; Theodor Eschenburg, *Die Deutsche Frage*, passim; Fritz K. G. Erler, "The Struggle for German Reunification," *Foreign Affairs* April 1956, pp. 380–93.

[13] Gablentz, *Documents on Berlin, 1943–1963*, pp. 132, 134, 138, 139, 142.

[14] Ibid., pp. 128, 132, 133, 145.

provide for these special contingencies and smooth the development of the legal structure because when adopting the Basic Law (*Grundgesetz*) in 1949, the Allies had been unwilling to incorporate the city of Berlin into the Federal Republic.

The Germans have never been entirely happy with these arrangements and do not always recognize that they are essential to the maintenance of Allied protection. They have agitated from time to time to have Berlin accorded full "*Land* status." The Allies have opposed this on legal and tactical grounds. A statement by Joachim von Elbe, legal officer in the American Embassy in Bonn, reads as follows:

> The term "Land Berlin" signifies that Berlin has the status of a "Land" as distinguished from the status of a "municipality," or a "district," or a "province." Under German public law, a "Land" is a political entity which is not subject to supervision by another public authority.
>
> Even though Berlin may be called a "Land" it does not follow that Berlin is a "Land of the Federal Republic," i.e. that it forms part of the Federal system as do the other German Laender (for instance cities like Hamburg and Bremen). In its decision of May 21, 1957, the Federal Constitutional Court declared that Berlin is a Land of Federal Republic. The Court added, however, that this is not the position of the three Allied Powers.
>
> The position of the three Allied Powers that Berlin is not a Land of the Federal Republic is based on a reservation in the Letter of Approval of the Basic Law by the Military Governors of May 12, 1949. (The reservation, incidentally, was specifically maintained upon the signature of the so-called Bonn Conventions whereby the Federal Republic achieved sovereignty). The reservation concerned "the participation of Greater Berlin in the Federation." It says in essence that Berlin may not be accorded voting membership in the Federal Parliament (Bundestag and Bundesrat), and that Berlin may not be "governed by the Federation." Berlin, nevertheless, may designate a small number of representatives to attend the meetings of these legislative bodies. The Kommandatura, without the Soviets, by letter of August 29, 1950, with respect to the Berlin Constitution, declared that dur-

> ing the transitional period envisaged in Article 87 of the Berlin Constitution (i.e., when the application of the Basic Law in Berlin is subject to restrictions) Berlin "shall possess none of the attributes of a twelfth Land."[15]

This summary differs slightly in emphasis from the exposition of Professor Plischke. The general significance of the two explanations is, however, the same: Berlin is isolated not only geographically but legally from all other jurisdictions.

The Berlin representatives in the *Bundestag* have no voting rights, but they work with the party leadership and with the *Bundestag* committees. For most casual observers as well as for active politicians, the distinctions involved in these and other special provisions make little difference in the governing of the city and its relations to the Federal Republic. Many of the services, for example post and telephone, are handled in precisely the same manner in the city as they are in the *Laender*. The arrangements and legal provisions are all written with a view to the inclusion of the GDR in the Federal Republic at some future time and the eventual transfer of the functions of the central government to Berlin as the capital. Meanwhile the city is occupied and still pays to the Allies approximately DM 300 million a year in occupation costs. Its citizens watch the troops and tanks on maneuver with a feeling of close involvement in the protecting presence of the Allies. Whatever the loss of prestige some may think they sustain by reason of their dependent status, this is for the most part offset by the extension of the Allied commitment there for their safety.

There has been almost no change in the legal and constitutional provisions, except for the exclusion of East Berlin which had been included in the original provisions as part of "Greater Berlin." The guarantees by the West were not limited to the Western sectors of the city in any formal statement before the speech by President Kennedy on July 25, 1961.

[15] Personal letter to the author dated July 1965, quoted in Dulles, *Berlin*, pp. 38, 39. After the Saar was incorporated in the Federal Republic on January 1, 1957, there were ten Laender; Berlin would have been the eleventh.

West German Criticism of Allied Policy

Allied firmness in the defense of Berlin has been questioned in many an informal conversation in Berlin and elsewhere. Many of the young men complained in 1965 and subsequently of the fact that the Soviet and GDR harassment was countered by words, not deeds.

The first disillusionment came after the revolt of 1953. At that time, according to many persons, there was a "last chance" to free the Eastern Zone. Although seasoned politicians knew that the Soviets could not then, as later they did not in Hungary, permit groups of rebellious youth and angry workers to defeat the objectives and the military might of Soviet Russia, these critics stigmatized the Allied nonparticipation as cowardice and termed it a severe setback to the German cause.

During the next eight years public opinion fluctuated. There were various special regulations with regard to access. There was the de facto acceptance of the 10,000-foot ceiling for the air corridors, making them in effect into air tunnels. There were skirmishes over the barges and delays on the *Autobahn*. In several cases the Western powers avoided a direct challenge by compromising over the papers required to enter and leave Berlin, allowing the soldiers on their trucks to be counted, or giving manifests to Soviet officers at control points on the access routes. In most respects they retained the substance of their position and put on a bold front in their statements. Meanwhile they allowed the impression to gain ground that in general they wished to avoid an open challenge. For some people this was statesmanship, for others it was erosion of policy and partial defeat.

One test of success or failure may be found in the economic situation. Berlin became during this period a magnet for visitors, a market place for goods, an active center for students and artists, and an increasingly productive industrial community. Confidence, though sometimes disturbed, was never destroyed.

CHALLENGES AND THE WALL: 1961 AND 1968

The Eisenhower-Dulles foreign policy had taken over the program and commitments of the Truman-Acheson years with little change. Leading Republicans had worked with the Democrats on the Berlin and German situations in various contexts for several years. During the mid-fifties the aid programs had expanded in type, but as aid to Europe tapered off the amounts appropriated began to decline. Khrushchev had tested U.S. policy in 1958 and found the position firm. By 1959 he was convinced that he would have to modify his tactics. But in 1961 he faced new men and new conditions.

The First Challenge

In June 1961 Khrushchev met the new President in Vienna.[16] John F. Kennedy had not been closely associated with the German policy of the past fifteen years. There was little to indicate whether or not he would turn in a new direction. It is not surprising therefore that Khrushchev tried again. On June 4 he handed Kennedy a new demand that the occupiers leave Berlin. The new President was shocked and discouraged by the encounter; his response was not immediate.

During the period that ensued, many recognized that Khrushchev had returned to his harder attitude and had sensed a possible opportunity in Washington's apparent hesitation. The three Western powers and Germany consulted together; in July they coordinated a strong and familiar position: they rejected the proposals contained in the Soviet note. During the interim however, some evidence of a partial shift had been perceptible in the tone of Washington's statements.

Meanwhile there were scattered signs of impending trouble. The number of refugees fleeing through Berlin mounted daily. The meaning of this for Ulbricht and his economy was noted in the United States. A number of leading political figures in Washington suggested that they would consider curbs on the flow of refugees justified.[17] Some observed that President Kennedy's speech of July 25 suggested that there were only two choices: local reaction or

[16] Kurt L. Shell, *Bedrohung und Bewaehrung*, p. 15.

[17] Dulles, *Berlin*, pp. 50–54, 56n. Speeches by Senators Fulbright, Mansfield, and Morse were widely quoted. In response to these statements, Herbert Wehner and Eric Mende reaffirmed the position that Germans had a complete right to travel back and forth.

nuclear war. The idea of a Western nuclear attack did not bring to the Germans any sense of dependable protection. In the absence of any proposal for cooperative countermeasures by NATO, perhaps affecting the Soviets' position elsewhere, there seemed to be little hope. It was noted that in Kennedy's July speech the response to Khrushchev referred to the defense of West Berlin—a weakening of the familiar formula. Thus, even though the President announced the call-up of 200,000 reserves to improve military readiness, the new Administration's exact intentions were for several weeks in doubt.

The Myth of American Foreknowledge

There will continue to be argument and disagreement about how much Washington knew in the early summer of the decision to build a wall. The difference of opinion is easy to understand. Even before the uprising in Berlin in 1953 the possibility of the GDR sealing off the communist part of the city had been considered. There appeared to be strong arguments against it: such a job would be for technical reasons difficult to do efficiently, and it would make the Ulbricht policy seem monstrous to outside observers.

There are three conclusions which can be regarded as incontrovertible: (1) Washington knew that something would be done to halt the exodus. (2) There was no "hard intelligence" or information that a wall would be built in August. (3) The Administration could have shown force, but this would only have altered, not eliminated, measures by the GDR.

The intelligence community was watching the signs and reporting them to Washington. These included Ulbricht's trip to Moscow, the meeting of the Warsaw powers on August 4, and scattered comments of refugees, but no evidence of the imminence of the wall. Robert Lochner, chief of Radio in the American Sector (RIAS) at that time, made the following statement to the writer:

> It has become apparent that on that fateful day in August 1961 when first barbed wire, then concrete blocks, were placed along the dividing line between East and West Berlin, that no one in the allied missions in West Berlin had the slightest indication of

what was happening. West Germans have frequently claimed since that the Americans knew all the time. This was not the case.

The rapid rise of refugees into West Berlin in preceding weeks had indicated something unusual was likely. But the consensus is that the Americans had not been able to figure out just what the end result might be. Even RIAS, usually the most reliable weather vane to reflect daily occurrences in East Berlin, had no indications of the extraordinary happenings to come.

Secrecy was such that *Neues Deutschland*, the leading East Berlin daily paper, was even able to come out with a special two-page edition to announce the event in the early morning hours of Sunday, August 13, simultaneously with the stringing of the first barbed wire.

The regular Sunday edition of *Neues Deutschland* was prepared as usual on Saturday night. On this particular occasion, however, a few hand-picked, hardcore Communist staff members remained after the regular crew had left, and, behind locked doors, put a second two-page edition together, announcing the wall.[18]

This view has been corroborated by other responsible officials as well as by indirect evidence of what the Western Allies and the Germans expected.

In this connection, a review of the German press is of interest. Even on the day after the Wall went up, it showed little awareness of the situation. This apparent slowness to react resulted from the facts that subsequent attention has focused on the date of August 13, although there was no actual Wall until about the 17th or 18th, and that the wood and wire barriers appeared to some at the time to be a temporary demonstration by Ulbricht and not the beginning of a permanent and effective structure across the entire city. The myth that Americans knew and condoned the plan can be dismissed.

American Inaction

The third contention—that there should have been a show of force in the second week of August—is more difficult to handle

[18] As quoted in Dulles, *Berlin*, p. 55.

since it involves general U.S. policy at that time. There is little doubt that U.S. troop carriers and tanks could have crossed into the East Sector which they still, in 1969, daily patrol in uniform. If they had done so, there might have been incidents, but in the absence of Soviet soldiers there would have been no serious opposition. A statement by General Clay, quoted from an interview by Deane and David Heller, reads as follows:

> Question: General Clay, when we were in Berlin shortly after the erection of The Wall, many Berliners expressed the opinion that the Western Powers should have "torn down The Wall" as soon as it was erected. . . .
>
> General Clay: I do not believe in second-guessing the decisions of military commanders on the spot. They conferred on the matter and did what they thought was right. It would be hard for anyone to say that they were wrong. One thing that might have been done . . . one thing I might have done . . . would have been to make a sufficient show of force to require the presence of the Russians in the building of The Wall. As it was, the East Germans handled the matter.[19]

It should be remembered that, although occasionally some have suggested that the Americans should go it alone, no significant step involving Berlin can be taken to meet a crisis without consultation with the French, the British, and the Federal Republic. It is doubtful if the British and French would have concurred in risking a show of force. In any case instructions from Washington had ruled out a local reaction. It was widely rumored that in the summer of 1961 word had been sent to Berlin to avoid, if possible, any tension in the city. The President had been shaken by the Bay of Pigs failure and was deeply concerned over conditions in Southeast Asia and particularly in Laos.[20] He was anxious to avoid a series of crises in various areas. He thought the Berlin problems could be contained and kept from boiling up. Thus, even though the

[19] Deane and David Heller, *The Berlin Wall*, pp. 237–38; Dulles, *Berlin*, p. 56. President Kennedy is reported as saying he was not advised to knock down the Wall (Lucius D. Clay, "Berlin," *Foreign Affairs* October 1962, pp. 47–58).

[20] Arthur M. Schlesinger, *A Thousand Days*, pp. 333–48.

troubles that the flight of the workers caused Ulbricht were widely noticed, American forces were not on special alert in early August.

The immense power of the United States and the often-repeated commitment to protect Berlin give ground for the perpetuation of the legend and the criticism levelled by many of the younger Germans. "You must have known," they insist. "You should have knocked it down." The seeds of distrust of Washington policy were sown in 1961. The United States had shown weakness. In the following year anti-Americanism flared in Berlin when the MPs failed to rescue Peter Fechter who was shot trying to escape and lay bleeding and helpless on the barbed wire. The communists had strengthened their position.

We must conclude that the Wall was a success for Ulbricht. As described in chapter 4, the East German economy made a spurt forward and has continued to grow; the drain of manpower has ended. The regime has survived the adverse propaganda to which he Wall gave rise. The shootings at the Wall, without which it would of course have been ineffective, are painful incidents in the minds of most people, who learn to forget.

Another Challenge

In June 1968 crisis loomed again. The East German authorities announced new regulations for Berlin traffic. These called for: (1) ransit visas costing 5 DM each for entry into and exit from West Berlin; (2) a charge of 15 DM each for West Germans entering he Zone; (3) for Zone residents visiting West Berlin or the FRG,[21] an increase from 5 DM to 15 DM in the amount of compulsory xchange; and (4) a new freight tax. These new demands were financially and even more politically disturbing. They were a manifestation of the continuing pressure by the GDR to assert its status s a "sovereign nation" surrounding and threatening West Berlin. The shock felt in Berlin and the apprehension in the Federal Republic were echoed in Washington. In a protest to the Soviets the three Western powers termed the new regulations an illegal move destined to increase tension and undermine efforts at friendly

[21] Occasional visitors of various ages and old-age pensioners are permitted to go to West Berlin.

East-West relations. Secretary Rusk flew to Bonn after the June NATO meeting in Iceland, to confer with Kiesinger.

Public reaction in West Germany called for more than official protests and diplomatic statements. The three Western Allies consulted together, but it soon became apparent that some Bonn officials did not wish the adoption of countermeasures. The Allies therefore keyed their position down to the policy of acceptance currently pursued by the Federal Republic. Bonn increased its subsidy to Berlin by approximately DM 150 million. The British, French, and American airlines increased their flights into Berlin, and the Federal Republic provided special subsidies to reduce the air fares. One journalist said to the writer cynically, "We can't do anything but pay."

This action by the GDR and the Western response to it illustrate the peculiar difficulties of the Berlin problem. Without the Allied commitment and particularly the American position, the situation would be perilous indeed. Even Washington's will to keep the city strong and to prevent encroachment from the East is limited by Bonn's plans for its *Ostpolitik*. Several newspapers, evidently supporting Bonn, said in June 1968 that reprisals were impossible and unjustified, and recommended acceptance of "temporary difficulties." Others criticized the United States and its allies for failing to take effective action. Then, as now, however the possibility of a vigorous Western policy depended increasingly on Bonn's view of the manner in which relations with the Warsaw Pact countries could best be handled. It is impossible for the United States to invoke strong measures in defense of Berlin if Bonn wishes less strong action.

The Wall Is Not Forever

The Wall cannot last indefinitely. It offends many communists as well as people in the Free World. It cuts off contacts which thousands desire. It is glaring evidence of the inferior status of those living under the communist system. Presumably the rising standard of living in the GDR will make oncoming generations in the ruling circles question its necessity. Before it is actually taken down, it will probably be pierced by holes, made less significant by a more liberal issue of passes, and be less brutally patrolled. It may be that in the future the tension will increase to a point where resistance will develop and the monolithic state of affairs will be altered from within; or it may be that a relaxation of tensions will lead the communists to adopt the tactic of seeking acceptance and more friendly relations. In any case the Wall cannot be kept indefinitely. The Wall is not forever.

BERLIN TODAY

Until the Wall was erected, Berlin had exerted an exciting and unsettling influence on the residents of the GDR. It had furnished information from the outside world, personal contacts with West Germans, and a striking comparison between the standard of living in capitalist Germany and in communist territories. The annual number of persons who crossed each way has been estimated at several millions. Among them were youths who went for vacations to recreation centers in the Federal Republic, churchmen, businessmen, and relatives of those who still lived in the GDR. Holders of GDR identity cards got cheap tickets or free admission to various Berlin amusements and cultural exhibits. Thousands of East Germans attended *Green Week* in winter and took part in the May Day celebration in the *Waldbuehne* each spring.[22] Here was an open book in which visitors could read the story of the free world with its strength and its weakness, its materialism and its ideals.

Nowadays the situation is vastly different. Some East Germans still of course visit the city; they are for the most part not citizens of Berlin but merely passing through the city. Officials at lower levels meet to arrange for emergencies and administrative problems in the city such as fire, crime, telephone connections, the maintenance of sewers, the subways, and the barge traffic. The interzonal trade authorities still confer in Berlin. There are dozens of formal contacts and a few informal relations.

Beyond the Wall one can see from the East the tower of the

[22] Green Week was an agricultural exposition held in January. The May Day celebrations in the outdoor theater in West Berlin were gay affairs. According to the German Embassy in Washington in July 1968, 3,545 persons went from West Berlin to East Berlin on "compassionate" passes.

Gedaechtnis Kirche, the white roof of the Congress Hall, the shining block of the Europa Center, and the colorful Hilton Hotel. The dead zone on the communist side contrasts with the free movement of traffic and groups of visitors who climb the special platforms to look over the Wall at the Brandenburg Gate, at Potsdamer Platz, and at Bernauerstrasse. The contrast is still obvious.

Its Continuing Importance

The importance of Berlin as a point of contact inside the barricaded line between the NATO and the Warsaw Pact countries remains. Whenever there is a crisis in the Far East or in Latin America, the watchful ask: "What will happen in Berlin?" The tripwire is there, the sensitive nerve of the free and of the captive people is still exposed. This political barometer, sometimes fogged over by Ulbricht's independent flourishes, still measures the degree of tension or of relaxation. The height of the Wall shows Ulbricht's vulnerability and failure to win the sympathy of the people. The significance of Berlin for the world still lies in its sharp etching of the difference between two societies.

For the West Germans, the city is at once a burden and a source of hope. It is also a human reality—a place where people live and work, listen to music and build houses, study and research, heal the sick, and debate the ills of the modern world. Here young men riot and old men pass laws. Here tax money from Bonn goes to support a hard-working and productive economy which of itself would not be viable. Here the committees of the *Bundestag* meet as a symbol of the city's status as the future capital of the Federation. Here newsmen compete for drama, and artists express their vital convictions. Without this teeming center of creative activity, the idea of reunification would be a thin slogan and an unconvincing debate between warring parties.

Without Berlin, Ulbricht's hold on the men and women under his regime would have become more effective a dozen years ago. There might have been an underground since the restless leader would have remained in the Zone, but revolt would have been harshly suppressed. Without Berlin, the doctrine of Marxism-Len inism would not have been contradicted by the known facts of another way of life. The differences are impossible to assess with accuracy, but one can guess that there would have been high-pressure indoctrination which would have molded thinking and closed the door to contrary ideas. As it is, most of the people give lip service to the regime. Had the Zone been early abandoned by the West and been without balanced information on world affairs, the result—at least among those who have never known freedom, that is, among all those under the age of forty—might well have been a general acceptance of communism.

There are three reasons why the Allies have held Berlin. For one thing, the challenge to the free world is clear and compelling. For another, the nature of the future Germany hinges on what happens to Berlin. When the residents in the Zone finally win self-determination, they will owe their capacity to do this to the influences that have emanated from the city. Finally, the people voluntarily stood with the West in 1948, when the blockade imperilled their existence, and afterward in voting, in working, in improving the quality of their democracy. We have told these people that we will not desert them. They have belief in our honor and in our ability to preserve their freedom.

The Economic Outlook

A few writers have recently taken a pessimistic view of the city's future. They have written of a "dying city."[23] Some of these writers have not had the experience of seeing the low point of bare existence in the early years and noting the will to survive. They report elements in the situation which have been known for two decades, and of these they make a story. The population has an unfavorable age structure, with fewer persons than normal in their active working years. The young men have a tendency to look elsewhere for their careers and so leave the city by the hundreds. The city authorities and the men in Bonn have faced these two problems since the Iron Curtain became a physical reality in 1952; they considered it even more intensively in 1961 after the Wall had

[23] *U.S. News and World Report,* December 4, 1967, pp. 81–82.

been built. Financial subsidies and special conditions have been developed for those who are drawn by the good living conditions and the well-rounded life which the city offers.

The result has been the steady increase in Gross National Product,[24] the rise in employment, the improvement of the living standard, the increasing number of tourists, the construction of impressive buildings, and the city's continuing high morale. Some few have wearied in the long period of isolation; some of the heroes

Table 9
Changes in GNP in the FRG and in West Berlin, 1960–1968

	FRG (*% change*)	*West Berlin* (*% change*)
1960	11.4	11.6
1961	6.3	9.8
1962	4.3	7.0
1963	3.4	5.2
1964	8.6	8.2
1965	5.3	10.3
1966	1.8	6.8
1967	−2.4	2.2
1968	11.9	7.9

Sources: For the Federal Republic, Statistisches Bundesamt, *Statistisches Jahrbuch fuer die Bundesrepublik Deutschland 1968*, p. 210; for West Berlin, U.S. Embassy, Bonn, *Handbook of Economic Statistics*, March 1968, p. 54, June 1968, p. 54.

have died. The city continues to have its ups and downs. It could stand a considerable depression without disaster, but in fact during the recent decline in the economy of the Federal Republic it suffered less than the Republic. Some firms shifted their management and some of their activities to West Germany, but the effect on the demand for labor has not been substantial. Both the Americans and the Germans are watching for signs of weakness. The decline in the population may continue, but, as Karl Schiller,

[24] U.S. Embassy, *Handbook of Economic Statistics*. The Bonn government increased the financial benefits for Berlin in July 1968.

minister of economics in Bonn and former economic councilman in Berlin, has said, the city is basically sound. Continued support from Bonn is however essential.

The *Frankfurter Allgemeine Zeitung* of March 13, 1968, reported the statement of Berlin Senator Koenig that more than a hundred new firms had been established in Berlin since the autumn of 1961. It estimated the resulting new investment at more than DM 500 million. Koenig urged further support for the city and stressed the unfavorable influence of the net loss of some 6,900 persons in the first ten months of 1967.

Table 10
Population Changes and Employment, West Berlin, 1963–1968

	Population (in thousands)	*Gain or Loss through Migration (%)*	*Industrial Employment (in thousands)*
1963	2,177	25.0	293
1964	2,193	25.0	287
1965	2,201	10.6	288
1966	2,191	1.5	280
1967	2,174	−7.5	255
1968	2,145	−0.9	253

Source: Handbook of Economic Statistics, March 1969, p. 62.

There has been a recurring loss of population in recent months, but there has also been an "in-movement" of workers to Berlin through special efforts of the Labor Office. The number of job openings has continued to exceed the number of unemployed. Unemployment was almost negligible in 1969.

Since attention is inevitably devoted to the question of population and *out*-migration, the figures given in table 10 may be of interest.

The *Berlin-ABC* gave the population of West Berlin for 1950 as 2,145,000 and for 1957 as 2,228,000.[25] There is said to be a slow

[25] Walter Krumholz et al., *Berlin-ABC,* p. 79.

out-migration, but it is likely to fluctuate, and no strong trend is noticeable. An increase in the labor force was reported to the writer in July 1968. In 1967 the decline in population was substantial, and the December total was below the average for that year. Concern over this drop occasioned comment in the press. Production in 1967 was slightly less than in 1966 but was recovering well in 1968.

Trade with West Germany held its ground, with total imports slightly above those in any previous year. The totals in millions of DM for the four preceding years were: 1963–10,220; 1964–11,430; 1965–12,815; 1966–13,370. The chart on page 53 of the *Handbook* shows almost identical amounts for 1967. The balance of trade with the Federal Republic is almost always unfavorable because of (a) the isolated location of the city which requires large shipments of commodities that would normally have been available from the surrounding countryside, and (b) the many services rendered by the Federal Republic. The Berlin budget shows the aid from the Federal Republic rising slightly each year and amounting to a total of DM 2,300 million in 1967. Other special help brought the estimated combined total to more in 1968.[26] It has been between 25 and 30 percent of the city's budget in recent years. A small portion of the total goes to the Allies as occupation costs.[27]

With the help of subsidies and various special arrangements in taxes and insurance as well as special efforts to encourage financial investments in the city, the standard of living has risen substantially, and the general atmosphere shows the well-being of the majority of the workers and visitors. The many hotels are crowded as thousands of visitors pour into the city to take part in a succession of conferences and to enjoy the varied cultural activities. In every respect it is a modern city with many luxuries to offer and a sophisticated night life in addition to its intellectual attainments.

[26] For Federal Republic aid, see *Handbook of Economic Statistics*, 1968, p. 60. For American aid, see Dulles, *Berlin*, pp. 147–57.

[27] The annual total for occupation costs has been DM 300 million, with two-thirds going to the Western Allies and the rest to the Germans for support costs. See Dulles, *Berlin*, p. 39.

Student Unrest

The workers, the government leaders, the businessmen, the professors, and all those who lived through the blockade months know and appreciate Allied support. When Acheson, Dulles, Kennedy, Johnson and Nixon have visited the city, the Berliners gathered in thousands to show their enthusiasm for understanding, for money, and above all for help in their special tasks. In recent years the attitude of the younger men has differed from that of their parents. As early as 1965 there was a questioning mood in the universities. When the writer went to speak at the sudents' request, they were courteous but somewhat insistent in their questions. A few months later they became strident. Recently they have been in revolt.

Disturbing though they may be, the student uprisings are a sign of strength rather than of weakness. These young men do not feel the menace from the East, and they consider that reform of the control of the universities is more urgent than the maintenance of an undivided front against communism. Meanwhile they grumble at times about the dependence on foreign support and clamor for more flexible relations with the Germans in the East. They look to the United States for models of revolt and feel that they can safely attack the Establishment without knowing clearly what they would put in its place. They may go further than their contemporaries in the West, but they have failed to cause serious damage to the city's life or to its economy, which is still impressive in the quantity and quality of its output. The city has permitted the activities of the communist party (the SED-West) without suffering any noticeable effect on its predominantly liberal democracy. Now there is a noncommunist New Left under student leaders.

This explosive problem is still especially dangerous in Berlin. But the great majority of students have a traditional and even actively pro-Western point of view. The extremists, with their shouts of "Mao" and "Castro," and a group of riot leaders that comprises a small but active minority (perhaps 5 percent) are countered by the protests of those who know that the city, without Western help, would be drowned in a wave of alien doctrines. The demonstrations so far have been against, not for, constructive plans. Those who have specific requests can be satisfied, at least in part, by those who value the future of the city and the society in which they have lived.

Some of its troubles the city shares with the Federal Republic; others are special and often acute. But life goes on. Surrounded, threatened, harassed, and aging, the city is still a good place to live. More than a symbol but less than a capital, it can endure in this situation as long as many a nation and can, even under stress, hold its ground for decades.

CHAPTER 7

The Federal Republic of Germany

THE RELATION BETWEEN INTERNAL AND EXTERNAL PROBLEMS

Internal political problems are of paramount concern in the Federal Republic of Germany and cannot be kept separate from foreign relations. No politician there can command widespread interest unless he has articulated views on contacts with East Germany, dealings with Eastern European countries, NATO, the European Common Market, the nuclear non-proliferation treaty, financial requests by the United States, and other key issues in foreign affairs.

A false move or unacceptable decision on any one of these problems could have shaken the Grand Coalition[1] and adversely affected the prospects of any of the parties and discredited the political leaders. Almost all Bonn's moves in its relations with other nations are closely tied to budget and economic decisions, to trade, national security, and action on emergency legislation (*Notstandsgesetz*) and voting reform (*Wahlreform*). A few politicians go further and introduce into their foreign policy the question of the significance of American action in Vietnam.

The situation is further complicated by the fact that the current and future status of the German Democratic Republic must receive constant consideration. This issue entails a certain paradox: it is not of urgent present concern to the majority of Germans, yet the public attitude to it is such that every politician has to bear it in mind in his handling of other issues. The politician's dilemma is aggravated by the specialized meanings that such terms as "occupation," "recognition," "contacts," "democracy," "co-existence," and

[1] The Christian Democratic Union/Christian Socialist Union (CDU/CSU) and the Social Democratic Party (SPD).

"peace" have come to have. It was difficult for Chancellor Kiesinger to write a letter to Willi Stoph, premier of the GDR, that will carry commonsense meaning to the outside reader, whether German or non-German, without seeming to yield ground. The delicacy of the recognition issue in particular sets traps for the party politician and in many instances paralyzes action. The German people want no door to reunification closed, although they do not anticipate any significant progress for decades to come. While they may themselves remain cynical and discouraged—or even indifferent—they will not tolerate any such attitude in their representatives in the cabinet or in the *Bundestag*.

There are thus in 1969 special hazards and grounds for unrest which increase the vulnerability of those who advocate more contacts with the authorities in East Germany, with the former satellites, or with Moscow. Moreover the attitude toward the United States is schizophrenic: there is a desire for partnership and close contacts, for support and understanding, but there is also an urge for independence together with a new, critical point of view that partially rejects the traditional reliance on American help. The extreme expression of the determination to shake off the traditions of the 1950s is found in the mood of the rightist National Democratic Party (NPD). The internal problems cannot be ignored, and they cannot be isolated from the whole complex of Germany's need to adjust to the troubled conditions resulting from the prolonged postwar crisis. In considering Germany's situation, it is sometimes difficult to decide whether the Cold War is a prolongation of World War II or the preliminary manifestation of a third world war. In this critical time Germany shares most of the economic, political, and security difficulties that burden other major nations.

For the new German nation, emerging from the ruins of the Third Reich, the crucial problem is psychological. It is the need to fill a political and spiritual vacuum created by the break with the past and to vitalize political life without giving grounds for extreme nationalism or aggressive policies. It is not easy to divert public interest into programs for international cooperation and still satisfy normal local concerns and materialistic aims. Such an effort raises problems that require subtlety and courage. And the Federal Republic has to make this effort in a period of conflict between generations, of frustration over the division of the nation, of emerging nationalism, of resentment over its special status in military and nuclear affairs, of an inadequate educational system, and of continuing sensitivity to the question of special guilt because of the iniquities of Hitlerism. The disorder created by revolutionary youth intensifies the conflict.

The German Problem

There is a unique "German problem," as Dahrendorf says.[2] Perhaps he is right in believing it to be more social than political. So far neither economic nor political problems of reconstruction have proved insurmountable. The alliance with the West has held firm, and the growth of industrial and financial strength has been gratifying. There has been a high degree of stability, and West Germany has commanded the respect of other major nations, including even the Soviet Union. The first years of reconstruction, under the strong leadership of Chancellor Adenauer, united the people in their quest for security and for an honorable place among nations. With the first goals achieved, the necessity of collaboration is less evident, and a growing unrest has stirred the people and given warning that the alliance with the Germans that is necessary to ensure a peaceful Europe cannot be taken for granted but must be actively cultivated. Reforms in education and in social outlook are urgently needed but difficult to accomplish.

The many different facets of Germany's social and political evolution are too complex to be covered in a single volume. The problems selected for mention here are all more or less directly concerned with Eastern Europe and with the developing relations of the Federal Republic with the United States. Even these cannot be treated in depth. Like people in other countries, the West Germans have characteristics which turn them in some cases toward traditional goals but which have undergone spectacular changes in a world of new speed and nuclear power, of rapid

[2] Ralf Dahrendorf, *Gesellschaft und Demokratie in Deutschland*, pp. 29, 480.

communication and scientific miracles. A hard-working and intelligent people has not ignored the facts of the modern world and the lessons of a disastrous war. The Germans have come to recognize their place in the community of nations and have adapted their policies to the support of international cooperation. Issues of local importance and the people's hunger for stability and prosperity sometimes foster and sometimes limit what the leaders can do. There is conflict between Right and Left as well as among the more moderate groups.

THE NEW POLITICAL CONFLICTS

The Rise of the National Democratic Party

For foreign observers of Germany's political scene the most startling development has been the recent rise of the NPD. Founded in Hanover on November 28, 1964, it has gained its strength for the most part since the Grand Coalition was formed. It is built on the remnants of several of the smaller parties. As Hans Maier noted, in the rapid rise of NPD membership in the last two years "one has almost forgotten that this party has in no sense come suddenly from nothing but has a long and complicated history."[3] It has been a response to the widespread complaint that when the Grand Coalition came to power there was no minority party and no means of protesting the decisions of a somewhat monolithic government. The fact that the Communist party was until recently outlawed in West Germany plays a part in the increase of the appeal of the NPD, even though the latter is clearly a *rightist* expression of nationalism. The NPD has also been stimulated by the student movement of revolt and reacts noisily to the criticism of the more violent leftwing youth groups.

The communists recently permitted in the FRG are still not a political factor. The Federal Constitutional Court in Karlsruhe had ruled on August 18, 1956, that under Article 21 of the Basic Law the German Communist Party (KPD) must be held to be illegal in the Federal Republic (Berlin being still occupied was not

[3] Hans Maier, NPD, p. 8; Fred H. Richards, *Die NPD*, pp. 23, 68.

covered by this ruling). The Socialist Party (SRP) had been outlawed on October 23, 1952. On the NPD, there was no serious consideration of a request for a court ruling until December 1968. The party worked within the law and without obvious extreme action to recruit members. Its success went largely unnoticed. In 1967 for the first time local elections showed a significant membership in the NPD which received more than 5 percent of the votes cast in four *Laender*.

As compared with 1963, the percentage of votes for the SPD declined. The CDU/CSU gained slightly; the Free Democratic Party (FDP) gained small percentages. E. P. Neumann estimated NPD membership in 1967 to have been distributed among the *Laender* as follows: Bavaria–29%; Baden-Wuerttemberg–17%; Lower Saxony–13%; North Rhine/Westphalia–10%; Hesse–9%; Rhineland/Pfalz–8%; Hamburg and Bremen–7%; Schleswig-Holstein–6%; West Berlin–1%.[4] The party is represented in the Hesse *Landtag* now but is said to have little influence. The relatively large membership in Bavaria is partly explained by the fact that the Federation of Expellees and Victims of Injustice (BHE) and the Sudeten Germans from Czechoslovakia were most active there. Fred Richards in 1967 estimated the growth of the NPD as follows:[5]

	NPD Members
1964	473
1965	13,145
1966	24,500
1967	27,000

The first opportunity for an NPD vote in national elections was in 1965. On that occasion the party won 2.1 percent of the votes, thus falling far short of the number required to secure seats in the *Bundestag*. It continued to work for representation in the several *Landtage* in various localities. By 1967 it was estimated to have gained a half million voters—less than 1.4 percent of the 37.4 million entitled to vote.

[4] Maier, *NPD*, p. 24.
[5] Richards, *NPD*, p. 69.

The Baden-Wuerttemberg Election

The jump in voting strength from 1964 to 1968 was notable. Even though there had been gains in 1967, the election in April 1968 in Baden-Wuerttemberg came as a surprise. Chancellor Kiesinger and others had waged a vigorous campaign, and yet the rightist party polled 9.8 percent of the vote and won 12 out of 120 seats in the *Landtag.* The *New York Times* reported that the loss of support for the SPD, which received only 29.1 percent of the votes, was regarded as a "crushing setback." The CDU lost slightly. The FDP, the minority liberal party, made minor gains.

The meaning of this vote, which distressed the government and was even more disturbing to opinion abroad, is that the coalition fails to satisfy the independents, the extreme Right or extreme Left groups. It indicates a feeling that the results of cooperation with other nations are not in line with true German interests, that a more independent nationalism is needed. The swing to the Right was definitely the result of reaction to the student violence and fear of the New Left, which does not appeal to the average German voter. It is clear that during the last few years the SPD has found it difficult to attract support among the less committed elements; by joining the coalition it has lost its distinctive issues.

The Baden-Wuerttemberg vote of April 28, 1968, was the more startling in that it was in a region where Kiesinger had many loyal supporters, where he had his home, and where he campaigned vigorously. He attacked the "arrogant, thoughtless and dangerous nationalism." He declared he would never capitulate by recognizing unconditionally a second German state. He stated that the *Ostpolitik* would help lead to a European peace settlement. Several journalists called his effort a "triumph"[6] and said he was an impressive, confident figure.

The meaning of this particular election is and will continue to be worthy of careful scrutiny. It now seems that the issues in the minds of new NPD voters were mainly four:

- Desire for a stronger foreign policy; a feeling that dependence on the Western Alliance and such issues as the non-prolifera-

[6] State Department Airgram of April 2, 1968.

tion treaty did not give Germany a sufficiently important role
- Desire for a stronger internal policy to prevent the excesses of the New Left, particularly among the youth
- Rejection of Brandt's statement on the Oder-Neisse line as a sign of weakness
- Dissatisfaction with the coalition and particularly with talk of a voting reform which, if carried through, would threaten the strength of the NPD by undemocratic legal means

These considerations, while nationalistic, have little similarity with the National Socialist program of the 1930s. There were few signs of economic discontent, and no clear call for a dictatorial leader.

Hans Filbinger, minister president and Christian Democratic leader of Baden-Wuerttemberg, ascribed the rightist gains "largely to the riots staged by the West German students during Easter after the shooting of the leftwing student leader Rudi Dutschke."[7] It is probable that the trend to the Right has deeper roots in the rejection of the coalition.

Nationalism that has been for a time suppressed is bound, as indicated by Klaus Mehnert,[8] to be a problem for the Germans. To some in the NPD President de Gaulle has provided an attractive model of nationalism. Others are less persuaded that his policy should be taken as a guide to international action, since he has blocked the European cooperation in which Germany played a major role. But his anti-Americanism and European (rather than Atlantic) outlook appeal to many in the party.

Potential Growth

In attempting to estimate the party's future strength, one must look back to its growth during the four years since its start. Some observers have underestimated this. In local elections that have been held since 1965 the NPD has received the following percentages of the votes cast:

[7] *New York Times*, April 29, 1968.

[8] Klaus Mehnert, *Der Deutsche Standort*, p. 206. Professor Mehnert at Aachen has wide knowledge of political tactics in communist and noncommunist countries.

1966	March	Hamburg	3.9
		Hesse	7.9
		Bavaria	7.4
1967	May	Lower Saxony	7.0
	June	Schleswig-Holstein	5.8
	June	Rhine/Pfalz	6.9
	October	Bremen	8.8
1968	April	Baden-Wuerttemberg	9.8
	September	Lower Saxony	5.2

There was to be no further trial of strength until the national elections in September 1969.

This four-year span is too short to indicate a trend in growth. The figures for 1964 to 1968 cannot take into account the changing political structure and the disappearance from the scene of the outlawed SRP and KPD, the transformation of elements of the German Party (DP) and the National Party of Germany (DRP), and the liquidation of the BHE. Friedrich Thielen, cement manufacturer from Bremen, was at first the national representative of the NPD. He came into conflict with Adolf von Thadden in 1967. From then on, von Thadden gained strength and became the unquestioned head of the party. The feeling of frustration among rightist groups had always been present but had not previously been organized into an effective party. The chance seemed to come with the coalition. The significance of the NPD will become clearer as the conflict sharpens in the months before the nationwide elections.

Hans Maier has stated that on general grounds in a healthy democracy one could expect approximately 15 percent to fall into an extreme rightist group, whatever its name and structure.[9] Helmut Schmidt, *Bundestag* representative and SPD *Fraktion* leader, expressed much the same opinion in early 1968.[10] He brushed aside the fears that are sometimes expressed and said that in a democracy it is healthy to have the extremes represented.

The view of many *Bundestag* members seemed to be that the NPD would not grow substantially. Some pointed to the fact that the representatives in the Hesse *Landtag* had been quiet and inef-

[9] Maier, *NPD*, p. 8.
[10] In a personal interview with the writer.

fective. All the Germans interviewed stated emphatically that it was unfortunate that the rightist party had so many votes because this fact alarmed foreign opinion. There is no doubt that Americans interested in Germany have been distressed and apprehensive. The misleading description "neo-Nazi," had caused commentators abroad to write of the danger of future German aggression. This fear is stimulated more by the use of intemperate language than by the party program. Nevertheless, it has cast a shadow over international relations.

Present Trends

In an article in *Der Politologe,* a magazine published by the Otto-Suhr Institut of the Berlin Free University, Dr. Klingemann states that there has been insufficient study of the radical right and that more research is needed to understand German democracy.[11] He describes one of the studies already undertaken. To the question, "Should an ideal party be nationalist?" 82 percent of the respondents replied "No." To a question asking whether a dictator is always a danger, replies from anti-NPD respondents were 79 percent in agreement, from pro-NPD respondents, 55 percent. The questions were structured to show variations in schooling, political involvement, preference for "Buy German" trade, attitude on civil rights, and so forth. The conclusions were in accord with the general view that the NPD has attracted people of illiberal opinions and that people opposed to the NPD have moderate inclinations. The research points the way to further studies involving larger samples, which are needed to clear the issues in a matter of grave international importance. There are not now signs of any real threat to German democracy.

Ferenc A. Vali in a thoughtful analysis of the German problem of the twentieth century has stated: "The appearance of another Hitler and the crossing of intense frustration and hyperbolic messianic nationalism may be considered an event not to be duplicated.

[11] Hans D. Klingemann (University of Cologne) *Politologe,* Otto-Suhr Institut, Free University. November/December 1967, pp. 23–31. (The percentages here have not been corrected for those not having an opinion.) The sample used was approximately 2,000.

Under present international conditions, even a united Germany would no longer be the superpower of 1939–45."[12]

Klaus Mehnert has referred to a "nation without nationalism" and suggested that it is not easy to restore a "normal" national consciousness.[13] German nationalism is still a minor political element, but the causes of its growth must be recognized. West German society is still burdened by a rigid class structure. Nationalism was accentuated by the lukewarm attitude which for a brief period followed the strong guidance of Chancellor Adenauer. It has been stimulated by the spectacle of *le grand Charles* in France and has been fostered by the feeling that dependence on the United States had been excessive and unduly prolonged. It has derived additional force and meaning from a sense of the injustice of the oppression of the Germans in the East Zone and from the absence of any practical and effective policy designed to reunite the two parts of the nation. As Vali has said, "Western obtuseness toward the German dilemma might hasten the choice of national priorities."[14] This choice might be to the detriment of European integration and other Western policies. Allegations of Western indifference and government inaction set the tone of the NPD doctrine in 1968. The deep roots of the issue of reunification and of the resentment of the injustice of the division perpetuated by the Soviets have been recognized by many political scientists and sociologists. Others however feel that reunification will not be attained for a long time to come and tend to deny its importance to the peace of Europe.

Psychological undercurrents explain the appeal of the new party to those who lack a sense of identity and have not found satisfaction in recent government policies. So far, emotion has played a larger part than political wisdom. As Tauber says, the absence of a comprehensive, rational ideology has been one of the key weaknesses of postwar nationalism.[15] The tacticians of the party have

[12] Ferenc A. Vali, *The Quest for a United Germany*, p. 273–74.
[13] Mehnert, *Standort*, pp. 206, 207.
[14] Vali, *The Quest*, p. 275.
[15] Kurt P. Tauber, *Beyond Eagle and Swastika*, vol. 1, p. 446. As one reviewer wrote: "Unfortunately, the book was completed before the present

however been astute in keeping the aims and methods clear of the danger of constitutional prohibitions; by clouding the nature of its long-term aims they have made it more acceptable to many who would undoubtedly have been alienated if they had recognized the more aggressive intentions of the few.

It is thus open to speculation whether the NPD will move toward German autarchic strength and capacity for deterrence, or whether it will move in the direction of neutralism and make a bid for compromise with the Russian communists in order to bargain for some form of reunification. The judgment of Freiherr zu Guttenberg in 1964 was that the tendency toward neutralism would predominate.[16] Adenauer was of the opinion that the Soviets did not wish to have Germany out of NATO since in the early postwar years they considered the West a restraining influence on German aggressive tendencies. The NPD can develop considerable support for an uncertain program by opposing past policies on the grounds that they have deprived Germany of a chance for greatness. The fear of being a second- or third-class power stirs the passions of the less rational Germans. This is a pattern made familiar by the nationalism prevailing in the rightist circles of other nations.

If at this time the Western powers—particularly the United States—should take an ambiguous or unfavorable stand on reunification, the forces of the West German Right, now diffuse and indeterminate, would crystalize into a hard line against those nations which have abandoned their pledge to support self-determination for East Germany. The danger of the NPD is that it might capitalize on mistakes made by German politicians or by foreign powers to fan into flame an issue which otherwise would merely have smoldered. Meanwhile constitutional provisions, which could be invoked by the Federal Constitutional Court if members of the NPD could be said "by reason of their aims or the behavior of their adherents to seek to impair or destroy the free democratic basic

---

resurgence of political nationalism in the NPD, and this most significant of all postwar nationalist parties is paradoxically left out of consideration, although many of its leading personalities are treated and its predecessors shed much light on it as well."

[16] Karl Theodor, Freiherr zu Guttenberg, *Wenn der Westen will*, p. 193.

order or to endanger the existence of the Federal Republic of Germany,"[17] are deemed to be a protection against a danger such as that which arose under the Weimar Constitution.

The reason for the lack of alarm in the Federal Republic is that political circles do not find any clear parallel with the past and cannot see any substantial erosion of the more moderate parties. There is no recent economic disaster, no racial fanaticism, no sense of isolation from the West, no notion that a nation could make gains by aggressive war—there are in fact none of the factors that in the early thirties were used as strong incentives to militant nationalism. Even if present-day Germany had not been ravaged by saturation bombing nor suffered the heavy penalty of airborne war, her knowledge of the nuclear strength—which she does not share—of several major powers has brought a restraint and cooperation which she had not learned before 1940.

The inexpert leaders of the New Right have used some of the slogans of the past, but the persons and the statements have little glamor. Moreover the slogans in party harangues that were loud in protest against the Bonn Government have not been supported by concrete proposals.[18] More than in the Adenauer era, the Right wing has felt the need for strength and has often expressed this feeling in irrational ways that have had little or no influence on practical politics. The present constitution gives much less opportunity for splinter parties than was the case under the Weimar Republic.[19] Those who find signs of the future health of the nation in its expanding industrial and political life do not fear the future. In any case, it was decided in early 1968 not to press for a revision of the electoral law until after the 1969 elections.

No discussion of the NPD can be isolated from consideration of general conditions. Professor Eric Voeglin, with whom I talked in Munich where he was teaching, expressed views[20] which others also

[17] Walter Hubatsch et al., eds., *The German Question*, p. 340.
[18] Maier, *NPD*, p. 18.
[19] James Pollock, "The West German Electoral Law," *American Political Science Review* 48:107–31.
[20] Personal interview.

have stated. The line of reasoning is as follows: The lack of continuity in Germany, the lack of any dependable institutional framework in education, in the family, in the church, in the press, and elsewhere accounts for a lack of meaning and guiding principles in German political life. This is in his opinion a serious situation and has led to a general deterioration of morale. There is thus no foreign or domestic policy of significance. Once the major task of reconstruction had been completed, the political leaders tended to drift in a vacuum. There has been no general understanding of past Nazism and little understanding of present conditions. Unless the minds of the politicians can be clear on the past and the present, they cannot move forward. The present danger, Professor Voeglin said, lies not in ambition for power but in the lack of goals. The youth of the land is frustrated because it has had no revolution. Moreover it is not likely to have one. The young people could build a good future; but at present they are not doing so.

This is a dark assessment of the situation by a learned scholar. Although not completely out of line with the facts or with general attitudes, yet when considered in the light of the improving democratic institutions and the genuine desire to foster international cooperation existing in many quarters, it is almost certainly unduly pessimistic. There is more vitality to be found than this gloomy appraisal would suggest.

The *Frankfurter Allgemeine Zeitung,* in a recent article on the NPD, urged more attention to the growing criticism of the political leaders and the danger of ignoring basic democratic principles. An excerpt states:

> The BRD [FRG] is beginning to experience the opposition to parliamentary government which accompanied and threatened Weimar from its birth. That is, the "extra-parliamentary opposition" has turned into "anti-parliamentary opposition" in radical groups.
>
> In the face of such radicalism there are many who still keep their eyes shut, and who until now have praised the "healthy discontent." . . .
>
> Although their numbers are not yet very large, they have suc-

> ceeded in putting the parliamentary democracy of West Germany in question, a democracy that has seemed for 20 years to be a matter of course. . . .
>
> Only when, and if, the parties are willing to continue being critical of their own actions, can they with any understanding look at their radical opposition critically.
>
> It is often agreed that the best democrats are those who are continually critical and questioning. The radical opposition does not fit in here, however, since they seek to destroy this democracy. They cry for freedom, but sound as though they want only the power to decide who should have what freedom. They cry gladly for the people to mobilize; when the people do not answer, the radicals call them dumb, worthless, and submissive. They want to be a lot of things, but one thing they aren't is democrats.[21]

The New Right and the New Left both pose problems which are important to the future of German political development and war against many of the practical elements in contemporary German society. Both display a streak of romanticism in their attempt to break the mold of established institutions and substitute vague and indefinite goals that are hard for the outsider to take seriously. Talk of Mao, Castro, and the earlier Marxist writers does not carry conviction to those concerned with concrete industrial, security, or diplomatic issues. This lack of understanding is one aspect of the gap between generations that exists not only in Germany but in the United States, Japan, and most other nations. There are traces of anarchism in the intent to flout the law and disregard the courts. At times the protesters seek publicity and arrest through the display of violence.

YOUTH FIGHTS THE SYSTEM

The swing to the Right apparent in the elections in Bremen and Baden-Wuerttemberg manifested the influence that the violent demonstrations of youth were exercising on the voting. Trouble over streetcar fares had resulted in a violent strike by students in January 1968. In April there had been student rioting in a dozen German cities. Hundreds were arrested, many were wounded, and

[21] *Frankfurter Allgemeine Zeitung, February* 8, 1968.

at least two died. Violence on such a scale had clearly gone beyond the range of local affairs and had become a national political problem. The disorders and the disruption of normal life were a deliberate and obvious challenge to government. The public response varied from calls for rigorous repression to regrets at the use of police force and the reiteration of statements that reforms were necessary.

The rioting students' most specific target was the press; there were bitter attacks on the Springer press in particular and widespread concern over its growing monopoly.[22] The *Sueddeutsche Zeitung* of Munich asked how far the Springer press had been responsible for the attempt on the life of Rudi Dutschke, but said that the blame cast on the federal government for "not having done anything about the Springer newspapers' smear campaign against the extra-parliamentary opposition" was unrealistic. While Dutschke lay on his hospital bed in Berlin, the demonstrators continued to interfere with operations in the Springer publishing houses in several major cities, including the glass-and-metal Hochhaus overlooking the Wall and the East Sector.

The Rise of Dutschke

Dutschke himself is said to have had "nothing but contempt for violence." His methods have allegedly been copied from the American Negroes' fight for equal rights. His rise to prominence in the student movement, which was already in ferment by early 1965, has been remarkable. He first attracted public attention when he spoke against the Grand Coalition at a meeting of the *Falken* youth group in Hasenheide, Berlin, in November 1966. His dramatic personality came to the fore at the time of Benno Ohnesorge's death in the riots against the Shah of Iran at the Berlin Opera House on June 2, 1967. He gained worldwide notoriety during the Christmas season of the same year when he seized the pulpit of the Gedaechtnis Kirche in Berlin and interrupted the services to de-

[22] Axel Springer had gained control over a large segment of the German press. This monopolistic influence over newspapers with varying and often low standards caused general concern. Demagogic tendencies with strong rightist tones emerged. The New Left was outraged by this development.

liver a revolutionary tirade. He became a leading symbol of the New Left. He calls himself a professional revolutionary, out to overthrow the "corrupt establishment," the manipulators of "late capitalism in the West and late Stalinism in the East."[23] He may not be the most able or the most attractive leader of West German youth; the names of Ekkard Krippendorf, the young *Assistent* from the Free University of Berlin, Mahler, Lefevre, Nevermann, Langhans, Kunzelmann, Teufel, Schlotterer, and others come to mind. He is however the most talked about.

Concerning his attitude and methods there is some difference of opinion, but it is clear that his exhortations led directly and indirectly to violence. His ideas are said to come from Marx, Engels, Lenin, Rosa Luxemburg, Mao Tse-tung, Herbert Marcuse, and Che Guevara. His speeches are almost incomprehensible, but his dynamic force is spectacular and perhaps pathological. The annihilation that he advocates of system and control, institutions and monopolies, and the rule of men over men would bring perhaps a fulfillment of dreams—perhaps chaos. In any case he carried the message of the new revolt from city to city.

Now, because of the shots fired by Joseph Bachmann, a deranged housepainter from Munich, Rudi Dutschke has become a symbol and rallying point which can be exploited in the interests of his Socialist Students' League (SDS) and of wider circles of revolutionaries which are thought by some to advocate the destruction of parliamentary order.

Meanwhile the various *Land* governments which hold the police power have conferred on the preservation of law and order, and state that they can control violence. The people of Berlin, even more than those elsewhere, are at the end of their patience. There has been a succession of demonstrations over a period of more than two years. The student riots in April 1968 were particularly violent. Many were injured, and at least one man (press photographer Klaus Frings) was killed. After a tumultuous week there was a pause in the demonstrations as the public, young and old, took account of the bloody conflict and tried to sort out the issues.

[23] *New York Times*, April 16, 1968.

The Attack on the Government and Education

The main target throughout the recent agitation was the rightist press, but there were other demands. There was clamor against the government, accompanied by vague accusations of corruption. There was opposition to the Emergency Law which would permit the government in certain types of emergency to govern by decree, and there were general demands for rights and privileges and from time to time proposals for closer relations with East Germany. Another object of protest was the U.S. fighting in Vietnam.

Criticism of the educational system was both specific and general, with demands for a larger share in the running of the universities, changes in instruction, smaller classes, and better conditions of study and living. Amid the welter of loud and confused student demands the changes in the educational system have tended to recede into the background, and the external and internal political issues have come to the fore. Of the urgent need for improvement in the universities, in the *Hochschulen*, and at the lower educational levels there is little question, but because of the legal and administrative conditions under which these institutions operate, reform is difficult to effect. It is beyond the range of the SDS and the more spectacular element of the student movement, although these elements can obviously create the sense of urgency to speed reform.

In Germany, as in the United States and throughout the world, the nature of the revolt of youth raises the question whether the segment of the population now between the ages of fifteen and forty will continue as a protest movement and become a political force, straining the limits of orderly democracy and taking direct action on what it considers to be the wrongs of established society and the rights of the weaker and more "reasonable-minded" masses. This revolutionary development may be limited to a particular decade, as was the Populist Movement in the mid-eighties. On the other hand the signs of revolution are there. It is possible that, as the young people of the present grow old and become conservative, the changing nature of education and communication, the economic abundance, and the loosening family ties will continue to cause succeeding generations of protesting youth to seek various means to seize power and drive their elders into defensive positions.

Resentment against the older generation is not confined to any particular nation. In Germany the parents are held responsible for Hitlerism. In the United States they are accused of responsibility for the Vietnam war and racial inequities. In no country, it seems, have they learned to keep the peace. They have created the technical systems that have made possible the economic, financial, and political complex of modern society. They are accused of making money their goal, of forgetting the essential rights of human beings. The young people in Berlin, New York, Berkeley, and Prague, even though they have no practical alternatives to offer, demand that their elders step down from their positions of authority in government, in the press, over the police, and in education, and make way for a new society. What that new society might be and how it could be kept incorruptible is not clear.

The violence of 1968 has demonstrated that the urgency of the demands of youth has been underestimated. Now the destructive methods used have brought fear to many in the older generation. The Federal Republic shares with other nations the difficult task of finding a moderate course.

THE NEED FOR REFORM IN EDUCATION

Few of the present troubles can be resolved until substantial changes have been effected in lower and higher education. The students in their recent protests against the Establishment seem to have forgotten the specific problems of educational reforms or at any rate to have given few of them priority. Nevertheless a number of major shortcomings in the educational system call for legislation and for financial and administrative changes, and merit urgent attention. These reforms, when accomplished, will inevitably affect the course of German democracy, party alignments, and the nation's role in the international world. Middle and higher education need to be more broadly based. This holds true for the liberal arts courses and for the technical branches of higher education. Democratic motivation should be strengthened and facilities increased.

Part of the lack of flexibility and democracy in the German

university system is traceable to the fact that the student is required to decide at ten or twelve years of age whether to go on to higher education or to turn toward trade school and technical training. This decreases the diffusion of knowledge and maintains the class structure that has characterized Germany during the past decades. The educational system in the GDR makes no such requirement; the children of the working classes are encouraged to continue their education. It is estimated that only 0.5 percent of the West German population goes to the universities and *Hochschulen*, as contrasted with 2.2 percent in the United States.[24] If this situation continues unchanged, it will accentuate the gap between West Germany and the United States in science and intellectual capacity. Wide opportunities for academic advancement, even in the early years, can greatly stimulate those with creative talent and enhance their number and standards. The present exclusion of the less privileged groups in the population tends to widen the technological gap between the two countries and to dampen enthusiasm for advanced science and research.

Thus German education, which served as a model for many American institutions sixty or seventy years ago and attracted scholars from many countries, has now ceased to be in the vanguard and lacks inspiration and imagination. Fine professors and able administrators exist, but they find it hard to reform a system frozen in an ancient mold. While the discussion of change goes on, preoccupation with problems outside the country, East and West, obscures for many the importance of early action. The issues cannot be indefinitely postponed, however, and recently a meeting of the prime ministers of the *Laender*, held in Hannover on October 30, 1968, reached agreement on a number of proposals for reform. It recommended a strong permanent executive in each university, more freedom in handling the funds, changes in faculty appointments and tenure, and more consultation between students and the academic body. In August the Berlin *Abgeordnetenhaus* adopted a new constitution for the Free University.

The students cannot as yet find any assurance of early practical

[24] Mehnert, *Standort*, p. 161.

action. They are aware of the shortcomings of the present system, but their unruly behavior and extravagant demands do little to facilitate concrete remedies. In view of the problems facing the German government and the present legal provisions, it will be more than a decade before any significant and comprehensive changes can be made. Meanwhile, dissatisfaction tends to feed the rightist groups; students blame the Establishment for educational shortcomings whose real causes they fail to discern.

The Educational "Catastrophe"

Georg Picht, seeking to shock the government into action in 1964, wrote a strong indictment of the school system.[25] He held that faults in the lower school system are at the root of the educational "catastrophe" as a whole. He cited studies and projections for different European nations made by the Organization for European Cooperation and Development (OECD) in Paris. These placed Germany at the bottom of the list of member nations with respect to the probable increase in the number of students of the *Abiturienten* type.[26] In all the other countries surveyed, the probable increase over eleven years was 100 percent or more; in Norway, for instance, it was 163 percent; in France, 154 percent; in Yugoslavia 148 percent. In Germany it was 4 percent. These estimates and the accompanying discussion had a shock effect. Although the statistics later proved to be inaccurate, most educational experts, sociologists, and political scientists have accepted the general significance of the comparison as a warning. There has been little doubt that the numbers of children continuing their education beyond the elementary school and the quality of the facilities, curriculum, and teaching provided have been unsatisfactory and present the Federal Republic and the *Laender* with serious problems. The situation can be remedied only by an emergency program of great urgency which would increase the number of students by several million and more than double the number of

[25] Georg Picht, *Die Deutsche Bildungskatastrophe*, pp. 27, 56, 71, 78, 87.

[26] The *Abiturienten* are students prepared for higher academic work and are generally considered to be on a level with college freshmen or even sophomores at American colleges.

teachers. In so far-reaching an effort the federal government would have to cooperate with the *Laender* in providing for the equalization of facilities between the different areas.

Picht concluded that the funds needed would be large but not beyond the capacity of the nation. He stated the obvious truth: "Every nation has the educational system it deserves. . . . If Germany does not undertake the task, the third breakdown in German history in this century will take place."[27]

Writing three years later, Professor Klaus Mehnert stressed the same theme and gave statistical comparisons (see tables 11 and 12) of the percentage of national income spent on education and of the populations and student enrollments in various countries.[28]

Table 11
Educational Expenditure in Ten Countries

	Percentage of National Income Spent on Education	*Year*
Israel	9.4	1962
Japan	7.2	1962
USA	6.8	1961
Netherlands	6.3	1961
USSR	6.1	1962
GDR	6.0	1962
Sweden	5.7	1961
Peru	4.9	1963
Taiwan	4.1	1962
FRG	3.7	1962

Source: Mehnert, *Standort,* p. 160.

Additional statistics comparing enrollments in higher education in America and Germany (see table 13) were provided by UNESCO. The differences between the different sets of figures are due to the different categories and definitions used.

Neither Mehnert nor Dahrendorf[29] explain the lack of motiva-

[27] Picht, *Bildungskatastrophe,* p. 42.
[28] Mehnert, *Standort,* pp. 160–90.
[29] Dahrendorf, *Gesellschaft,* pp. 88–94, 341, 359, 451–64.

Table 12
Population and Student Enrollment in Four Countries

	Number of Students Enrolled in Hochschule and Universities	*Total Population (in millions)*
USA	4,174,936	190
USSR	2,943,700	220
Japan	827,376	95
FRG	344,102	58

Source: Mehnert, *Standort,* p. 160.

tion behind the small number of advanced students. It is clear that the feeling in many families that higher education is an unjustified luxury and the lack of disposable funds tend to prolong a long-outdated tradition among peasants and workers. In spite of the changing economic and social picture, class distinctions still persist, with their tendency to separate intellectuals from blue-collar workers and farmers. Only recently have the differences between social groups been seriously challenged.

The attack on the hierarchical society that has now begun will certainly affect the educational picture and could well become a political issue. Meanwhile many critics of the West German system have noted the contrast with the classless approach to education in the GDR. The contrast is sharper in the number of students than in the content and quality of education, but there are clearly branches of learning in East Germany that are on a high level.

The failure to modernize the educational system in West Germany has brought with it political dangers which will plague the Federal Republic for some years to come. It is not the main or the only cause of the young people's dissent, but it does make it more difficult to moderate the demonstrations against the constituted authorities and the prevailing political attitudes. A sound and progressive educational system would open up economic and cultural opportunities to many protestors who at present see little hope for advancement by peaceful methods.

James B. Conant, former president of Harvard and U.S. ambassador to Bonn in 1953, wrote an article in the form of a letter dated

Table 13
Student Enrollment in Higher Education in the USA, FRG, GDR, and West Berlin, 1950–1965

	Year	Students Enrolled in Higher Education: Total	%	Number of Students per 100,000 Inhabitants
USA	1950	2 296 592	32	1 508
	1955	2 664 375	34	1 606
	1960	3 582 726	37	1 983
	1964	4 950 173	39	2 577
	1965	5 526 325	39	2 840
FRG	[a]1950	122 668	20	256
	1955	175 353	19	350
	1960	265 366	23	499
	1963	342 760	25	611
	[b]1964	254 961	24	455
	[c]1965	372 929	24	632
GDR	1951	27 822	23	162
	1955	60 148	29	358
	1960	69 129	32	428
	1964	75 578	31	475
	1965	74 418	31	466
West Berlin	[a]1950	12 032	23	563
	1955	18 499	24	843
	1960	25 860	21	1 176
	1963	31 590	23	1 451
	[b]1964	26 371	21	1 203

Source: UNESCO, Paris, personal letter to author, April 3, 1968

[a] Not including engineering schools (*Ingenieurschulen*) and postgraduate teacher training

[b] Not including engineering schools (*Ingenieurschulen*)

[c] Including West Berlin

February 10, 1967, and addressed to Ralph Becker of the Max Planck Institut in Berlin, in which he stated that there had been little change or improvement in the universities and high schools in the preceding 40 or 50 years.[30] He added that the necessity for

[30] J. B. Conant, "Krise in der deutschen Bildungspolitik. (Open letter to Ralph Becker.) In *Zeitungen, Zeitschriften und Buecher*, No. 1. Berlin: Max Planck Institut, 1967.

change was pressing and made a number of practical suggestions. The fact that the rector was usually chosen for a one-year term indicated that the development of long-range planning was hampered and the exertion of personal influence from the top was weak. The curricula of the past, he continued, were no longer suitable for the present, yet little modernization had been attempted. The slow promotion of the younger teachers had kept them in subordinate and ill-paid positions. The students complained of the excessively large classes. An outstanding professor at the Free University was said not to have given his lectures at all during the first five or six weeks of the 1967 fall term.

Another recent statement criticized the universities in the following terms:

> The inflexible hierarchical system of the German universities must invite the students' opposition. In the midst of a pluralistic liberal society are islands with a constitution which provides the Professors with almost autocratic powers. Reform slogans fire the rank and file of the student body which has hitherto been lethargic. The minority now endeavor to use this theme as a booster. The Academic youth is to be carried into the orbit of an extremist political engagement.[31]

Student Protest

The Free University of Berlin was founded at the time of the blockade in 1948 and is thus one of the most recently established of the West German universities; there are a few more experimental modern universities including Konstanz on Lake Constance.[32] It has however failed to free itself from the more traditional ways and, perhaps because of the special tensions in the city, it became the first in which student dissidence was evident. The radical Executive Committee of the General Students Association (ASTA) asserts that the students—not the professors or the government—founded the university and claims that they should be

[31] *Atlantik-Bruecke*, December 4, 1967, p. 36a.

[32] New universities have recently opened in Regensburg, Bochum, Dortmund, Bielefeld, and Duesseldorf.

given more participation in administration and control. There were three students among the sixteen members of the university senate, but some claim they should have a majority control over such matters as the hiring and firing of professors and major financial decisions. It is not clear what aims determine the tactics of Krippendorf, Teufel, Mahler, Lefevre, and Dutschke. Their activities and their speeches appear disruptive; nevertheless they do represent a considerable segment of the Berlin youth, a vocal minority of probably more than 5 and less than 20 percent. The student body, which used to comprise approximately 30 percent from the East Zone and to be much more strongly anticommunist, now contains a large number of young people from West Germany whose residence in Berlin makes them free of the German army draft. Others have been attracted by the special Berlin situation and the excitements of the divided city. Even so, most of the students ignore the occasional riots and devote their attention primarily to preparing for their examinations. They may complain about the quality of teaching and living accommodations and about old-fashioned ideas, but few of them vote in the student elections or parade with banners. The faculty and administration, being somewhat freer under the constitution than those in the provincial universities, are endeavoring to search out the weaknesses and to respond to the more legitimate criticisms.

The problem of education is everywhere, but it is notably different in Germany. One of Germany's most distinguished diplomats who had met in Berlin in July 1967 with the children of those executed after the July 20, 1944, attempt on Hitler's life philosophized with me one evening on their attitudes. He said these young people were arrogant, rebellious, and difficult; but that they must be listened to. Older people who have lived through earlier phases of German history must be tolerant and patient with them and must endeavor to gain their confidence. He said that a revived Germany cannot be as strong as in the past and that this is disturbing to the young. The older people are not ashamed to be grateful for the magnanimous treatment by the United States, but the young find this difficult. They look at their parents and say: "*You* were silent. No one can say *we* did not speak out." Thus the sound and fury increase, but the purpose and direction are not easy to determine.

Its Future Effect

It is difficult to anticipate the future influence on education of rebellious youth, whether on the Right or on the Left. Some assume that as they take on family, business, and political responsibilities they will find their place in the system and become a part of the existing political parties. There is no clear indication that the majority of those now protesting will become extreme nationalists. There are strong international overtones in most of their pronouncements. There are even traces of procommunist leanings. Certainly the Berlin students are anxious for reforms, for better educational facilities, for more contacts with people in East Germany. In some of their meetings they have urged recognition of the GDR. I heard this idea in Munich, in Tuebingen, and elsewhere. To those who worry about the submissive attitude of Germans to a strong leader the present mood of revolt should bring some consolation. Many of the younger men say that there will never be any ground for the accusation that they "accepted the orders and the programs of the older men without question and without criticism." It is safe to forecast a more independent and skeptical public in the decades to come.

Meanwhile the impatience of many of the older people and most of the workers over the unbridled agitation and clamorous protests of a minority of the students was evidenced on February 20, 1968. Some 7,000 to 10,000 persons were said to have been in the February 18 march in protest against the authorities in general and the Americans in particular. In impressive reaction to this demonstration, more than 100,000 persons met in the John F. Kennedy Platz in front of the Schoeneberger Rathaus carrying banners that proclaimed gratitude for American help and a desire for continued American support. There were some clashes between participants, yet on the whole both gatherings were orderly and impressive. Emotion ran high at this time, but most students were busy with their studies.

In Berlin and in the Federal Republic the problems of the

German educational system are complicated by the relations between state and church, the ancient traditions, the subtle changes in the attitude of youth, and the practical problems of finance. Foreign observers with different backgrounds can only agree with German critics on the need for early and comprehensive action.

SOME PROBLEMS IN GERMAN-AMERICAN RELATIONS

In spite of the fact that it faces several insoluble problems, the Federal Republic is prosperous and conscious of its recently regained strength. The complaints and the criticism of political leaders are those of a strong, not a weak nation. The solidity of the *Deutsche Mark*, the increase in the Gross National Product, the importance of German officials in international conferences including the councils of NATO and the European Common Market, are generally recognized. The increase in its capacity in all fields of international action tends to arouse in the Republic feelings of frustration over the barriers on its eastern flank.

The Non-Proliferation Treaty

In this general mood of unrest, the resentment over the nuclear non-proliferation treaty (NPT) has permeated political opinion. Some state that the treaty relegates Germany to the position of a second-class power for twenty-five years. They object to any action that would freeze conditions for so long a time. Others, in spite of the revision of the earlier text of Article III, fear that the treaty makes inadequate provision for industrial uses of nuclear power, for the European Atomic Community (EURATOM), and for research in vital areas. Officials in Bonn still say they were not adequately consulted in the preparation of the treaty.

The new wording of Article III, together with the explanation by Adrian Fisher, counsel to the U.S. Disarmament Delegation in Geneva in 1967, has satisfied some but not all the doubters. Others say that there is no assurance of what the Soviets think of Article III. They are still concerned about interpretation and hope that India, Switzerland, Italy, and others will argue the points of disagreement on nonmilitary use of nuclear potential as well as a possible drastic revision of nuclear strategy in the defense of Europe. These matters are being discussed in the Federal Republic but are matters not so easily urged by Germans burdened with past history.

Prominent businessmen and industrialists are reserved in their comments, but politicians speak strongly against the manner in which the treaty was developed and its contents. One outstanding cabinet member referred to it early in 1968 as a prison which no minor improvements could make acceptable to those under restraint. Several *Bundestag* members said the whole action was immoral and deprived small countries of basic rights, without consultation or consideration.

The new Article III, which has resulted from months of negotiation, reads in part as follows:

1. Each nonnuclear weapon state party to the treaty undertakes to accept safeguards, as set forth in an agreement to be negotiated and concluded with the International Atomic Energy Agency in accordance with the statute of the International Atomic Agency and the agency's safeguards system, for the exclusive purpose of verification of its fulfillment of its obligations assumed under the treaty. . . .
2. Each state party to the treaty undertakes not to provide a) source or special fissionable material, or b) equipment or material especially for the processing, use or production of special fissionable material to any nonnuclear weapon state, unless the source or special fissionable material shall be subject to the safeguards required by this article.
3. The safeguards required by this article shall be implemented in a manner designed to comply with Article IV of this treaty, and to avoid hampering the economic or technological development of the parties or international cooperation in the field of peaceful nuclear activities. . . .[33]

The following excerpt from Article IV extends the meaning of the foregoing:

IV. Nothing in the treaty shall be interpreted as affecting the inalienable right of all the parties to the treaty to develop

[33] *New York Times*, January 19, 1968.

> research, production and use of nuclear energy for peaceful purposes without discrimination and in conformity with Articles I and II of this treaty. . . .[34]

Adrian Fisher said that the International Atomic Energy Commission in Vienna, in order to avoid duplication, should make "appropriate use of existing records and safeguards." This is interpreted to mean that the Vienna agency can negotiate an accord with EURATOM to assure itself the safeguards that EURATOM applies to all members that meet the requirements of the treaty.

Franz-Josef Strauss, West German minister of finance, stated in 1968 his definite rejection of the idea of Germany producing or controlling atomic weapons. He recalled the incident in October 1954, cited in the memoirs of Chancellor Adenauer, at the time of the renunciation of ABC weapons in the nine-power London conference. Adenauer wrote that Foster Dulles, then secretary of state, had added the proviso *nur rebus sic stantibus.*[35] He added that only the complete destruction of the alliance with the Western powers would change the circumstances. Reports to the effect that Strauss would resign and endeavor to take the CSU out of the coalition if the treaty were signed were discounted in high circles, and the more responsible opinion seems to be that after lively discussion in the *Bundestag* the Federal Republic will sign. The willingness to sign was further reduced, however, in August 1968 by the Soviet invasion of Czechoslovakia.

Current official and lay attitudes toward atomic weapons and West Germany's role with regard to them appear to be consistent and in line with the renunciation of ABC weapons accepted in 1954 at the time of the agreement to bring the Federal Republic into NATO. Even the rightwing leaders hold that Germany should not seek either production or control of nuclear arms. What they

[34] Ibid., August 25, 1967.

[35] " 'Herr Bundeskanzler, Sie haben soeben erklaert, dass die Bundesrepublik Deutschland auf die Herstellung von ABC-Waffen im eigenen Lande verzichten wolle. Sie haben diese Erklaerung doch so gemeint, dass sie—wie alle voelkerrechtlichen Erklaerungen und Verpflichtungen—nur rebus sic stantibus gilt!' Ich gab ihm zur Antwort, ebenfalls mit lauter Stimme: 'Sie haben meine Erklaerung richtig interpretiert!' Die uebrigen Anwesenden schwiegen" (Konrad Adenauer, *Erinnerungen, 1953–1955*, p. 347).

do object to is what is called the U.S. monopoly, and they urge a multilateral system with more than one "finger on the trigger." There is much agitation among politicians for changes in this field and much discussion in the press. The attitude of the general public, in contrast, is one of resignation; it neither expects nor, with the exception of the small nationalistic groups, wishes any significant change in the treaty.

In this, as in other questions, the NPD has taken a position so far to the right of responsible and experienced legislators and bureaucrats that it has no perceptible influence on action. Its position is one of protest; it has failed to develop constructive proposals. Its spokesmen are spectacular in their public statements but negative in their attitude toward acceptable programs. Even their demands for increased national strength are not formulated in concrete terms. They will, therefore, have little influence on the serious debate on the NPT.

The desire in various West German quarters to demonstrate independence of American influence has deeper roots than the NPT, although it has been accentuated by what is considered to be Washington's neglect of Bonn's opinion. It is a predictable result of the far-advanced reconstruction of economic and parliamentary institutions and an expression of the growing influence of the men who were born after the war. There is a diminishing awareness of GARIOA[36] and Marshall Plan aid to the Federal Republic and to Berlin.[37] There is a fading appreciation of the moderation of the Western Allies in the postwar settlement. There is a resentment of the failure of the United States to assure a united Germany. There is a sense of betrayal on the part of those who thought the East Zone could have been liberated from communist rule and are insufficiently informed on the delicate balance of relations in a world threatened with a nuclear explosion in a period of continuing tension.

In the young men the Vietnam war stirs a sense of outrage,

[36] Government Administration and Relief in Occupied Areas.

[37] "Figures for the American aid granted to Berlin vary with the inclusion of cultural, military and private contributions to the city. The sixteen-year total exceeded a billion dollars" (Eleanor Lansing Dulles, *Berlin*, p. 156).

which is fed by propaganda of various types. There is a restive feeling that the guilt which they have been asked to face should not be placed on their shoulders, that other nations too are guilty of crimes against humanity. As Professor Mehnert has said, the young people insist that "Our fathers were not crazy," and that in any case they themselves were not there.[38] Television programs showing the horrors of war in Vietnam have led by natural reaction to the conclusion that Americans who had for years accused the Germans of atrocities have now themselves perpetrated crimes. Young people who had been bewildered by their inability to account for Nazi crimes have thus turned to emphasis on the wrongs committed by Americans. The views of the students and the NPD are not shared by the experienced leaders in Bonn, but they have cast a shadow over the friendly attitudes which had characterized the first two postwar decades. These expressions of doubt and sometimes of hostility are magnified by the press and give the impression of a major change in the orientation of the people.[39] Such a major change has not taken place.

Support for the Dollar

The second problem to become involved in the external and internal affairs of the Federal Republic has been the request for German financial support for the dollar. Washington had for some time sought the aid of the Federal Republic through the Offset Agreement to buy American equipment for the army. This was pressed by the Dillon-Anderson mission in 1960. Bonn agreed to make such purchases to the extent of approximately $700 million a year and reluctantly carried out the terms of this agreement for three years. The gradual improvement in the military equipment produced in Germany and the adequacy of materials available led to a decline in demand and an increase in resistance to dependence on American supplies. As of 1968, there were large unspent balances for this purpose in the United States and no substantial need

[38] Mehnert, *Standort*, p. 117.

[39] Chancellor Kiesinger on February 20 "decried what he described as a 'certain climate of anti-Americanism' " (*New York Times*, February 21, 1968).

for the transfer of further funds. This changed financial situation limited the manner in which the Federal Republic could come to the aid of the dollar. The measure most commonly discussed was the purchase of short-term government bonds to the extent that the budget of the Federal Republic could support such a move. The wish of the United States for long-term bonds was not favored in German circles. The constant and consistent efforts of Dr. Karl Blessing, head of the *Bundesbank*, and others to lessen European pressure on the dollar and the gentlemen's agreement not to take gold to satisfy claims indicated recognition of the importance of a stable dollar in a world of expanding trade and uncertain monetary prospects.

The German financial experts in the *Bundesbank*, in the government, and in business have been watching the American financial position with apprehension. Dr. Blessing has continued to maintain close and constant relations with William McChesney Martin, chairman of the Federal Reserve Board. German economists, more aware of the dangers of inflation than economists in other countries and conscious of the importance of the dollar as the world's key currency, have urged action by the U.S. government and monetary authorities to lessen the outflow of gold and stabilize the value of the American currency. Some, while hoping for such action, still found the program of January 1968 disturbing. The *Bundesbank* was apparently in full sympathy with the proposal of President Johnson to restrict foreign investment and raise taxes. Even the *Bundesbank* however registered doubts as to the extent of the help which Germany could extend. Others, less sympathetic with the goals and sharply critical of some of the methods, tended to add this problem to those which were already stirring dissatisfaction with German-American relations.

While Germany's *Deutsche Mark* is a sound currency and West Germany has ample financial reserves, Eurodollars, and a dependable trade surplus, Bonn cannot contemplate extensive support of the dollar if this would put undue strain on the budget. When the German economy was emerging from a mild depression in 1967, the issues of higher or lower taxes, budget needs, and the state of the economy caused controversy in the cabinet and the *Bundestag*.

In January 1968 the conflict between Finance Minister Franz-Josef Strauss and Economics Minister Karl Schiller became acute. Strauss threatened to resign over the tax issue but won the contest when Schiller's plan to reduce taxes on business failed to pass. Strauss thought that the economy was already gathering sufficient momentum and that the importance of a conservative budget policy was overriding. The economic worries which came with the mild decline in production stirred anxiety, but they were those which come normally after a rapid rise as production and prosperity reach a temporary plateau and yearly increases in the standard of living fall below public expectations.

American Investment in German Companies

The amount and direction of U.S. investment constitute a third problem in American-German relations. Business quarters were not seriously concerned by the curbs on U.S. investments abroad proposed in President Johnson's January 1968 message. They recognized that this program might adversely affect some industries but knew that they were protected by the provisions for the fulfillment of past commitments. Their attitude toward the inflow of American funds was in any case ambivalent. Objections to increasing foreign control of German companies have been gaining momentum. The unacceptable type of American business action came to the fore early in 1968 when the American Gillette Company took over the Braun Corporation, buying out the German interest. This transaction, which was barely mentioned in the U.S. press, occasioned serious German criticism of American imperialism. Many valued the gains effected through the introduction of advanced American techniques that tended to mitigate the much-discussed "brain drain," but the loss of control in industry was regarded as too high a price to pay for them. Views varied with the varying positions of the commentators, and there was considerable inconsistency and uncertainty. There will be a number of special cases in the field of investment, based on the nature of contractual arrangements between businesses and banks and the plans of German corporations. The exact legal provisions on which the decisions as to funds from America will be based are not yet known.

In matters of security, diplomacy, finance, and investment West Germany is considerably preoccupied with her relations to the United States. She also pays continuous attention to American technical developments and educational exchanges. The troop issue, which had caused some misunderstanding, seems now to be of relatively minor interest. In 1968 it was apparent that there was no responsible or significant desire for the withdrawal of American troops. Some brigades which had been withdrawn earlier were returned to Germany in that year after the invasion of Czechoslovakia. Government spokesmen and experienced observers said that minor reductions would be compatible with Germany's security interests but a continuing military presence of reasonable size—perhaps 150,000 men—was desirable. Only a few extreme rightwing Germans advocated the complete withdrawal of troops, and even they admitted the special significance of the small Allied military forces in Berlin.

THE SOVIET NOTE ON BERLIN, JANUARY 1968

Early in 1968 the Soviets caused a flurry of concern in an episode which shed light on the attitude of the younger officials and some students toward the Berlin situation and an Allied occupation which had lasted for twenty years. On the initiative of Soviet Ambassador Semyon K. Tsarapkin, conversations were held on January 6 between him and Foreign Minister Willy Brandt (representing the chancellor, then absent from Bonn) concerning a Soviet note about Berlin. Since the Russians asked that this aide memoire not be published, it was only after some ten days that detailed information about it became available to newsmen and Allied authorities.[40] Thus it was not until the week of January 14

[40] "Bonn/Washington/London. In Bonn wurde am Mittwoch bestaetigt, dass in dem Gespraech, das Bundesaussenminister Brandt am 6. Januar mit dem sowjetischen Botschafter Zarapkin gefuehrt hat, die Berlin-Frage eine wesentliche Rolle gespielt hat. Es wurde auch bekannt, dass Zarapkin ein entsprechendes Aide memoire uebergeben hat, in dem vor allem eine Einschraenkung von Aktivitaeten der Bundesregierung und des Bundestages in Berlin gefordert wird. In Washington und London wurde zu dem sowjetischen Vorstoss erklaert, es seien darin keine Anzeichen fuer eine neue Berlin-Krise zu sehen. Auch der Bonner Regierungssprecher Diehl sagte, der

that the press began discussing its contents. Even then the exact wording was a matter of speculation. State Secretary Guenter Diehl, speaking for the government, said the Russian ambassador had expressed objections to visits to Berlin by the chancellor and other high officials of the Federal Republic and to meetings of *Bundestag* committees and of political *fractions* in Berlin. In addition he had proposed direct Soviet-Federal Republic conversations, bypassing the three Western Allies, on the Berlin "problem."

A few persons, impatient at the restraints on action in the Berlin situation, saw in this idea the opportunity for an attempt to end the stalemate and reach for a new status for Berlin. A small group in the Foreign Office urged this view. In informal conversations its proponents indicated a restiveness over the "Berlin Clause."[41] Why, they asked, should the Berlin Clause have to be imposed automatically on, for instance, an agreement with Switzerland over water rights on the Rhine? Such complications, they urged, delayed negotiations for weeks in many cases. On the other hand, a modification of this provision would carry the risk of weakening the Berlin position. The United States at this juncture called the attention of the West German government to the sensitivity of the Berlin problem and to the importance of avoiding a crisis and of refraining from weakening the position by one-sided concessions.[42]

The basic danger of an alteration in the legal and diplomatic arrangements with regard to Berlin was immediately recognized. Mayor Klaus Schuetz, who returned from talks with Willy Brandt on January 12, had the Tsarapkin aide memoire in mind when he spoke to the Merchants Association of West Berlin on January 12. He indicated that he expected diplomatic problems, with efforts by the GDR to change the situation of the city in the course of the coming weeks; but he said emphatically that the status of Berlin

---

Status Berlins sei in Zarapkins Darlegungen respektiert worden. Diehl teilte mit, dass Bundeskanzler Kiesinger den Sowjetbotschafter empfangen werde, 'wenn es die Umstaende erfordern.' Brandt habe das Gespraech vom 6 Januar nicht als Aussenminister, sondern als Vertreter des damals im Urlaub gewesenen Kanzler's gefuehrt" (*Tagesspiegel*, 18 January, 1968).

[41] See chapter 6, p. 139.

[42] *New York Times*, February 10, 1968.

would not be changed.[43] He made clear at this time and later his full appreciation of the Allied occupation which from a legal point of view prevails for all Berlin. He took the same position as that taken by Brandt in his speech on December 22, 1967. He indicated that he was willing to talk with communist authorities and on January 18, accompanied by his wife and an aide, he went to dinner at the East Berlin home of Soviet Ambassador Pyotz A. Abrasimov. No progress on basic issues was reported.

Its Objective

The Tsarapkin note was regarded as a clever attempt to exploit differences between the Western Allies and the Federal Republic regarding the relations of Berlin to the FRG. Few seem to have been deluded by this move, although it appears to have induced an increasing and noticeable restlessness and criticism of the lack of progress under long-established policies. Although the communists were endeavoring to fish in troubled waters, it is by no means clear that they wished a change in the status of Berlin or East Germany at that time. They were aware of the legal theory of the occupation that took effect in 1945, and they were not anxious to have the eastern part of Germany fully established as an independent nation, unrestricted by the control the Soviets now exercise. Such a drastic change could be expected to further unsettle the Warsaw Pact system and accelerate a loosening of ties that had already been observed in Czechoslovakia, Romania, and Yugoslavia, each of which followed in some respects a separate path.

The problem of the status of Berlin has been explored in chapter 6. The combined force of the three Western occupying powers and the more solid core of Bonn's leadership continue to withstand assaults of this type. Berlin is occupied under accepted legal terms that will not be replaced until sweeping changes have been made in Europe. The Tsarapkin note was not answered for almost two months.

Kiesinger's Reply

Kiesinger replied to the January note on March 1. The reply was not published but was reported in a general way in the press. It

[43] *Die Welt,* January 13, 1968.

rejected the accusation that the Federal Republic was endeavoring through forceful means to annex West Berlin, stated that the West German government maintained the existing status and relations of Berlin to the FRG, took cognizance of the manner in which, by the Wall and otherwise, the Soviet Union had infringed on the four-power status of the city, and asserted that a new communist party could be considered in West Germany if it could function within the framework of the constitution.[44] Earlier, in January, Kiesinger in a demonstration of resistance to Soviet threats had gone to Berlin to meet with the association of refugees and escapees. At no point did the leaders weaken in their response to the communist demands. Thus another menacing flourish came to nothing.

THE STRENGTH OF THE ECONOMY

The German situation offers no basis for an extreme reaction against the government. The alliance with the West is firm, the economy is strong. Thus the average voter is likely to support the more moderate wings of the CDU/CSU and the SPD unless catastrophic events should shake general confidence. The high degree of prosperity, the absence of spectacular political issues, and the growing status of the FRG in the European community, all tend to dampen the activities of the rebels, who are estimated to be still a small minority. Not all even of those who vote with the NPD are nationalists; some, in fact, tend to the Left.

Most observers agree that in the next decades only two changes could lead to a dangerous increase in nationalism. A severe economic depression, with unemployment higher than 10 percent, would admittedly lead to a reaction against prevailing policies. And a complete breakdown of the Federal Republic's relationship with the Western Allies and, in particular, evidence of anti-German policies in the United States could bring a revulsion of feeling and turn what is now only a disturbing murmur into a clamor for an independent line. Neither of these two calamities is considered likely by experienced German politicians. There is no prospect of

[44] Such a party (the Deutsche Kommunistische Partei) was in fact formed late in 1968 and was permitted by the Federal Constitutional Court on September 26 of that year.

clumsy and hostile action in Washington. And in an era when the interdependence of trading nations is an accepted fact, the German economy, inherently strong, is sure to receive help in times of stress from the European community as well as from the United States. It is admitted however that the economic situation could be crucial to political developments.

By early 1968 the Federal Republic was emerging from its only significant postwar recession. Unemployment, which had never been severe (being below 2 percent in most of the preceding five years) was cushioned by the presence of over a million guest laborers, some of whom returned home. These workers could disappear from the labor force without seriously affecting the German economy. Although the rate of growth declined from a high of 9.9 percent in 1961 to 0.9 percent in 1967, there was still some expansion of production, and there was no conspicuous decline in the

Table 14
Economic Growth of the FRG, 1965–1968

	Increase in Growth (%)	*Increase in Personal Consumption* (%)	*Total Labor Force (in thousands)*	*Unemployment Rate* (%)	*Job Openings (in thousands)*
1965	9.5	6.4	27,153	1.3	609
1966	6.1	3.5	27,082	1.2	584
1967	0.9	0.6	26,292	3.1	276
1968	8.9	3.6	26,655	0.8	609

Source: Handbook of Economic Statistics, March 1969, pp. 2, 3, 43, 44.

standard of living or in general consumption.[45] Although an economic slump, with significant unemployment, always presents political problems, the short period of decline in the FRG occasioned little alarm except among those who looked for a continuous rapid increase in growth and prosperity.

[45] *Handbook of Economic Statistics,* December 1967. This quarterly (formerly monthly) publication is the source of the figures given in this section.

Even during the recession there was growth in all the major categories of production reported under the Gross National Product (see table 14).

Foreign Trade

In the field of foreign trade, there were substantial changes between 1965 and 1966, with a favorable balance in commodity exports of DM 71.7–70.4 billion in 1965 and DM 80.6–72.7 billion in 1966, thus increasing the foreign reserves and giving significant support to German currency on the exchanges. A review of the main statistics reveals certain weak spots; but there was no overall decline in reserves and no serious setback. The concern during the recession was caused by the fear of a decline in living standards, by a slight decline in wages, and by the existence of visible unemployment rather than by any widespread industrial setback. None of the bankers interviewed in 1967 and 1968 were pessimistic. All expected a favorable recovery at a moderate pace.

Most German products are competitive with those of other advanced nations, and German exports to Common Market and other countries are substantial. The surplus of exports over imports was 7.9 billion in 1966. While perhaps the larger part of this trade was with Europe, more than 10 percent was with the United States. In the quality and price of its goods the FRG continues to hold its competitive position and thus maintains one of the most stable exchange rates in the world.

The Financial Situation

West German holdings of foreign reserves and Eurodollars are large. German ability and willingness to help support the dollar in periods of stress caused by the unfavorable American balance of payments has been a major factor in maintaining the international payments system. While the Federal Republic in common with most other countries has difficulty in balancing its budget, its revenues are dependable and, like its expenditures, have increased each year. The deficit for 1967 showed the effects of the economic setback but was estimated to be smaller in 1968. The contribution to the City of West Berlin has increased since the termination of

American aid and in 1969 probably will exceed three billion DM out of a total budget expenditure of approximately 77 billion DM. Wages have increased about 40 percent in the past six years, while prices have risen more slowly.

The Overall Picture

Optimism with regard to the economic situation is based in part on the substantial increase in industrial orders, which have already passed the 1965 level. Some estimates of the 1968 growth in production are as high as 8 or 9 percent. The countercyclical measures instituted earlier are expected to have considerable impact on large government investments. The cabinet rejected the proposed tax reduction because it considered the stimulus already adequate and the budget deficits likely to cause strain.

On the whole the picture is one of stability coupled with a high degree of economic control. There is nothing in prospect to cause alarm or to lead to pessimistic forecasts. The Germans, who learned the horrors of inflation in 1921 and 1922, are not likely to forget the importance of moderation. They continue to manifest a willingness for hard work and efficient production.

The most serious problem during the 1966–1967 recession was concentrated in the Ruhr area and particularly in the coal mines. Economics Minister Schiller developed a plan which subsidized workers for a transitional period and endeavored to transfer labor to other jobs and areas. Such a program necessarily entailed strains on infrastructure, housing, schools, and other supporting elements, together with changes in retail trade and consumption that called for special relief measures. The resulting demands on the budget sharpened the conflicts between Schiller (SPD) and Finance Minister Strauss (CSU). On January 25, 1968, Strauss defeated Schiller on the tax reduction issue. The cabinet then held that maintenance of a conservative budget policy, especially in the light of evidence of improvements in employment and production, was the correct course. Those who are familiar with the recurrence of periods of readjustment in investment and trade that characterizes our modern society do not expect uninterrupted rapid growth.

The change in the West German GNP from year to year is reported as:[46]

	Percent Change
1963	+6.5
1964	+9.6
1965	+9.5
1966	+6.1
1967	+0.9
1968	+8.8

Statistics indicate that West Berlin suffered less than the Federal Republic during the 1966–1967 recession: the rate of unemployment was lower, the decline in production less marked. These facts have been ignored by several writers, who picked up the chronic difficulties of the city and noted several shifts in well-known economic enterprises that moved their headquarters from the city.[47] These aspects of the picture combined with the admittedly adverse age distribution of the city's inhabitants were a basis for a sad story of a "declining city." This unduly pessimistic picture has been discussed in chapter 6. It exaggerates problems of which Washington and Bonn have been aware for two decades.

The Effect on Politics

The main significance of the brisk recovery from the 1966–1967 recession lies in its effect in dampening dissatisfaction at home and strengthening the position of the more moderate parties, thus relieving some of the pressure on internal and external policies. The overall economic potential of the West Germans to handle their financial and industrial problems is sufficiently impressive to offer hope of a reasonable and intelligent political evolution. The typical worker is conservative and not aggressively concerned with party politics. The businessmen are sophisticated and practical. Members of the *Bundestag* have kept their differences within healthy limits. The programs of Adenauer, Erhard, and Kiesinger

[46] Ibid., March 31, 1969, p. 2.

[47] Siemens, for example, moved some of their main offices to Munich. The "textile" or garment industry was also expanding in that area.

have met with wide acceptance. In 1969 the Federal Republic stands firmly on its resources and productive capacity and is the most stable and prosperous nation in Europe.

The Germans in Bonn are still solidly behind European integration, but their position is complicated by the desire and intention of maintaining good relations with France. They would therefore like to urge leaders of other nations, particularly Italy and The Netherlands, to take some of the burden of persuasion in matters of concern to President de Gaulle. They are still optimistic, in spite of Kiesinger's reported admission in his talks with de Gaulle that Great Britain's membership cannot come quickly.[48]

Germany's strength in the Atlantic Community as well as the vigor of her *Ostpolitik* depend in no small measure on the favorable development of her economic system. The internal strength that comes with sound industry and finance facilitates cooperation in NATO, in the EEC, and with other nations with which Germany desires trade and diplomatic ties. Even such political problems as the *Notstandsgesetz* and the *Wahlreform* become more manageable if growth continues and the standard of living improves. The political importance of recovery from the mild recession of 1966–1967 has generally been recognized as crucial. There is an awareness that with the expansion of opportunity for scientific, economic, and intellectual advancement the young men can be brought into meaningful and constructive relations to the problems of Germany, Europe, and the world. Even the interaction of protest and conformity can stimulate onward progress.

Bonn's capacity to reshape relations with nations to the East depends on confidence in the internal workings of economic and political democracy; without this, it would have no platform from which to operate. Fortunately the strength created in the first decades after the war has now made West Germany capable of independence, experimentation, and new initiatives. These capacities are likely to become more evident in the future than they have been in the recent past.

[48] Statement by Kurt Georg Kiesinger, February 15, 1968, after his return from Paris (*New York Times*, February 17, 1968).

Issues have sharpened as the struggle preceding the election grows more compelling, but activity will not be repressed. Younger men, coming recently into politics, will undertake reforms in education, the press, business structure, transportation, labor relations, negotiating tactics, and security measures and in liberalizing the social traditions of a nation which in the past has been prey to centralized power and dominating ideologies. The new measures and alliances may be different—perhaps as sharply different as the present is from the twenties and thirties. Changes are already taking place in attitudes toward other nations as well as toward domestic problems. Only a small number of those born in the twenties are now in positions of control. The fluidity of the ideas that are shaping in the *Bundestag* and in the *Landtage,* in the universities and in industry is already evident.

CHAPTER 8

Soviet Policy and Plans

FIRST SIGNS OF SOVIET AIMS, 1945–1949

The Soviet leaders, always conscious of the strength of Germany and doubly so after the bitter battle of Stalingrad, have made Germany the focal point in their European policy. Their frequent changes in tactics are not easy to follow. However the goals of Stalin and Khrushchev during the twenty years after World War II were clear. And since Khrushchev's fall in 1964 there have been no dependable signs of change.

At Yalta Stalin appeared genuinely convinced that his desire to suppress and control Germany and Austria was more or less approved by his colleagues. The agreement to study the feasibility of dismembering Germany was consistent with the general determination of the wartime allies to prevent German aggression, and gave the participants little basis for anticipating what was to come. Many facts that were soon to be revealed were not evident at the time of the German capitulation in May. The Katyn massacres[1] had not been made known to the planning committees, although an account of the incident had been given to President Roosevelt. The behavior of Russian troops, as they moved forward, was not held to indicate the continuing brutality of the Soviet occupation. The Morgenthau Plan, aimed in a direction similar to that proposed by Stalin, was still a guiding influence.[2]

[1] The bodies of 4,000 Polish officers were found in a mass grave in the Katyn forest in 1943. The Soviets in 1944 claimed that they had been killed during the German occupation of the area. A Select Committee of the U.S. Congress in April 1952 declared that the Soviet Security Police were responsible for the murders (U.S. Congress, House, Select Committee on the Katyn Forest Massacre, *Hearings on the Katyn Forest Massacre, 82d Cong., 1952*. Washington, D.C.: U.S. Government Printing Office, 1952, pp. 2214, 2217, 2218, 2266, 2267).

[2] U.S. Congress, Senate, Committee on Foreign Relations, *A Decade of American Foreign Policy: Basic Documents, 1941–1949*, pp. 502–505.

The Soviet leaders had not expressed objections to the treatment of Germany as an economic unit. There was in fact little comprehension of the inherent contradiction of talking about an economic entity while discussing dismemberment and disunity in political and security matters. The Allies turned their attention to practical issues of administration and gave too little thought to the Russian occupation policy which even in 1945 was starting to destroy German and Austrian institutions and values. At first Soviet dismantling of German industry had appeared justified in view of the large losses the Russians had suffered during the war, but it soon passed beyond the limits indicated by useful application to reconstruction in Russia.[3] It became increasingly punitive and destructive of economic potential. What appeared at first to be a natural hatred of the German enemy soon became a more far-reaching policy toward Europe and a sign of the forward movement of communism toward the Atlantic. The Russians twisted the de-Nazification program into a largely opportunistic policy of persecuting capitalist leaders as they cleared many of the friends of communism for jobs, regardless of their record under Hitler. The leaders of the Left were given predominant preference, but others willing to cooperate also benefited.

Russian eagerness in 1945 to forge ahead with the creation of a central government for Austria seemed on the whole to be a constructive attitude and was paralleled by other efforts not fully understood at the time. The socialist Karl Renner was established as president of Austria; the "Ulbricht group" was brought into Berlin. Thus Moscow misjudged the situation in Austria at the same time that Washington was misled about the early developments of the Socialist Unity Party (SED) in Berlin. It was not until 1946 that the true situation and the divergence of aims began to be recognized in the two capitals.

The Struggle for Berlin

The Soviet goal was domination of Germany as a whole, but the party leaders in Moscow recognized the importance of Berlin. The

[3] The needs were enormous but useful transfer of machinery could only be accomplished in a few cases.

work of organizing the socialist groups in that city went ahead. Prime attention was given to labor and to the problem of choosing an *Oberbuergermeister* and a *Magistrat* (the executive branch of the city government) for the whole city that would be acceptable to the Kremlin. No serious question of the division or reunification of Germany arose at this time. The Soviets assumed that with the help of the leftwing socialists and the strong anti-Nazis they could quickly and effectively organize a subordinate apparatus for the conquered nation, as they hoped to do in Austria. Such an apparatus would hold all Germany under their control. There is reason to think that they did not expect American opposition to this program. American troops were going home. Moreover the Western Allies had suffered at the hands of the Germans and feared their resurgence.

In these critical months in 1945 and 1946, as the Soviets tried to form a government and a unified party which would give them the controlling voice in the nation, they invited to Pankow many men who were later to take a prominent part in the fight for a free Berlin. They ignored the Social Democratic (SPD) vote on March 31, 1946, against merger with the German Communist Party (KPD) and allowed the KPD to assume control as of April 21. In fact for a brief time the SPD and KPD functioned side by side in Berlin. In August the Allied Kommandatura restored constitutional government and arranged for secret elections. This was followed by rejection of the anomalous SPD-KPD situation on October 20, 1946, when the last—and only—all-Berlin election was held.[4]

Thus by the end of 1946 the divergence of policy between the USSR and the democratic forces of the West with the support of the aroused and watchful SPD became evident to those close to the day-to-day problems. Meanwhile the Russian failure in Vienna shed light on the Soviets' program in Germany, where they avoided the conditions which led eventually to Austria's independence and sovereignty.[5] The continuing struggle for control was sharpened by the fight against Ernst Reuter, the SPD candidate who in June

[4] Walther Hubatsch et al., eds., *The German Question*, p. 251.
[5] See chapter 8.

1947 was chosen by the city assembly for Governing Mayor. The Soviets particularly objected to Reuter who had been a communist during a brief stay in Moscow and had returned recently from exile in Istanbul,[6] and used their membership in the Kommandatura to veto his election. Louise Schroeder was elected as acting mayor and served ably despite her frail health. Reuter was her helper and was, in the minds of many, the real mayor.

Another problem—which was to bring the first outright challenge to the Allied position in Berlin—was the currency reform which the experts were developing as an effective instrument of economic integration and as a spur to reconstruction. The importance the Soviets attached to rejecting the technical arrangements for the introduction of a new currency in Germany was a result of the success of conversion in Austria. The significance attached by the West to this economic reform was obviously not lost on the Russians. It was partly responsible for their preblockade harassment of the city and for their leaving the Berlin Kommandatura temporarily in April 1948 and definitively in June of that year.[7]

In trying to discern the outline of communist policy at this time, it is worth noting that the United States had not appeared to raise any significant objection to the communist seizure of power in Czechoslovakia in February 1948 or made any show of strength in the Pacific when China fell to the communists. The Soviets apparently expected by a combination of offers to the Berliners and threats to the Allied position in the city to loosen the Western hold on the three occupied Zones reaching beyond the Rhine. Negotiation of a German peace treaty in Moscow had made no progress in March and April 1947 or in London in December. The Truman Doctrine had been announced on March 12, 1947, and the Marshall Plan speech was delivered on June 5, but the consequences of these crucial Washington decisions were not immediately obvious. The expenditure of American funds and the movement of goods took time, and the Greek and Turkish problems were not solved overnight. Soviet policy in Europe reached a criti-

[6] Willy Brandt and Richard Lowenthal, *Ernst Reuter*, pp. 37, 111, 113, 204, 349, 377, 380.

[7] W. Phillips Davison, *The Berlin Blockade*, pp. 70, 118.

cal turning point when Moscow prevented Czechoslovakia from joining other nation's accepting U.S. aid under the European Recovery Program. The decision taken in Moscow in 1948 to cut off Berlin from the Western zones of occupation was a bold challenge for which the United States was only partially prepared.

The Blockade

It was not certain at the outset that this action was intended to be lasting; it might have been only another case of short-term harassment. The Soviets were endeavoring to dominate the city government or, failing that, at least drastically to affect its operations. Accordingly they engaged the Berlin leaders in long and difficult interrogations. W. Phillips Davison reported their tactics as part of a plan to bring chaos to the city and thus induce violent clashes in which the Americans, attempting to maintain order by force, would be thrown into an unacceptable militant position.[8]

The disagreement among American experts and advisers on means to counter the blockade, once it had started, was sufficiently obvious to lead the Russians to hope that they would win their gamble. Few of them considered the airlift to be more than a stopgap measure. On the assumption that the United States would not go to war, they felt they had little to lose. They had high hopes of intimidating the Germans.[9] In view of the vulnerability of the city and the general skepticism about the continuation of the airlift that had been begun on a small scale at the end of June, their action appeared to have succeeded. As Davison wrote, "Soviet plans for taking over Berlin were well considered. The amazing thing is that they failed."[10]

The Berliners took their stand even before the Western powers had consolidated their views and determined to solve the technical problems of supplying Berlin by air; they refused the food and fuel offered by the Russians. Soon, to escape the unbearable pressure on individual officials, the city government left its offices in the eastern part of the city and moved to Schoeneberg in West Berlin.

[8] Ibid., p. 147.
[9] Ibid., pp. 323–79.
[10] Ibid., p. 145.

For the communists the year 1948 did not end as propitiously as it had begun. The airlift had captured the imagination of the world as planes flew into the hard-pressed city every minute or so, discharging large amounts of food, fuel, and raw materials. The Marshall Plan was moving from hope to reality. Austria was holding firm. Yugoslavia had taken an independent line. The Italian elections had not gone to the communists. France was turning to the Right. The Allies hardened their attitude toward the Soviet Union, urged cooperative security measures and a stronger alliance, and finally joined together in a strong defensive posture in NATO.

So it came about that early in 1949 the Soviet representatives signified their willingness to discuss the Berlin situation. At the request of Jacob Malik, Soviet ambassador to UNO, he and Philip Jessup, his U.S. counterpart, held informal discussions in New York on the question of access to Berlin. Afterward the Paris meeting of the foreign ministers of the four powers on May 23 spelled out a new statement on Berlin and the blockade was ended. The planes that had flown for eleven months in good and bad weather had demonstrated Western determination to stand by the Germans. The first phase of the Soviet attempts to push the West out of Germany was over. Berlin had gained new vigor and support, and the rearmament of West Germany had become inevitable. The Kremlin took a new approach in its European policy. A new attack on the Allies and on the position of the free world was to begin in the Far East. The first chapter on Germany was closed.

A ZIGZAG COURSE, 1949–1955

World opinion had been captured by the stand of the Berliners. The Soviets, after the partial defeat they had suffered, took a more complicated course, and their intentions became less obvious. Since they could no longer anticipate easy acceptance of their demands after the Berlin airlift, the establishment of NATO, and the response to the attack on South Korea, they modified their tactics which became more difficult to interpret. The zigzag course of probes alternating with retreat, of demands for American withdrawal alternating, after the death of Stalin on March 5, 1953, with requests for conferences was confusing. They fashioned new instruments through the creation of Comecon in 1949 and the Warsaw Pact on May 14, 1955, and turned their attention to other parts of the world while keeping a concerned and watchful eye on the development of German industry, trade, political institutions and armaments.

In the years following the abortive Berlin blockade Ulbricht's proven capacity led the Soviets to give him more scope and support in the administration of the East Zone.[11] They rejected the concept of a "German road to socialism" that some had held since 1945. Stalinism was to prevail in the GDR even after most communist lands had been de-Stalinized following the 1956 Twentieth Party Congress. They also further enhanced Ulbricht's status by liquidating the Soviet Military Occupation Administration; its place was taken by the Soviet Control Commission in Germany which had much the same functions.[12] The declared Soviet policy was the campaign for world peace and total disarmament, but this only rendered their real intentions more inscrutable as they continued with varying intensity their harassment of Berlin and pressure on Germany.

One element in this complex policy was the communist acceptance of the Oder-Neisse line as the border between Poland and Germany. This step was part of the continuing Soviet effort to consolidate their position with their satellites. In June 1950 Warsaw and Pankow reached an agreement in Moscow that this line constituted the *peace border* between their two nations. Soviet use of such terms as peace, democracy, freedom, voting, the people's will was so distorted that their communications are difficult for the inexpert to understand. The agreement of June 1950 ignored the legal condition embodied in the four-power agreements, that the final borders must wait on the conclusion of a peace treaty. The theory of a single German state still obtained and was reflected in the platform of the Soviet-sponsored National Front of October 4, 1949, designed to protect the interests of all Germans. It emphasized the concept of the whole of Germany

[11] See chapter 4.
[12] Hans Hartl and Werner Marx, *Fuenfzig Jahre sowjetische Deutschlandpolitik*, p. 255.

lying under the fascist domination of American imperialism, from which the entire nation must be freed.

Propaganda Moves

In the early 1950s the Soviets made various threatening statements against NATO and, as Allied policy veered more and more toward bringing Germany into the Western defense community, they intensified their propaganda attacks. In October 1950 the GDR participated in a conference of Soviet bloc foreign ministers in Prague and for the first time played a distinctive role in an international meeting.[13] The communique issued at the conclusion of the conference called for the withdrawal of occupation troops from Germany and the creation of an all-German constitutional assembly to govern the entire nation. The proposed body was not to be established by a free election. Since it would be the creation of the Communist party and thus not based on self-determination, it was obvious to Moscow that the Western Allies would have to turn the proposal down. However the plan seemed to offer opportunities for propaganda and accordingly was for some years the official Soviet line in discussions of German reunification.[14]

On March 10, 1952, the Soviets made what purported to be an attempt to resolve the German question. This took the form of a proposal that was vague on all important issues such as elections and could not be given serious consideration after the blockade. Its terms would have had more appeal at an earlier time. This note was perhaps Stalin's only comprehensive attempt at a German solution.

The Switch in 1953

The year 1953 was a time of changing leadership. The overthrow and subsequent death of Beria in June saved Ulbricht from a potential fall from power,[15] and Ulbricht gained greater control over German policy. Economic policy in Moscow changed following Stalin's death and may have reflected to some extent an aware-

[13] Ibid., p. 272.
[14] Ibid., pp. 273, 274.
[15] Ibid., p. 316.

ness of the brilliant recovery taking place in West Germany. In any case, after 1953 the Soviets not only ceased their large-scale dismantling and reparations inside the Zone but also extended a credit of 485 million rubles and put a limit on the amount to be paid by the Ulbricht regime for the cost of the troops occupying East Germany.[16] Hans Hartl and Werner Marx refer to these changes as attempts to strengthen the position of the SED regime and to "popularize" it.[17] Living standards had been miserably low for the preceding ten years; the reports of the thousands of refugees streaming out of the Zone were ample evidence of this, and there were many other signs. Thus Moscow's economic policy became more benign after the Berlin revolt of 1953. Its political and diplomatic position however showed no significant change.

The Berlin Conference, 1954

An exchange of notes in 1953 led to an agreement for a meeting of the Soviet and Western foreign ministers, to be held in Berlin in January 1954. The subjects discussed at this conference included the relaxation of tension, the German problem, and the Austrian State Treaty. It was at this time that Secretary Dulles, discouraged by the lack of progress on Germany and Austria, spoke in the following terms about the interminable meetings on the Austrian State Treaty:

> For about 2,000 years now there has been a figure in mythology which symbolizes tragic futility. That was Sisyphus, who, according to the Greek story, was given the task of rolling a great stone up to the top of a hill. Each time when, after great struggle and sweating the stone was just at the brow of the hill, some evil force manifested itself and pushed the stone down. So poor Sisyphus had to start his task over again.
>
> I suspect that for the next 2,000 years the story of Sisyphus will be forgotten, when generation after generation is told the story, the tragic story, of the Austrian State Treaty. Austria was promised its independence 11 years ago. When our forces moved into Austria 9 years ago they announced that they were

[16] See chapter 4.
[17] Hartl and Marx, *Fuenfzig Jahre*, p. 316.

> there only to liberate. Now, year after year has gone by, when we have repeatedly been almost at the point of concluding an Austrian State Treaty, and always some evil force manifests itself and pushes the treaty back again. So we have to start again from the bottom of the hill. That is again the tragedy being repeated here today.[18]

The Austrian treaty required ten years of negotiation; the German treaty is still not in sight after twenty-five years.

On January 29, Anthony Eden, with French and American concurrence, introduced his plan for a five-stage reunification of Germany.[19] On February 4 Soviet Foreign Minister Vyacheslav Molotov categorically rejected the Eden Plan and proposed the speedy conclusion of a German peace treaty and a general European security pact. In commenting on Molotov's proposal, Secretary Dulles referred to the "mysterious '32' nations of Europe" and to the fact that the United States was to be an observer. He asserted that if the Atlantic Charter, the Yalta agreements, and the United Nations Charter, to which the Soviets had adhered, had not succeeded in assuring constructive measures and peace in Europe, a new, inclusive organization such as the proposed pact could not be expected to accomplish this objective.[20] It was apparent that this Russian move was diversionary rather than designed to bring a change in the Cold War which had already been aggravated by the communist attack on South Korea. The Russian proposal was termed an ineffective formula for the settlement of a great problem.

The various communiques issued at the end of the meeting reflected the wide divergence of views among the participants. The three Western powers stated their insistence on free elections and added that they were forced to the conclusion that the Soviet Government "is not now ready to permit free all-German elections, or to abandon its control over Eastern Germany. . . . Offers were made to discuss how the undertakings which already protect the

[18] U.S. Department of State, *American Foreign Policy: Basic Documents, 1950–1955*, p. 1864 (hereafter cited as *Basic Documents, 1950–1955*).
[19] See chapter 5.
[20] *Basic Documents, 1950–1955*, p. 1864.

Soviet Union against aggression could be reinforced. The Soviet delegation made no response to these offers."[21]

The joint communique issued by the four foreign ministers stated flatly that they "were unable to reach agreement upon these matters."

The Western Allies' insistence on the importance they attached to an Austrian State Treaty, Khrushchev's mounting desire for a summit meeting in order to advance his ambition as he stood behind Premier Bulganin, and consideration of the questions of Korea and Indochina led to the scheduling in May 1955 of a summit conference to be held at Geneva the following July.[22] A meeting at the summit proposed in 1953 had been put off owing to the illness of Winston Churchill. These events resulted in one of those puzzling and unpredictable shifts in Soviet policy.

In other respects also the year 1954 had been one of varied pressures and changes. In August the French for a number of reasons turned down the European Defense Community to which they had earlier agreed; some of these reasons related to the defeat in Indochina. The decision to bring Germany into NATO by other means was taken as the British acted under the Brussels Pact and Western European Union (WEU). The Paris Agreements in October were another step in this direction.[23]

The Austrian State Treaty, 1955

The question of the neutralization of Austria appeared to become increasingly important to the Soviets in 1955. They were consolidating their position in the satellite countries and in East Germany. They saw no way of persuading the Western Allies to abandon Austria or of winning Austria's favor. Their keen interest in a summit meeting is generally considered to have been a decisive factor in their diplomatic game. Perhaps they were thinking of the success won at Yalta and at Potsdam. Perhaps Khrushchev's internal maneuvers to gain greater control influenced their action.

The unity of the NATO powers was impressive. In a note dated

[21] Ibid., pp. 1870, 1871.
[22] Ibid., pp. 2372, 2373.
[23] Ibid., pp. 1881, 972–79.

November 29, 1954, the United States had suggested direct conversations between the Austrians and the Russians; a three-power declaration on April 5, 1955, included the same idea. On April 22 the Western foreign ministers welcomed "the Soviet Government's view, that the possibility now exists of concluding the Austrian State Treaty."[24] It noted that preparatory work between the Austrians and the Soviets was still incomplete but could be carried out by the ambassadors of the four powers in Vienna. The treaty was signed in Vienna on May 15. This episode constituted the first major shift in Soviet policy with regard to a conquered nation.

West German Rearmament

Just before the NATO treaty was signed, the divergence of views between the CDU/CSU and the SPD with regard to German neutrality and rearmament came to a sharp issue in the exchange of letters between Chancellor Adenauer and Erich Ollenauer, head of the SPD.[25] But in March the *Bundestag* ratified by a large majority membership in the Brussels Pact and NATO. In recalling this phase of negotiations Adenauer was to state in his memoirs that "the SPD had put the German Government in a false light."[26]

The question naturally arises whether the Soviets were misled by the internal German differences. Yet the possibility of German neutralization had no place in Allied strategy or in Bonn's thinking. Secretary Dulles said in his press conference on May 24: "I do not believe that anybody realistically believes that the German people, 70 odd million of them, are destined to play the role of a neutral country."[27] He pointed out also that neutrality of the Austrian type permitted an unlimited army and that this could be allowed to a country of seven million but was not applicable to Germany. Thus the four nations approached the summit conference in Geneva with policies unchanged with respect to Germany. The meeting took place on July 18–23.

[24] Ibid., p. 1885.
[25] Konrad Adenauer, *Erinnerungen 1953–1955*, pp. 410–20.
[26] Ibid., p. 439.
[27] *Basic documents, 1950–1955*, pp. 1885, 1886.

The Geneva Summit Conference, 1955

The Geneva summit meeting illustrates the sharp difference between the tactics of the communists and the aims of the Western Allies. The Soviets wished to give priority to the creation of an inclusive European security pact and disarmament and then to consider the solution of the German question. The West wished to tackle the concrete and practical issues involved in bringing the two parts of Germany together. President Eisenhower and his colleagues and the French and British heads of government, Edgar Faure and Anthony Eden, all considered the larger proposal to be impossible, vague, and remote. They felt that the same limitations which hampered the United Nations would make so wide-reaching an approach impractical.

Many have forgotten that in Geneva the Soviets agreed that Germany should be reunited through free elections.[28] They made it clear however that they thought the arrangements could only be worked out with official representation of the GDR and the FRG. The conference decided to study the questions of a security pact for Europe, the limitation of armaments, and the establishment of a zone in which armed forces would be disposed by mutual agreement. The decision to explore these matters led to the meeting of foreign ministers in Geneva in the autumn. The common agreement about the reunification of Germany was ignored by the Soviets.

NEW DEALINGS BETWEEN BONN AND MOSCOW 1955–1958

The Geneva Conference left the official pronouncement on German reunification by free elections unchanged but offered little hope of speedy progress. Meanwhile in a note, dated June 7, 1955, to the West German ambassador in Paris the Russians had indicated a desire to "normalize relations with the Federal Republic"[29] and invited Chancellor Adenauer to visit Moscow. In thus seeking

[28] Hartl and Marx, *Fuenfzig Jahre*, pp. 346–48; *Basic Documents, 1950–1955*, pp. 1886–97.

[29] Hartl and Marx, *Fuenfzig Jahre*, p. 343.

relations with the FRG they were presumably operating on the thesis of two Germanys. On September 20, immediately after the agreement between Bonn and Moscow for the exchange of ambassadors, the treaty on the relations of the Soviet Union and the GDR was concluded. It stated that the GDR was free in interior politics and foreign policy. This agreement was acknowledged in the often-cited letter of the same date from Lothar Bolz, foreign minister of the GDR, to Valerin A. Zorin, Soviet deputy foreign minister. The letter stated that the GDR was assuming control over access to and from West Berlin, except for Allied military traffic.[30] Moscow abolished the Soviet High Commission to Germany and stated that questions pertaining to Germany as a whole would be handled by the Soviet ambassador to the GDR.

A few days later the foreign ministers of the United Kingdom, France, and the United States, meeting in New York, declared that Moscow's agreement with East Germany could not affect the responsibilities the Soviets had accepted in earlier four-powers agreements.[31] Thus the harassment continued and the diplomatic struggle went on; but Soviet personnel continued to handle the Allied papers at the checkpoints on the access road to Berlin.

The Geneva Conference of Foreign Ministers, 1955

The meeting of the four foreign ministers, called for in a directive issued by the heads of government at the summit conference in the spring of 1955, was held in Geneva October 27–November 16, 1955. In the interest of European security the Western powers proposed consideration of the Eden Plan, which had been submitted at the Berlin conference in 1954 together with various provisions designed to reassure the Russians with regard to any presumed danger of German aggression. These included renunciation of the use of force, withholding of support from aggressors, limitation on armaments and forces, inspection and control, consultation, and other steps which would make all parties to a proposed general European treaty on collective security responsible for keeping the peace. Preparations for implementing the Eden Plan would

[30] Hubatsch et al., eds., *The German Question*, pp. 177, 178.
[31] U.S. Department of State, *Documents on Germany, 1944–1959*, p. 485.

involve four-power planning in consultation with the Germans, East and West, and a supervisory commission to carry out the plans.[32]

Foreign Minister Molotov's stated objections to the plan were summed up by Secretary Dulles as being (a) that a reunited Germany would be bound to join NATO, and (b) that the "sanctions of the treaty were mere 'consultations.' "[33] Dulles agreed that European security and German reunification were closely linked and of great importance. In speaking of Molotov's objections he emphasized the fact that, with proper elections, the Germans would choose their future course.

> In this connection I recall a provision of the Eden Plan which forms a part of the proposal submitted last week, which reads "The All-German government shall have the authority to assume or reject the international rights and obligations of the Federal Republic and the Soviet Zone of Germany and to conclude such other international agreements as it may wish."[34]

In commenting on this exchange, Fritz Erler, SPD policy leader until his death, said that both sides knew that in a free choice an all-German government would join NATO.[35]

In the course of the ensuing discussions various unsuccessful attempts were made to meet Soviet fears of a new German aggression. On November 4 Dulles made the following statement:

> Yesterday, Mr. Molotov, just returned from Moscow, made a statement on behalf of the Soviet Union. It has such grave implications that I asked that we should suspend our meeting until today, so as to be able to give his statement deliberate thought. I am now in a position to express the views of my government.
>
> My first observation is that the Soviet position if persisted in will perpetuate conditions which put in jeopardy the peace of Europe. My second observation is that it strikes a crippling blow

[32] *Basic Documents, 1950–1955*, p. 1902.
[33] Ibid., p. 1906.
[34] Ibid., p. 1916; Hartl and Marx, *Fuenfzig Jahre*, p. 357.
[35] Fritz Erler, "The Struggle for German Reunification," *Foreign Affairs*, April 1956, pp. 389–92.

> at the possibility of developing relations of confidence with the Soviet Union.[36]

A communique issued on November 16, 1955, reiterated the July agreement of the four powers, to which Bulganin had been a party, on "common responsibility of the Four Powers for the reunification of Germany" and that this should "be carried out by means of free elections." It added that the negotiations had failed because of the Soviet refusal to accept the security measures and other plans brought forward.[37]

Secretary Dulles reviewed the history of the two Geneva meetings, including the November failure, on radio and television from Washington on November 15. A salient passage in his address concluded:

> Some thought that the Soviet Union might be willing to allow Germany to be reunified by free elections if a reunified Germany would not enter the North Atlantic Treaty Organization. But in fact, the Soviet delegation made it abundantly clear that it would not permit Germany to be reunified by free elections even on such terms.[38]

Molotov's assertions with regard to the German menace sprang from a certain historical determinism. His statements at this time reflected an expectation of the inevitable progress of a resurgent and aggressive Germany, devoid of any awareness of the many basic changes brought by the nuclear age. He expressed firm belief that the dynamics of German development were a threat to the existence of communism. From these premises he arrived, by a logical extension of his Marxian ideas, at the inescapable conclusion that Germany must be either communist or divided.[39]

In the Wake of Failure

The failure of the meeting meant the closing of the door to reunification for many years. All subsequent maneuvers were of

[36] *Basic Documents, 1950–1955,* p. 1922. The statement of November was for an All-German Council without prior elections, to coordinate the political, economic, and cultural life of the two Germanys.

[37] Ibid., pp. 1926, 1927.

[38] Ibid., pp. 115, 117.

[39] Hartl and Marx, *Fuenfzig Jahre,* p. 358.

little significance, except as they demonstrated the Western powers' determination not to abandon the principle of freedom for the German people or to weaken in defense of Berlin or the support of German democracy.

The presence of a German ambassador in Moscow and a Russian ambassador in Bonn did little to affect the relations between the two governments. The dialogue was limited to official statements which showed no discernible easing of the two positions. In the Soviet Union the two main events—the Khrushchev speech at the Twentieth Congress and the forcible repression of the Polish and Hungarian uprisings—did nothing to alter policy toward Germany. There was no notable confrontation until 1958. In East Germany steps were taken to establish a ministry of defense and to build up a people's army.[40]

One element in the Kremlin's tactical approach to the German problem was an increase in Pankow's independence, in the hope of a nationalistic type of rapprochement between the two Germanys and a consequent infiltration of communism into the western part. The instrument for this policy was to be an all-German council.[41] Nikita Khrushchev was to furnish the drive for "normalizing" the situation.

These years were also a time of great improvement in Berlin's economic condition, of rearmament in West Germany, and of further steps toward European economic cooperation. Khrushchev declared the new policy of de-Stalinization in February 1956.[42] The concern of most Germans for reunification was probably subordinated during this period to their increasing involvement in Western policy and commerce. The strength of the new Germany was becoming evident even to the most doubtful observer. Ulbricht was worried because of the lag in his economic programs yet actively pursuing rearmament with a variety of military formations. At the same time contingents of Russian soldiers, estimated at more than 200,000—perhaps as many as 300,000—remained on East German soil.

[40] Ibid., p. 367.
[41] Ibid., p. 351.
[42] Malcolm Mackintosh, "Three Détentes," in *Détente*, ed. Eleanor Lansing Dulles and Robert Dickson Crane, pp. 103–120.

KHRUSHCHEV'S BATTLE FOR BERLIN

In 1958 Khrushchev became established in the party and the government. During this year he enjoyed almost unlimited power as he pressed hard on the perimeter of his empire and probed for weakness among the democracies. He had urged the calling of another summit meeting at which he hoped his preeminence would be more conspicuous than it had been in 1955. He instigated action in the Middle East. In the Far East this was a year in which he could insist on a Chinese attack on Quemoy and Matsu—and then call a halt. Throughout this year there was a running debate between Khrushchev and Dulles, and a notable degree of brinkmanship in the Far East, Middle East, and elsewhere. As regards Germany, it was the year of the Khrushchev ultimatum to the three Western powers over Berlin.

A Year of Intense Diplomatic Activity

That Khrushchev's desire for a summit meeting was related to the German question was manifest in the series of communications that started with Premier Bulganin's letter of December 10, 1957, to President Eisenhower on the Rapacki Plan for neutralizing Central Europe and Eisenhower's reply of January 12, 1958. It continued throughout the year. This was a period of active diplomatic communications between Bonn, Washington, Moscow, and elsewhere. These activities were variously interpreted as pointing up the danger of growing German strength, indicating a wish on the part of the Soviets to placate a more active GDR, an increased awareness of the significance of nuclear weapons, or an intention of capitalizing on the success of Sputnik and other achievements in the field of missiles and space. Their divergence from the statement on reunification made at the conclusion of the Geneva Summit Conference was evident in the proposal for an agreement between the two German states contained in Bulganin's note of December 10.[43] In his reply, President Eisenhower reminded Bulganin of the directive agreed on at the Geneva Summit Conference in July 1955 and said that, if suitable preparations were made, he would be

[43] U.S. Department of State, *Documents on Germany, 1944–1959*, pp. 44–59, 225, 233, 264, 265, 277, 281, 291, 300.

willing to have a meeting of heads of government.[44] Consultations preparatory to such a summit were initiated but bogged down for months when difficulties arose over the agenda. These difficulties were mainly connected with the German issue and a continuing debate over "reunification," a "peace treaty," "confederation," the "security" issues, and the apparent Soviet propaganda efforts. The summit meeting itself was not scheduled until May 1960, and then it was to be broken up by Khrushchev's angry gesture in leaving Paris.

In September a Soviet note urged early conclusion of a peace treaty and dealings between the two German states but ignored the question of free elections.[45] It was therefore rejected by the three Western powers. This note differed in no essential respect from the earlier notes, but it emphasized Khrushchev's growing determination to make gains along the lines he had been pursuing since the Geneva Conference. All the moves in this attempt to force the Allies to compromise their position rested on the tacit assumption that Berlin could be used as a pressure point. Tension was mounting.

Khrushchev's Ultimatum

In early November 1958 Khrushchev delivered a speech at the Sports Palace in Moscow which foreshadowed the demands he was to make on November 27. He said that only the German people, working together as two separate states, could settle the question of reunification. This statement, following as it did the failure to gain acceptance for the Rapacki Plan in 1957 and the discussion of an all-German council in the weeks immediately preceding, occasioned much talk of the German question in all major capitals. Secretary Dulles was asked in a press conference what Washington would do if the Soviet personnel at the checkpoints were replaced by East Germans. He said that while Washington would not accept any situation that gave recognition to the East German regime, it might consider such an arrangement if the persons at the

[44] Eleanor Lansing Dulles, *John Foster Dulles*, pp. 96–109. The chapter "Promises Are Pie Crusts" contains a comment on summitry.

[45] U.S. Department of State, *Documents on Germany, 1944–1959*, pp. 44–59, 301.

checkpoints were acting as the *agents* of the Soviets. In spite of its probable legal validity, this statement caused considerable agitation in Bonn.

These discussions and forewarnings did not prevent the harshly worded ultimatum of November 27 from coming as a severe shock to the Western powers. They had no thought however of accepting the ultimatum; they recognized that if the Kremlin had finally decided to make Berlin an issue, they would have to stand their ground, whatever the risk. An immediate press statement made this clear. After the first few hours of panic, the Berliners showed their understanding of the Allied position by the speed with which they returned to the savings banks the funds they had hurriedly withdrawn; and the economy moved on in high gear. Within a few days Khrushchev showed his understanding of the Western position by stating at an Albanian Embassy reception that he had not intended an ultimatum.[46] The ultimatum itself was not mentioned again, although the six months' span it had set forth continued to worry some diplomats.

These events brought another change in Soviet tactics. Khrushchev began to show interest in an invitation to visit Washington. He delayed action on a unilateral peace treaty with the GDR. There was no substantial change in the Berlin situation after 1958 until the Wall. In spite of occasional harassment, access to Berlin was not seriously disturbed, and, with a feeling of reasonable security in the city, the economy continued to improve. The Allies, having shown their firmness, could accept the status quo for years to come.

The United States still maintained its willingness to meet with the Soviets. Secretary Dulles, in his press conference on January 13, 1959, spoke of the Soviet demands in these terms:

> That proposal highlights what I just referred to as the two different philosophies about dealing with Germany. The Soviet Union has consistently believed that Germany should be isolated, segregated, to a large extent demilitarized and neutralized and separated from close association with the neighboring countries.

[46] Jean Edward Smith, *The Defense of Berlin*, p. 185.

> We don't believe that that is a sound approach to the problem. On the contrary, we take the view that Germany and the German people are too great, vigorous and vital a people to be dealt with in that way and that that way is fraught with very great danger for the future. We believe that the future is best served by encouraging the closest possible relations between Germany and other Western European countries which are peace-loving and having such a close integration, military, political, economic, that independent, aggressive, nationalist action by Germany becomes as a practical matter impossible and also something that would not be desired.[47]

In order to make sure that there was common understanding at this crucial time, Dulles made his last trip to Europe. Impressed by Western unity, the Soviets abandoned their November demands. The dangers of a serious East-West conflict due to miscalculation had been averted.

The Geneva Conference, 1959

The Geneva meeting beginning in May 1959 brought no agreement and no change in the German situation. Although the Russians had been offered a greater opportunity than they realized, no substantial ground was lost to them.

On June 16 the West proposed a limitation of the garrison to 11,000 men, reduction of the garrison if "developments were to permit," conditional East German control over access to Berlin, and a curb on intelligence and propaganda in the city. Presumably this proposal would have meant the closing of RIAS. These conditions, if adopted, would have led to a continuing wrangle. Professor Jean Smith has indicated the pitfalls that seemed likely to result. The various proposals offered were however rejected by Gromyko, who failed to realize that they would have meant significant concessions by the West and major gains for the communists. As Smith has stated: "The final Soviet proposals were a repeat of the earlier recommendations. . . . [They remained] unacceptable. . . .

[47] U.S. Department of State, *Documents on Germany, 1944–1959*, pp. 371, 372.

Had Gromyko accepted the final Western proposals. West Berlin's hope of survival would have been destroyed. . . ."[48]

The battle for Berlin, which was in fact the battle for Germany, tapered off as Khrushchev looked to Washington and his coming visit. His talks with Eisenhower outside Washington, which have been frequently regarded as leading to a relaxation of tensions called the "spirit of Camp David," did not in fact bring any changes in Russian policy toward Germany. The last years of the Republican Administration were relatively undisturbed as Khrushchev, interested in Cuba, Africa, and the Middle East, strove to expand his foreign relations and twice appeared in the United Nations (1959, 1960). The ultimatum served on the Western powers and the threat of a unilateral peace treaty melted away. There was an appearance of harmony and acceptance of the status quo until after the American elections in November 1960.

THE WALL

The changing of the guard when John F. Kennedy took over the leadership in Washington naturally led to curiosity and excitement on both sides. Kennedy was eager to meet with Khrushchev and to take his measure.[49] The Soviet chairman for his part wished to test the firmness of the new young man. The meeting was scheduled for Vienna in early June. The American President had expressed his optimism as he started his journey, but the talks in Vienna left him depressed and apprehensive. Before the 1961 meeting in Vienna ended, Khrushchev presented Kennedy a note similar in some respects to that of November 1958. Earlier, on his return from Paris through East Berlin in 1960, Khrushchev had again spoken of a separate peace treaty for the GDR.

Worried about Laos, shocked by the misadventure in Cuba, and distressed by his failure to make any constructive moves with

[48] Smith, *Defense*, p. 208. See also chapter 5 above.

[49] The Soviet ambassador gave the German chancellor a nine-point note on February 17, 1961, urging recognition of the realities of defeat. It seemed to close the door to reunification. Little attention seems to have been paid to this Soviet effort in the free-world capitals (Otto Martin von der Gablentz, *Dokumente zur Berlin-Frage*, 1944–1962, p. 412; Hubatsch et al., eds., *The German Question*, p. 280; Hartl and Marx, *Fuenfzig Jahre*, p. 488).

Khrushchev, Kennedy did not present to the world the strong image that was later to be his. Weeks elapsed between his receipt of the note and the rejection of the Soviet demands on July 17. The American reply reemphasized the priority of German reunification and self-determination. In a news conference on July 19 and in a speech on July 25 Kennedy stressed the importance of the Western military presence in Berlin.[50] It was at this time that he referred to the protection of *West* Berlin, ignoring the fact that four-power rights applied to all four sectors of *Greater* Berlin. Meanwhile for a variety of reasons fear mounted and the outflow of refugees from the Zone increased to proportions not witnessed since 1953. The flight from the GDR was discussed by several American senators, in a manner which left doubt as to the clarity and firmness of the position in Washington.[51]

Its Significance

Built in the week beginning August 13, 1961,[52] the Wall was an expression of Soviet readiness to support Ulbricht. It has also an indication of Soviet calculation of the possibility of defying the American government with impunity. Some have concluded that American inaction at the Wall led to the missile crisis over Cuba a year later.

The significance of the Wall for Berlin and for the GDR has been discussed in chapters 4 and 6. Its meaning for the Soviets is less clear. The Wall creates a situation for East Germany which does not exist in any other Warsaw Pact nation. It constitutes a visible expression of communist policy from which it will be difficult to retreat. The manner in which it will be eliminated will tax the ingenuity of the men in the Kremlin and in Pankow.

At the same time the Wall represents a major Soviet concession to Ulbricht. It could not have been established in any period when the Allied position was recognized as firm and might have been beyond Ulbricht's reach after Kennedy's stand in the Cuban Mis-

[50] Ferenc A. Vali, *The Quest for a United Germany*, pp. 194, 195.
[51] Eleanor Lansing Dulles, *Berlin*, pp. 53–57.
[52] See chapter 6.

sile Crisis of 1962 had caused the communists to make a new assessment of his will.

The rapid economic progress in the GDR, following the walling in of the workers and Ulbricht's consolidation of his position, presented the Soviets with a dilemma which they were not to solve in the next few years. On the one hand, they wished the East Germans to be so far controlled and pacified that they would not object to the conditions under which they lived or develop an underground that worked for revolt. On the other hand, they did not wish a nation on their western flank, peopled by Germans whom they feared, to develop enough strength to manifest independence of Moscow and develop Titoist tendencies. As of 1969, they had achieved a tolerable balance between the two possibilities. The question was bound to trouble them increasingly, as the signs of change in Romania, Czechoslovakia, and Poland challenged the prevailing leadership and stirred revolutionary groups in the Warsaw Pact countries generally. Estimates of the future direction of German attitudes affected the Soviet intention of signing a separate peace treaty and explain to some extent the delay after repeated threats to act unilaterally.

There has been no basic change in Soviet policy, only variations in the way it has been stated and in the tone of its expression over the years. Thus the threatening words about intervention in West Germany to protect communist interests after the invasion of Czechoslovakia in August 1968, and the enunciation of the Brezhnev Doctrine[53] in September have led to fears of increased aggression. However the action has not diverged from a line which reflects on the one hand support of Ulbricht and on the other cautious respect for Allied commitments.

THE KEY TO SOVIET POLICY IN EUROPE

The short-term expectations and intentions of the Soviet leaders, in contrast to their basic aims, changed several times in the quarter century between 1943 and 1969. Tactics altered as Khrushchev followed Stalin after an interval of shifting power, as Eisenhower

[53] See chapter 3.

succeeded Truman, and as Kennedy took over in 1961. They altered also as world conditions changed and Soviet concerns became worldwide.

In the first period that included the years just before and just after the close of the war, Russia expected to move westward with the help of left-wing Germans and the acquiescence of the Western Allies. This hope began to dim following the Byrnes speech in 1946 as the Americans indicated that they were reversing their position and would leave significant numbers of troops in Europe, aiding Germany to regain a decent economic existence. The clash over small matters of administration grew into the more serious conflict of the Berlin blockade and airlift. After the Truman Doctrine and the Marshall Plan, the men in the Kremlin came to comprehend Western support of Germany; and after the formation of NATO in April 1949 and their setback in Berlin, they came in May 1949 to a temporary agreement with the Allies in Paris which seemed to promise a resolution of some of the difficulties between them.

From 1949 until the Geneva Conference in 1955, the Russians continued to probe American firmness and to follow an opportunist path in their changing attitude toward their zone of occupation and the Federal Republic. On the surface their policy here, as often elsewhere in foreign affairs, pursued a zigzag course designed to throw the adversary off balance and marked by sporadic harassment of Berlin and a fluctuating intensity in pressure on the West. The basic intention however was to drive the NATO powers back and even to persuade the Federal Republic that its alliance with the West was unproductive. Repeated Washington reaffirmation of its pledge to the Germans together with its continued economic support, particularly of Berlin, and cooperation in the Atlantic Community began to impress Moscow. Neither the 1954 conference in Berlin nor the 1955 summit meeting in Geneva caught the Western powers off guard. Nor did these meetings uncover any serious Soviet intention to permit German reunification, even though the Russians had subscribed to the Four-Power Declaration in July 1955 that German reunification would come through free elections.

The situation changed slightly in September 1955 following Chancellor Adenauer's visit to Moscow. The agreement to exchange diplomatic representatives brought the Federal Republic more clearly into the picture and sharpened Russian perception of the differences between the two parts of Germany. Reconciled, at least for the time being, to its failure to convert the West Germans to communism, Moscow hoped to widen the gap between East and West through further isolation of Berlin.

In the third period distinguished here, Khrushchev gained control in Moscow, strengthened Russian military capacity, and engaged in 1958 in the battle for Berlin. In an aggressive confrontation with the Eisenhower Administration, he issued his most insistent ultimatum—only to withdraw it immediately, at the Albanian Embassy reception on November 29, when he was met with an unequivocal rejection. The strong Allied rebuff did not fit his plans for world influence, so he shifted his tactics. For a time the Berlin situation became quiet, as did the foreign relations of the Federal Republic.

Shortly after the change from the Eisenhower to the Kennedy Administration Khrushchev reasserted his intention of signing a peace treaty with the GDR and again demanded Allied withdrawal from Berlin. On this occasion he was not so sure of the American will to stand by Berlin and, even after the exchange of notes which showed that the Allies would not surrender, he still risked the danger of countermeasures or an armed clash by allowing the construction of the Wall. Not until the confrontation over Cuba in 1962 was he persuaded that the West was still determined to maintain its strong position in Germany.

Guiding Principles of Moscow's German Policy

During these years and to the present day the Soviets have followed certain guiding principles in their German policy. First, their actions as well as their words show that they consider Germany, including Berlin, to be the key to the problems of Europe. Here both their defensive and their offensive interests come to the fore, and their security is engaged. They cannot extend their sway if West Germany maintains her democratic government and remains a partner of the West. At the same time, in spite of all offers for joint security measures, they profess to fear a recurrence of aggression.

Second, they show in their dealings with both East and West Germans their fear of any increase in genuine freedom, their distrust of elections, and their unwillingness to allow a liberalization of the press, the arts, education, or labor. In Ulbricht they have found an effective instrument for this principle.

Third, they have shown their persistent hope that the Western powers would weaken and be willing to change their attitude toward Germany—that they would cut their costs and narrow their responsibilities; that, fearing the consequences of confronting the communists, they would seek a relaxation of tensions and close their eyes to declared expansionist tendencies. The shifting tactics of recurrent probes and withdrawals and their propaganda use of diplomatic language, enticement, or abuse, all suggest that the Soviets expect that America may weary of its burdens and seek any easy way out of its commitments. In these hopes they lean on anti-German feelings in Europe and even in America and on the expectation in the communist world that the long-continued separation of the two Germanys and the isolation of Berlin will create a widespread desire to recognize realities in a way which will help them consolidate their power. The reality of Berlin's recovery seems to them less meaningful than the reality of the Wall, and they overlook the forces for change in their sphere which are even more real.

At the July 1966 meeting of the Warsaw Pact nations in Bucharest, Soviet Premier Alexi N. Kosygin said:

> The main prerequisite for the achievement of European security is the unreserved acceptance of the existing borders, including the Oder-Neisse line and the line between the two German states, the denial of atomic weapons in whatever form to West Germany . . . and a German peace pact on the basis of the existence of two German states.[54]

[54] Hartl and Marx, *Fuenfzig Jahre*, pp. 602, 604. Two German states would presumably mean three, with Berlin an entity apart.

Throughout the past twenty-five years Germany's importance to the Soviets as a geographic area, as a people, and as an element in the contest between the great powers has been obvious. Germany, in fact, has been a crucial element in the shaping of Russian policy. In their view of the significance of Germany, if in no other matter, the Soviets are in agreement with the United States.

CHAPTER 9

Allied Policy

THE SEARCH FOR PEACE

The basis of Allied policy toward Germany is the search for enhanced security. International peace has been the aim of all the measures adopted, whether the theory behind them has been that of deterrence, containment, avoidance of miscalculation, mutual security, or capacity for retaliation in various forms. Except in a very minor degree, the policy has not been one of retribution or vengeance–nor has it been a result of benevolence or charity. Its motive force has been the determination to stop aggression and prevent war.

In its first phase Allied policy was governed by the resolve to prevent new German aggression. This phase came before the major changes in East-West relations were evident, before the awareness of nuclear weapons, before the hardening of the communist intentions, and before it had become clear what attitudes a conquered Germany would take. In early 1945 Soviet and Western aims seemed, at least in the minds of President Roosevelt and some British leaders, almost parallel. Fear of Germany was widespread.

Gradually during the years 1945 and 1946 the brutality of Soviet actions in Germany and Austria came to be understood as being the expression, not of spontaneous disorders on the part of undisciplined soldiers, but rather of an inherent attitude and of ruthless plans to establish communist rule over new territories in Europe and beyond. The threat to peace was seen as coming from an expansionist Russia rather than a resurgent Germany. The heart of the problem was still in the center of Europe, but Germany now appeared as a potentially useful partner instead of a menace. This change in public and private attitudes was not immediate; but it was evident in the discussion about NATO in the late forties and became a military reality after the admission of the Federal Republic into NATO in May 1955. The new attitude took almost ten years to develop. It was accentuated by the Russian attacks on Berlin and particularly by the blockade of that city. At this point the divergence of aims had become glaringly apparent and forced the Western Allies into open conflict with the Soviets over policy and action.

The Consistent Western Policy on Germany

Since 1946–1947 the general direction of Western policy on Germany has changed little. In spite of Soviet destructive action, the West Germans, buoyed up by hope and spurred on by the need for economic reconstruction, have built a new nation. They are destined to exert leadership among the nations cooperating in NATO, in the EEC, in OEEC (now OECD), and in the IMF. Germany has not been reunified, the Soviets are still a threat to peace, but the transformation of the Federal Republic has been spectacular. This achievement is now taken for granted; but in 1945 it could not have been foreseen. Critics who focus attention on objectives that have not yet been attained tend to forget that in 1945 Germany was in danger of being totally engulfed by hostile forces and crushed in the conflict between the democratic and the communist states.

From the days of the Berlin airlift to the present time, Allied policy toward Germany has been well coordinated. It has received most frequent enunciation in connection with the pressure on Berlin and the maintenance of the Western position there. During these twenty years unofficial opinion has undergone a number of changes, but the overriding policy has remained unswerving. A recent statement, written to counter the "agreement signed by the Soviet Union and the so-called 'German Democratic Republic' on June 12, 1964," dealing with Berlin and Germany and their "frontiers," sets forth the formulation used in recent years. It reads in part:

> The Three Governments consider that the Government of the Federal Republic of Germany is the only German government freely and legitimately constituted and therefore entitled to

speak for the German people in international affairs. The Three Governments do not recognize the East German regime nor the existence of a state in eastern Germany. As for the provisions related to the "frontiers" of this so-called state, the Three Governments reiterate that within Germany and Berlin there are no frontiers but rather a "demarcation line" and the "sector borders" and that, according to the very agreements to which the agreement of June 12 refers, the final determination of the frontiers of Germany must await a peace settlement for the whole of Germany.

The charges of "revanchism" and "militarism" contained in the agreement of June 12 are without basis. The Government of the Federal Republic of Germany in its statement of October 3, 1954, has renounced the use of force to achieve the reunification of Germany or the modification of the present boundaries of the Federal Republic of Germany. This remains its policy.

The Three Governments agree that the safeguarding of peace and security is today more than ever a vital problem for all nations and that a just and peaceful settlement of outstanding problems in Europe is essential to the establishment of lasting peace and security. Such a settlement requires the application in the whole of Germany of the principle of self-determination. This principle is reaffirmed in the United Nations Charter, which the agreement of June 12 itself invokes.[1]

AMERICAN POLICY AND LEADERSHIP

Official Washington action and attitude have differed from those of the other two Western Allies only in detail and emphasis. Since the end of the occupation Washington's policy has also been closely coordinated with that of Bonn. The phases through which American policy has passed are similar to the phases of the French and British policies. Although in recent months the French have tended to depart from the accepted line in their dealings with the Kremlin, they have continued to join in the concerted expressions of policy.

[1] U.S. Department of State, *Background Notes, Federal Republic of Germany*, Department of State Publication No. 7834, updated July 1967, pp. 7, 8.

Early Planning

Analysis of the goals and methods of American policy distinguishes six different periods since 1945. In the first phase, the major preoccupation of planning was, as indicated in the preceding section, the prevention of future German aggression. Within each nation there were conflicting views with regard to reconstruction and the economic and political future of Germany. Gradually however the question of dismemberment receded into the background and became of no practical consequence.

In this connection, it should be noted that the impression given by George Kennan in his memoirs is misleading. He says that, because of President Roosevelt's well-known aversion to anything that resembled a discussion of postwar political problems while the war was on, no serious consideration was given at that time to the problems of postwar European unification," and there was no analysis of these coming issues.[2] As one who worked on several committees that from 1942 to 1945 considered economic, financial, and political unification, I can attest to the serious and comprehensive work done on these questions. Several plans for European unification, including that developed by the eminent Belgian statesman Paul van Zeeland, were studied. Methods of cooperation in commerce, transport, labor, investment, and finance were explored at length. The result of this work was made concrete in the regional and worldwide organizations set up in the early postwar period: IMF, IBRD, GATT, and UNRRA.

Detailed studies laid the groundwork for the loan of $3,750 million to Great Britain, and careful consideration was given to the regional associations to be permitted under the United Nations

[2] George F. Kennan, *Memoirs 1925–1950*, p. 417. Because of the large number of readers whom this book rightfully attracts, Kennan's statement on Germany should not go unchallenged. Light is thrown on the work of the Americans on the European Advisory Commission in London by several articles in *Foreign Affairs* and elsewhere and by the recently published *European Advisory Commission: Austria, Germany* (U.S. Department of State, Historical Office, *Foreign Relations of the United States: Diplomatic Papers, 1945*, vol. 3, Department of State Publication No. 8364 [Washington, D.C.: Government Printing Office, 1968]).

Charter. Kennan was not stationed in Washington and so may have remained unaware of some of these matters. The work of Dr. Leo Pasvolsky and others in the Department of State, organized on a comprehensive scale and coordinated with that in other agencies, merits recognition. It continued for several years. Mention should also be made of the overseas work of Philip Mosely and James W. Riddleberger and others associated with them, as well as of such British experts as John Maynard Keynes.

Another important and regrettable omission from Kennan's story on Germany is Secretary Byrnes' speech of September 6, 1946. This omission is the more surprising because, without the change of policy developed in the spring and summer of 1946 and expressed in this speech, the Truman Doctrine and the Marshall Plan on which Kennan did such notable work would not have been possible.

In fact, the account of policy on Germany given in these memoirs needs both modification and expansion. It fails to reflect the importance attached to plans for Europe and to the central issues with regard to Germany's position in Europe.

To the outside observer, the first phase of policy, colored as it was by war emotions, was confusing. The policy planners were however persons with an objective sense of issues who held to a steady line which finally emerged as accepted policy. Some of these men and women are still working on policy for Germany.

The Change of Course

Byrnes' speech in 1946 ushered in the second phase of American policy with its expressed determination to support reconstruction, keep troops in Europe, and work actively for European cooperation in economic and security programs. The nature of the Soviet aims was not yet clearly defined, but the need for the Western powers to develop an independent policy was obvious.

Strengthening of European Cooperation and the FRG

The third phase was marked by the decision to create NATO, to admit Germany to membership, and to allow her limited rearmament and full economic participation in the European Coal and

Steel Community[3] and other international bodies. The Berlin Conference in January and February 1954 and the presentation of the Eden Plan represented a strong effort to secure some basis for reunification. This meeting was followed by the equally unproductive Geneva Summit Conference. The Western powers then turned to other measures to strengthen European cooperation. West Germany was given a large degree of independence and an international status. As a result Chancellor Adenauer went to Moscow, hoping perhaps that diplomatic contacts might improve his bargaining power with the Russians.[4]

In its fourth phase, lasting from 1955 to 1959, American policy took a strong line. Faced by the challenges of the Cold War, it integrated German politicians and statesmen into its efforts to strengthen and enhance Germany's position in the councils of Western Europe and in relation to Russia and Eastern Europe. This phase ended with the termination of the demands and ultimatum issued by Khrushchev in 1958.

An Uncertain Interlude

The next phase, running from June 1959 to the Cuban crisis of October 1962, was a time of uncertainty, changing attitudes, rumors, and personal conflict. With the death of Secretary Dulles on May 24, 1959, and a number of personnel changes in the Department of State, rumors of a softer policy had disturbed German politicians. Shortly thereafter President Eisenhower invited Premier Khrushchev to visit the United States. The superficial interpretation of the "spirit of Camp David" as a complaisant atmosphere stimulated yet more talk. The Russian attitude became somewhat confusing to the outside observer when the Paris Summit Conference was broken off in May 1960. The American election of November 1960 ushered in the Kennedy Administration

[3] Under the Schuman Plan of 1950, a coal and steel community was outlined for Germany, France, and Belgium. It began functioning in 1952. John Foster Dulles in January 1947 was sent by Secretary Marshall to Paris to talk with Schuman and Jean Monnet (Eleanor Lansing Dulles, *John Foster Dulles*, p. 114).

[4] See chapter 5.

and a period of uncertainty as to what, when the chips were down, the new President's policy would be.

In their search for future trends, the German commentators in 1961 may have attached undue importance to various statements made by the incoming President. On December 9, 1959, for instance, in an interview with John Fischer Kennedy had discussed the German problem and Berlin. There is no serious indication that he thought there could be a corridor to Berlin, although in his interview he did mention the concept as worth talking about. He stated that "the chances are dim for a permanent solution of Berlin. . . . German reunification which is a long-range goal, is certainly not in the cards for many years."[5] In answer to a question by Mr. Fischer about neutralization he said, "I do not believe that disengagement represents a reasonable alternative to our policy now."[6] Until Kennedy's Vienna meetings with Khrushchev, there was considerable confidence in Europe that he would hold to a hard line on German problems. Chancellor Adenauer visited the White House in the course of his trip to Washington in early spring of 1961; in a personal talk immediately afterward he expressed an optimism he was later to abandon.

In the months to come, particularly in Germany, the atmosphere was to be troubled by various discussions; some ideas were put forth by the planning staff of the State Department, some by the quadripartite task force in Washington,[7] and some by the White House. At this time Sir David Ormsby-Gore became British ambassador in Washington. His close and longstanding friendship with President Kennedy led to conversations on Germany and other questions that were not coordinated with decisions made through normal channels. It was at this time that the queries about the possibility of a neutralized zone, considered and discarded on various previous occasions, came to the fore and were taken by some

[5] Wilhelm Cornides, "President Kennedy's Engagement in Berlin," *Europa Archiv* (June 25, 1963) vol. 18, no. 12, p. 428; John F. Kennedy, *The Strategy of Peace*, ed. Allan Nevins, pp. 212–16.

[6] Kennedy, *Strategy of Peace*, p. 215.

[7] Composed of German experts from the Department of State and the German, French, and British Embassies.

officials in Bonn and elsewhere as indicating a possible new Kennedy line which would reverse established policy. In the whispering of newsmen and foreign policy experts, West German Ambassador Grewe was caught in a situation which led to criticism by the White House and his transfer out of Washington.[8]

The article by Julius Epstein (now of the Hoover Institution, Stanford) in the *Rheinischer Merkur* of August 31, 1962, discussed an episode in Paris and the change in policy said to have been initiated on October 3, 1961. On that date, Thomas K. Finletter, U.S. Ambassador to NATO, talked with his German counterpart, Gebhardt von Walther, in Paris about policy. He asked von Walther what Bonn's attitude would be if Washington were to propose the creation of a partially controlled and demilitarized zone. Asked how such an idea could be discussed, Finletter replied that in Washington "people are living as if on the moon." The reports of this conversation shocked the Germans in Bonn to whom it suggested the end of NATO, and had strong repercussions in Germany where there had been concern that the new President might be willing to scrap the traditional policy.

These ideas, which were not accepted plans in the Department of State, echoed through the German councils as well as in Paris and excited doubts in many quarters. Disturbing information regarding a statement by Assistant Secretary of State Foy Kohler on October 7, 1961, to the NATO Ambassadors' Steering Committee, led to the conclusion that the West was prepared to accept the temporary frontiers as permanent before a peace treaty had been agreed. Other concessions, including "respecting the authority of the GDR," were discussed in the Steering Committee and also in bilateral United States-Soviet talks. President Kennedy talked briefly with Foreign Minister Gromyko in the White House; further talks by Ambassador Llewellyn Thompson in Moscow were envisaged. These conversations, though reported at length in the *Rheinischer Merkur* article, were not featured in the American press. The first time they were outlined in a U.S. publication was in

[8] Wilhelm Grewe was recognized as a scholarly and experienced diplomat, but he was reported in 1961 to be less congenial in White House circles than other ambassadors. He was assigned to NATO in Paris in 1962.

an article by a young German, Paul J. Friedrich, in the winter 1967 edition of *Western Politica.* Friedrich wrote: "The American decision to reverse wholly the traditional Dulles strategy . . . was made largely without consultation among its European partners. . . . In Germany the report received [considerable] attention."[9]

The reason these reports were ignored in the United States may well have been that the experts knew that these ideas had no solid roots in continuing American policy. Much of the discussion was forgotten when the views of the State Department again flowed in familiar channels. The brief interlude of 1961 was a low point in American postwar policy on Germany.

The end of this fifth phase came in 1962, when the strong U.S. stand over the Cuban missile crisis restored confidence in Washington policy. In the meantime U.S. unwillingness to take action over the Berlin Wall in August 1961 and the sharp reaction over U.S. failure to attempt the rescue of Peter Fechter in August 1962,[10] added to the Bay of Pigs fiasco in Cuba, and the discouraging Kennedy-Khrushchev talks in Vienna, had led to a sense of frustration and disappointment over American policy.

Guiding Principles

American encouragement of West Germany's independence and loosening of restraints on her foreign policy were increasingly evident after the admission of the Federal Republic into NATO. Throughout the period that started with Adenauer's visit to Moscow and covered the emergence of the *Ostpolitik* ten years later and the active pursuit of this policy by both parties in the Grand Coalition from November 1966 on[11] the Federal Republic has shown an increasing initiative, which has been quietly supported by the West. This initiative has included the attempts to broaden and deepen relations with Germany's eastern neighbors and was not abandoned after the Czech crisis of August 1968.

[9] Paul J. Friedrich, "Germany: Reunification through Detente," *Western Politica,* Winter 1967, pp. 24, 25.

[10] See chapter 6.

[11] See chapter 3.

Unless the principles governing Western treatment of Germany since World War II are considered in historical perspective, no understanding of Germany in 1969 is possible. There was no lack of sympathy for the suffering of the people during the miserable years of privation after surrender. The efforts to rebuild destroyed industries and cities won the admiration of those who knew the almost insurmountable difficulties that the workers had to overcome. These memories of past suffering and the hard years of reconstruction, long though they remained, were not the major forces behind Allied policy in England, in France, or in the United States. Rather, the central idea was, as it still is, mutual security. This is the fundamental issue that has justified the plans for reconstruction, the funds for assistance, the development of defense measures, the military cooperation, and the joint commercial and financial efforts. The heart of Western philosophy and actions is the preservation of peace and the extension of freedom and justice to those in East Germany who live under an oppressive system of government. Only such high considerations can justify the risks that have been taken in defense of West Germany and Berlin.

Those who are inclined to be cynical about this interpretation of American policy overlook the fact that peace in this nuclear age is one and indivisible, that although every nation must look to its own security, that all nations that are bound together under the United Nations Charter have an added obligation to preserve the general peace. A good understanding with the Germans was essential to the shaping of specific programs to this general end. Such an understanding was begun under Truman and Acheson and brought to a high level by the friendship of Dulles and Adenauer. After Germany's self-respect and confidence had been restored, her economic capacity and military potential had to be strengthened. Some Germans, misunderstanding the interrelationship of conventional defense and nuclear retaliation, raised the cry that Europe was being prepared as a battleground, ripe for attack by Soviet missiles, while the United States, sheltered by distance, would survive the first clash and even a second strike. They ignored the fact that from a security point of view there is now no such thing as distance. They overlooked the imminent danger that the Soviets would hope to extend their power by means short of nuclear war and thus would strive by direct or indirect means to take over areas not armed with every type of defensive weapon.

In summary, the Allied policy which in the case of each major power was oriented toward the defense of the heartland was nonetheless the best for general protection. The existence of competent armies in being was the surest safeguard against those lesser incursions which might well bring in their wake a nuclear holocaust. It was firmly believed that a strong Germany would not only help protect frontiers vulnerable to Soviet armies but also constitute an important element in the system of deterrence which would save the peace. These elements of defense could be ignored only by persons unaware of Soviet intentions.

In this dimension of Western policy Germany is not unique; but her role is more urgent and her geographical situation more vulnerable than those of others. The capabilities of the FRG and its future contribution to mutual defense should be viewed in the light of the renunciation of the ABC weapons and of the policy of limited rearmament that allows Germany no finger on the nuclear trigger. Consideration should also be given to recent misunderstandings over the multilateral nuclear force,[12] the Nuclear Test Ban Treaty, the nuclear non-proliferation treaty, and the attitude of France toward American dependability.

Moreover the German program for the development of commercial and diplomatic relations with the Warsaw Pact countries and Yugoslavia is now a factor in security planning for Europe. Given moderate German leadership and the spirit now prevailing in Bonn, American policy can accept this program within the elastic framework of cooperation. As understanding between Germany and the West grows stronger and the fear and hostility inherited

[12] Proposals for a multilateral nuclear force as a deterrent and the provision of Polaris missiles under joint control were announced in January 1963 after the Kennedy-Macmillan meeting in Nassau (U.S. Department of State, *Current Documents, 1962*, p. 636; Ibid., 1963, p. 38).

from the Hitler regime grow weaker, relations between East and West may run less risk of miscalculation, and the chances of eventual cooperation in areas of common interest may improve.

Security is the paramount issue in the initiation, execution, and support of Western policy for Germany. For the past twenty-five years it has been the goal toward which the thinking and choices of policymakers have been directed. This aim helps to explain the specific programs and formal agreements which have made up the warp and woof of Western policy. Unless the underlying assumptions of this policy are accepted as valid, the German program would look like an expensive gamble for uncertain gains. During the years since the war however these assumptions have proved to be dependable guides.

In major outline there has been a remarkable consistency in the United States policy over the last few years.

In 1969 Germany is an independent partner, with the freedom and the will to criticize where her own national interests are affected or other nations' proposals seem unacceptable. American policy now requires even greater delicacy and skill than previously. Germany has much to offer the United States including cooperation in economic, defense, and fiscal matters and in relations with communist countries. There are few areas of foreign affairs in which Washington cannot benefit from consultation with and assistance from Bonn. Similarly, it is important for Bonn to know the American attitude and to have American cooperation in tasks of mutual interest and concern.

As one looks back, it is apparent that by the time of the Berlin Conference of 1954 five cardinal principles had been set forth. These principles, which still apply, are the following:

- The four major powers concerned with German affairs are legally and morally bound to seek a peace treaty for all Germany by the Yalta agreements and, again, by the communique issued after the Summit Conference in Geneva. The link between reunification and security must be recognized.[13]

[13] U.S. Department of State, *American Foreign Policy, 1950–1955: Basic Documents*, pp. 1851, 1861, 1918.

- In light of the Soviet Union's aggressive words and deeds that threaten West Germany and Berlin, the Western powers must furnish special support and binding commitments to protect Germany and Berlin.
- In the task of developing mutual security and increasing deterrent strength, German armed forces are needed. Neutrality that created a vacuum in the center of Europe would endanger the entire structure.[14]
- An economically healthy and productive Germany can avoid extremism and can play a constructive role in world development and scientific progress.[15]
- Since Germany is essentially oriented toward the West and will endeavor to preserve the legal, cultural, and social values that are consistent with the liberal democratic system under which the West lives and which it wishes to defend, the Western Alliance must include Germany.[16]

Obstruction to action along these lines and under the UN Charter has come not from the Germans but from the Soviets. It is the Soviets who have acted counter to their agreements and put forward demands and false allegations that have disturbed the peace and brought dismay. In spite of attacks of varying degrees of sharpness, the principles stand, the work of rehabilitation goes on, and the Federal Republic has progressed in all spheres, extending its action and its influence in new directions, its confidence unshaken, its place in the Alliance firm.

BRITISH POLICY

As members of the Western Alliance, the British have worked closely with the Americans on German policy. Together, they fashioned the bizonal arrangements designed to improve the eco-

[14] Ibid., pp. 1859, 1885, 1886.

[15] The philosophy behind this principle was made real in the extension of the Marshall Plan to Europe. See also Secretary Marshall's Report of December 19, 1947, in U.S. Department of State, *Documents on Germany, 1944–1959*, pp. 51–55.

[16] U.S. Department of State, *American Foreign Policy, Basic Documents, 1950–1955*, p. 1869.

nomic situation and to lay the basis for an eventual government.[17] This agreement came into effect in January 1947. On April 8, 1949, the French adhered to the agreement. Thus was created Trizonia which as a result of natural evolution and much Allied planning and consultation developed into the Federal Republic.

On January 22, 1948, British Foreign Secretary Ernest Bevin, who was in a considerable degree responsible for the realization of the ideas expressed by Secretary Marshall in his Harvard speech of June 1947, called for the formation of a Western Union.[18] This move led to the Brussels Treaty that was later to prove so important in providing a way for bringing Germany into NATO after the French had rejected the European Defense Community (EDC) in 1954.

In spite of their close working relations with Berlin and in Bonn the association of the British with the German leaders was never as intimate as that of the Americans. There were two reasons for this. The practical execution of the American Marshall Plan and the many agreements and programs involved led to a more active working collaboration between Americans and Germans; and the British had for a time imprisoned Dr. Adenauer and thus caused a coldness in their later relationship with him that was in marked contrast to the close friendship between Adenauer and Dulles, which lasted from 1953 until the Secretary's death.

Prime Minister Churchill, in his Iron Curtain letter to President Truman on May 12, 1945, had warned of the danger facing Europe and the difficulties of dealing with the Soviets.[19] There had been harsh Soviet protests over the attempted American negotiations for the surrender of the German armies in North Italy,[20] and hostile arguments over the Polish question, reparation payments, and the situation in the Balkans. The British took the differences over these issues more seriously than did the Americans who, being less closely involved, were not equally quick to recognize their significance. Both governments however realized in the early months of

[17] Walther Hubatsch et al., eds., *The German Question*, p. 25.
[18] Ibid., p. 28.
[19] Winston S. Churchill, *Triumph and Tragedy*, p. 573.
[20] Allen W. Dulles, *The Secret Surrender*, p. 147.

the occupation the specific problems in Germany; on these there was no division between them.

Dulles-Eden Teamwork at Berlin Conference

The Western Allies made no progress toward a German treaty in Moscow in 1947 or in subsequent meetings. Discussions on an Austrian State Treaty had also bogged down. The death of Stalin in 1953 and the revolt in East Germany made it imperative to urge a German settlement in that year. A proposed summit talk might have provided a suitable forum, but it was postponed after Churchill suffered a slight stroke in late spring. Following this cancellation a note was sent to the Soviets asking for a foreign secretaries meeting to discuss a German peace treaty. The Soviets replied that such a meeting would be useless. In December, Churchill, Secretary Eden, Secretary Dulles and Foreign Minister Georges Bidault met in Bermuda. Dulles is reported to have said that the Congress of the United States was becoming restive over the failure to make progress in Europe on the German question and the EDC.[21] Anthony Eden has stated that the word "reappraisal" in connection with American policy was first used at this time.[22] Meanwhile Moscow, reversing its earlier stand, proposed a meeting for January 1954. The site proposed was Berlin. Eden flew to Bonn to talk to Konrad Adenauer, particularly about the possibility of Germany issuing a statement on security, if it seemed that this would be likely to affect the Soviet attitude. Adenauer, understanding the nature of the issue, was cooperative.

At this time, Eden and Dulles collaborated closely and found a good understanding on both the substance and the tactics of the struggle with Molotov. As Eden wrote in his memoirs:

> I had some dealings with Mr. Dulles over the Japanese Peace Treaty, but the Berlin Conference was the first occasion when I negotiated with him as a partner. We were able to keep closely

[21] Sir Anthony Eden, *Full Circle*, p. 55.

[22] In December, Dulles used the phrase "agonizing reappraisal" in connection with French hesitation over EDC. He feared an isolationist return to hemispheric defense in Washington.

in step with each other and with M. Bidault, with good results, I think, for our countries.[23]

The record bears out this statement. When the British foreign minister introduced the Eden Plan Secretary Dulles vigorously defended it. It was a reasonable and constructive effort to move toward a German peace treaty and German reunification and offered adequate protection for various international interests.[24]

At the Berlin Conference Eden was mainly responsible for putting the Western case, and Dulles argued continuously and cogently in favor of the points made. From the acceptance of the Soviet agenda to the final communique no divergence of view was expressed. In this conference the three powers set the lines of a position that was to be held through the years. There has been no official alteration of it—only modification of details. In his attempt to appraise the handling of the issues at this time, Richard Goold-Adams, although criticizing Dulles in some respects, has written that "nearly everyone who observed him at this conference agreed that he handled Molotov extremely well."[25] In fact, Dulles' various statements on this occasion constituted the most effective formulations of the American as well as the British and French positions on the German question, and "established the formal pattern."

This occasion is notable in that the British and French agreed wholly with the American position. In fact, the British took a more active part than they had taken before or were to take after.

[23] Eden, *Full Circle*, p. 63. He added that he was "not so fortunate" later. British leaders, including Eden, did not differ with Acheson, Dulles, Rusk on Berlin policy. When Sir David Ormsby-Gore (later Lord Harewood) was ambassador to Washington, he is said to have taken an anti-German attitude in talks with Kennedy.

[24] Konrad Adenauer, *Erinnerungen 1953–1955*, p. 247.

[25] Richard Goold-Adams, *The Time of Power*, pp. 124–28. Professor Goold-Adams' discussion of the conference is strangely ambivalent. He gives praise to Dulles and then sharply criticizes him. It is of special interest because the Dulles-Eden relationship had been of importance in a number of crises and has not been adequately interpreted. Goold-Adams' statement that Dulles gave the impression he did not genuinely want reunification should not be allowed to stand unchallenged, since a mere impression on such an important question should not override the written record.

A Loyal and Consistent Course

In all practical working relations in Bonn, Berlin, Washington, and London, the Anglo-American cooperation was impressive even though many of the British feared the Germans. There were indeed signs that they were more concerned than the French about future relations with Germany. Speculation about background attitudes in England cannot cast any real light on either the past or the future. The British leaders, having chosen their course, were to pursue it loyally even when plagued by emotion and memories of the past. The evidence of Anglo-American unanimity in a long series of conferences and the consistency of the British stand during two decades have been more important for the Allied position, for NATO, and for the future course of European cooperation than the criticisms of the established policy voiced by various writers and members of certain minority groups. In fulfillment of their solemn pledge, the British have kept their troops in Berlin, and they have concerted with the Americans the means of countering threats from Moscow and the manner of replying to the many diplomatic maneuvers or measures of harassment that have disturbed the city of Berlin and brought apprehension to West Germany. In the meetings of 1949, 1954, 1955, and 1959, America and Britain have agreed on tactics and pursued the same goals. The solid front has not been broken.

FRANCE

The French attitude has been more fluctuating and complex than the British. It is no secret that the degree of enthusiasm with which the three governments have viewed their common objectives has varied from time to time. They have recognized the importance of holding the agreed line, but in a number of ways they have questioned the desirability of German reunification. France, in particular, has not been fully consistent over the last twenty years. Her actions in leaving the NATO organization while still adhering to the treaty, in holding separate talks with Russia, and in stirring up uncertainty in the European Common Market on basic issues have raised doubts about her future course of action with regard to Germany.

In the early postwar years the four occupying powers were responsible for the foreign relations of occupied Germany. During this time German economic prostration and lack of trained government personnel facilitated a unity of approach and willingness on the part of the Allies to protect German interests. After the creation of Trizonia, the approval of the Basic Law in 1949, and—with the conclusion of the Contractual Agreements—the establishment in 1952 of a fully sovereign government in Bonn, the situation changed. West German independence increased each year, and Bonn was brought up against the more complex problems of special relations with a number of different capitals. Maintenance of coordinated commercial, financial, and diplomatic policies became increasingly intricate. Even in this second phase of postwar development, however, there was remarkable unity among the three Western powers, each of which still held its own special responsibilities.

De Gaulle's New Policies

When in 1958 Charles de Gaulle took over the Presidency of France and developed new ideas about the balance of power and the exertion of leadership in running the world, his impact on German policy introduced into the European alliance a new element which diverged in some respects from the American line. There were even some who taking a superficial view said that Germany would have to choose between France and the United States. De Gaulle did not go so far as to pose this issue in cultivating his friendship with Chancellor Adenauer, which led to the Treaty of Friendship in January 1963. He supported Adenauer and endeavored to tie the Federal Republic closely to France thus lessening the danger of unacceptable German action in matters of interest to France.

In pursuing this policy, France was not in fact raising difficulties for the United States, although some felt that the future relationship between the two countries had become somewhat uncertain.

Certainly the potential for trouble was there. But it would have become real only if Germany, out of weakness, had ever felt it necessary to make concessions to France. Even serious consideration of such concessions could have undermined the European community. These concessions have never been proposed. Through the years after France had excluded Great Britain from the European Economic Community in 1963 Germany stood steadfastly for Britain's entry and followed the course which Washington had outlined in the previous decade.

Even the problems raised by the French withdrawal from NATO have not materially affected Germany's defense posture. A statement made by President de Gaulle on February 4, 1965, however did cause considerable concern in German circles. The French President declared that the solution of European problems was up to the Europeans themselves; the suggestion was that the role of the United States should be reduced.[26] A subsequent explanation failed to erase entirely the widespread impression made by this statement, which was a natural offshoot of de Gaulle's desire for French domination of Europe with Germany as junior partner.[27] This goal was the cause of French nuclear policy and the result of de Gaulle's view that in the final analysis the United States would not employ nuclear weapons or effectively defend Europe; that only an attack on the *heartland* could lead to the use of the ultimate weapons of defense.[28] In creating the *force de frappe* France was seeking means of defense over which she herself could exercise control and at the same time casting doubt on the reliability of America's commitments to Europe.

Here again, in the development of new policies, it appears that Germany occupies a midpoint of defense strategy in NATO, somewhat to the consternation of those who sought a simpler solution, relying on the American deterrence to protect Europe's vulnerable territories but recognizing the value of its conventional forces. De

[26] Alfred Grosser, "France and Germany: Divergent Outlooks," *Foreign Affairs* October 1965, pp. 29–31.

[27] Karl Theodor, Freiherr zu Guttenberg, *Wenn der Westen will*, p. 168.

[28] Pierre M. Gallois, "Nuclear Strategy: A French View," in *Détente*, ed. Eleanor Lansing Dulles and Robert D. Crane, pp. 215–40.

Gaulle could at least have forced the action of the countries guaranteeing the safety of the communities.

Proposal for a Three-Power Directorate

French policy for Germany was thus at variance with the original intention of the Western Allies to emphasize cooperation among equals. The new trend had been obvious as early as July 1958, when de Gaulle suggested to Secretary Dulles that power in the West should be vested in a three-power directorate which should plan for all the weaker countries.[29] This proposal was later incorporated in a letter to President Eisenhower, who did not answer until October 20; the reply rejected the proposal as contrary to the spirit and principles of the great democracies.[30] The substance of the plan was an attempt to restore the glory of France by joining her in a superior position of control with England with its traditions and skills and the United States with its strength and economic potential. Germany would have been a valued junior partner. This proposal did not involve any abandonment of Berlin or surrender of the two Germanys to Soviet domination.

Since a three-power directorate of this dimension and scope was completely unacceptable to Washington and London, the French President sought power in different directions. He developed the *force de frappe* and reached out for new connections with Russia and China. The ultimate effect of French policy on the future of Germany is difficult to gauge. The desire of Germany for good relations with France is genuine. The willingness of Paris to cooperate with Bonn in most current European arrangements is evident. Differences over the British membership in the European Common Market (blocked in 1963) have not yet alienated the political leaders in the Federal Republic. In 1967 and subsequently murmurings have been heard against de Gaulle's more flamboyant statements about Israel, Canada, and nuclear potential. His sallies in strange directions have diminished his popularity in Germany.

[29] Eleanor Lansing Dulles, *John Foster Dulles*, pp. 135–38.

[30] U.S. Congress, Senate, Committee on Government Operations, Subcommittee on National Security and International Operations, *The Atlantic Alliance*, ed. Henry M. Jackson (New York: Praeger, 1967), pp. 285–86.

All things considered, however, the friendship between the two countries is reassuring in a world where understanding is of paramount importance.

Thus both France and Britain show divergences between popular sentiment and the stated official position with its continuing cooperation in working groups. In both countries different circles differ considerably in the degree of confidence they feel in Germany. This situation makes it difficult to evaluate French and British attitudes and policies. American attitudes are less of a problem. And since America has taken the lead in most policy matters, in extending aid and making public affirmation of support, the American policy of friendship with Germany is paramount in all international meetings concerned with German problems. Any serious conflict between the official positions of the three Allies is unlikely; if it occurred, it would be most disturbing. In the past twenty years there has been no such conflict.

CHANGING PRIORITIES

Time and changing priorities have brought the West to a different attitude toward the German question. Any attempt to formulate this change in words and rephrase Western policy, risks destroying some of the delicate balance of forces essential to the protection of Germany's future. Any assertion in Washington—or in London or Paris—that the NATO countries had abandoned their support of a strong and united Germany as a goal of policy would result in a cynicism and opportunism in Germany which would undermine the Atlantic Alliance. Yet the Germans themselves have come to recognize the length of time and the many other factors required for any substantial progress toward reunification. They have renounced force as a means of uniting Germany. They have placed self-determination ahead of the more classical type of union. They hold out no promise for the near future—nor does NATO.

Different countries in the Western Alliance show different gradations of opinion; but all agree that there has been a change both in the timetable and in the approach to practical measures. In his speech in October 1966 President Johnson expounded an attitude which had begun in spring 1959, gained momentum in 1961, and was destined to set the tone for later thinking about Germany's future. He reaffirmed the belief that German unity remained a vital purpose. He said:

> A just peace remains our goal. But we know that the world is changing and our policy must reflect the reality of today. . . . Europe is partitioned. . . . History warns us that until this harsh division has been resolved, peace in Europe is not secure. . . . In a restored Europe, Germany can and will be united.
>
> This remains a vital purpose of American policy. It can only be accomplished through a growing reconciliation. There is no short cut.

In describing what he meant by a restored Europe, he urged policy makers to move ahead to further and speedier integration, to make progress in East-West relations, and to provide a framework in which "a unified Germany could be a full partner."[31]

The shift in emphasis suggested in the Johnson statement was reflected in Paris, London, and elsewhere. It can be summarized in the statement frequently heard in some quarters that the solution of the German problem will come not from a Western position of strength, but as the result of the easing of tensions. In the main this formulation begs the question, since easing of tension can come only with balanced power; it was only because Germany had recovered a remarkable amount of strength and because the United States had for twenty years remained firm in its European policy that the question of reunification could arise. In fact the present stress on relaxation may be said to be a distortion of Allied intentions; it takes Western defensive capacity for granted and assumes that the only thing subject to alteration is the way in which this capacity is to be used. The changed manner in which policy is now stated is the result of an effort to allay the fears and change the atmosphere of East-West relations. Without the earlier Dulles-

[31] Lyndon B. Johnson, "Making Europe Whole: An Unfinished Task," *Department of State Bulletin* October 24, 1966, pp. 622–24.

Adenauer achievement of a powerful Germany, no easing of tension would have been possible.

The Risk of Miscalculation and Misinterpretation

How far can the Atlantic nations now go in shifting the emphasis away from a powerful Germany, without risking retreat? This question is central to world security. It is also at the heart of the changing NATO policy. To deny the importance of a capacity for deterrence would lead in the future, as it would have led in the past, to tragic miscalculation. Similarly, those who are watching the East-West struggle and those who wish to press communist ideologies would regard any weakening with respect to Berlin as a sign of fear or incapacity. Unless the policy on Germany rests on principles, as Professor Kissinger says, the communists will transform "the question of recognition from a matter of principle into a question of negotiating expedients."[32] If the Allies stand firm on principles, the communists will interpret these principles in the light of the determination of those who hold them. Since in this nuclear age deterrence and the avoidance of miscalculation are essential to security, it follows that the position of the NATO powers with respect to Germany (East and West) and to Berlin must be of a first order of importance. As more than one American president has said, no amount of talk about a thaw in the Russian attitude or about close relationships between communist and free-world countries can banish this issue.

The *Berliner Tagesspiegel* on October 8, 1966, stated that the Johnson speech assigned a new priority to the improvement of the political climate between Washington and Moscow, and gave this issue clear precedence over the unification which Johnson still supported. The *Sueddeutsche Zeitung* suggested that the game between the United States and Russia might be played at German expense.[33] The *Stuttgarter Zeitung* on October 11 stressed the idea that the speech constituted a change in Washington's policy. These journals linked this appraisal of American policy to de

[32] Henry A. Kissinger, *The Necessity for Choice,* p. 144.
[33] *German Press Review,* October 12, 1966.

Gaulle's attitudes and ignored the series of statements in which Secretary of State Rusk, Undersecretary Ball, and others affirmed the American intention of increasing the strength of NATO. This misleading interpretation of the President's speech sprang from exploration of the strength and cost of American troops in Europe and from a too-ready assumption that Vietnam was sapping the official interest and material capabilities which might otherwise have been devoted to Europe. Unfortunately some senators, particularly Stuart Symington and Mike Mansfield in July 1968, spoke as if most American troops in NATO should be brought home. As regards de Gaulle's utterances, Washington, intent on smoothing relations that had been ruffled by differences with the French President, had never considered it wise to emphasize the serious anxiety which many of his statements about European defense have occasioned.

The Security of Europe the Paramount Consideration

There was never any doubt in the State Department or in the White House that the security of Europe was paramount. However, because of the complexity of relations with France, with Russia, and with America's allies in the Far East, strategies which government circles in Washington took for granted were given less than their proper importance in public discussion. To have done otherwise would have wrecked some relations, though it might perhaps have improved others. In some instances the press was responsible for obscuring the long-range policies. Approximately three quarters of the questions in recent State Department press conferences, for example, were concerned with Vietnam, and few with Germany.

Misplaced German Fears

The Germans, always eagerly looking for American statements about their importance and expecting the reiteration of the significance of their position in Europe and appreciation for their contribution to Western programs, were disappointed by the turn which had been taken. The nuclear policy, the proposed multilateral nuclear force (MLF), the discussion of the Nuclear Test Ban

Treaty, the pressure to secure a non-proliferation treaty, combined with discussion of the financial burden of U.S. troops in Germany, compounded fears which were scarcely justified by Congressional action or Administration statements. The United States does not intend to turn its back on Germany or to take its troops out of Berlin. For a long time Germany had been a favored nation in the amount of attention she had received from the Department of State. More recently she had come to take a relatively less prominent position. Now she was standing on a par with other nations. Having regained much of her former capacity, Germany is no longer treated as a convalescent patient. This is a normal and healthy development which should lead to a sound international partnership.

In spite of some suggestions in editorial comment, the *Ostpolitik* of the Federal Republic has excited no adverse official or public reaction in America. Support of such a policy was clearly forecast in the Johnson speech of October, cited above. Such support was in line with the encouragement of German independence and seemed to offer some hope of breaking a stalemate in East-West relations in Europe. Both Washington and Bonn considered the broadening of the diplomatic base and the increase in contacts and understanding to be sound.

Any account of Allied policy on Germany would be incomplete without the mention of the (Harmel) NATO Report of December 1967,[34] and the NATO communique of December 14. The communique stated:

> No final and stable settlement in Europe is possible without a solution of the German question which lies at the heart of present tensions in Europe.

After a brief mention of the purpose of detente in East-West relations and of bilateral and multilateral contacts between European countries it continued:

> The problem of German reunification and its relationship to a European settlement has normally been dealt with in exchanges

[34] Named after the Belgian Foreign Minister, who chaired the plenary meetings of this special committee.

> between the Soviet Union and the three Western Powers having special responsibilities in this field. In the preparation of such exchanges the Federal Republic of Germany has regularly joined the three Western Powers in order to reach a common position. The other Allies will continue to have their views considered in timely discussions among the Allies about Western policy on this subject, without in any way impairing the special responsibilities in question.[35]

The main goal, as the communique indicated, is to "achieve a just and stable order in Europe, to overcome the division of Germany and to foster European security."

Few have made the attempt to *study in depth* or to analyze thoroughly the problems of European security for which the German issue is so important. The present is a time of flux. In Germany, in NATO, and in the Warsaw Pact countries and elsewhere swift and profound changes are modifying existing relationships and demanding new adjustments in government action and in public attitudes. There is not space in this survey to include—nor does the writer have the capacity to summarize—the results of the studies of the scores of experts who combine to cover the many varied facets of the European problems. Without a tour of the horizon however little understanding of the difficult questions here outlined can be gained. The dangers of future trouble have been indicated. Emphasis has been given to the continuing position of the United States: that Germany is a central issue that calls for prime attention. With this conclusion, this outline of policy and attitudes toward Germany must rest. It has focused to a considerable extent on the first twenty years after the war. It has not attempted to present the main elements of NATO redirection or of recent world-stirring political convulsions. It calls for a note of caution but also of exhortation: it points to a revitalizing of the German-American partnership. Weakness in Berlin and failure to support West Germany's fight for democratic survival now would plunge American policy and prestige to a disastrously low level.

[35] Department of State for the Press, No. 295, December 15, 1967, p. 2.

CHAPTER 10

Germany and U.S. Policy

THE WESTERN ALLIANCE

As we face the final decades of the twentieth century, we note swift and momentous changes in Asia, Africa, and elsewhere; but Europe is still at peace. In the course of the twenty-five years following the collapse of Hitler's armies, an interval longer than that between the two world wars, there has been a growth of European economic cooperation and hope for freedom from war. In the unpredicted and unexpected cooperation the Federal Republic has played a major role. By effective participation in programs of the Western democracies and with their financial and other assistance, it has become one of the outstanding contributors to economic stability and to the forces for the defense of the free world. And yet the struggle at the heart of Europe coutinues.

Moscow's Unwitting Assistance

In the 1940s Stalin played an unexpected part in the process of advancing West Germany to equal partnership in the Western Alliance. The change in the Western attitude toward Germany was accelerated by Soviet acts and pressures after 1945 and in 1948 and 1949. At the same time the acceptance of Germany into the Western community was facilitated by forces within Germany that worked toward moral as well as economic recovery. Germany was not passive. The Federal Republic developed a new philosophy: turning away from past nationalist ambitions and violent methods, it joined in a sincere effort to build collective security. The leaders of the new republic were fully in tune with the hopes and intentions of statesmen in Washington and in other major capitals of the free world.

The importance and urgency of West Germany's entry into the Western Alliance can be understood only by those who recognize the threat posed by the attitude and growing capacity of Soviet

Russia throughout the postwar decades. No renunciation of aggression by Moscow has paralleled the desire of men in the West to turn away from war efforts and devote themselves to peaceful pursuits. The dangers of the situation were visible to the more farseeing in the early forties but did not become generally evident until the communists took over Czechoslovakia and blockaded Berlin. Yet even before 1948 a change in American policy toward Germany had become imperative. The stalwart pro-democratic stand of the Berlin population and the firm pro-Western position of Konrad Adenauer and his associates made this change easier to effect. The early signs of a genuinely democratic spirit were the more welcome because of the increasing menace from Eastern Europe.

West Germany's Entry Into the Western Community

By 1955 West Germany had been brought into NATO, and rearmament had become a reality. Following lines fully approved by the United States, France, Benelux, Italy, and West Germany entered the European Coal and Steel Community. This organization joined together in mutual interest the industries which were basic to military resources and was designed to strengthen the defense position of Western Europe. These measures effected a shift in the balance of power in Europe and brought West Germany forward as a significant element in the defense of the free world.

Those responsible for the new position of the Federal Republic were not unaware of the need for the reformation of political attitudes and basic drives. There were and still are those who fear Germany's ultimate intentions. There are some who believe that there is a "German temperament" which leads to aggression and that the German will to power does not tolerate confinement in cooperative international systems. To such observers the outlook must be grim indeed, since without Germany the Western position is weak. Any sober, unemotional analysis of the European situation makes it obvious that West Germany, though limited by postwar losses and barriers to the East, is—and is likely to remain for decades to come—the most resourceful, dependable, and productive member of the West European alliance. Neither England nor

France, weakened by economic losses and mistaken policies, can provide the financial, economic and military help that Germany can supply.

There are others to whom the present situation appears to promise a constructive future. They are those who believe that German cooperation in the Atlantic Community is genuine and that German leaders are as worthy of confidence as those in other lands. This belief has been the basis for most American planning and reconstruction since 1946. It was one of the ideas behind the Marshall Plan and the Truman Doctrine and was a justification of West Germany's position in NATO. It supplied the keynote of the Dulles-Adenauer friendship and of the strong support that Dean Acheson accorded Germany. It has been expressed by Presidents Truman, Eisenhower, Kennedy, Johnson, and Nixon. Any diminution of sympathy and understanding, any development of suspicion and distrust now would lead the Western policymakers into dangerous territory.

The Indispensable Ally

The statesmen who have shaped policy since 1946 have known that the continued freedom and democracy of the Federal Republic and Berlin are essential to the maintenance of the Western position in Europe. There is no substitute for the German alliance. German manpower, industrial capacity, location, and will are all of paramount importance to the United States. The capabilities of the Federal Republic are unparalleled among the other allies of America and are thus of central importance to the continued operation of the Atlantic Alliance. From the point of view of both conventional and nuclear defense the Ruhr, the Rhineland, the central territories of Germany, and the stamina of a nation, strong to counter aggression, have an importance sufficiently obvious to render explanation superfluous.

The paramount aim of U.S. foreign policy since the end of World War II has been the protection, prosperity, and cooperation of Europe. And for more than two decades the foundation stone of this policy has been close collaboration with Germany. Now, with West Germany's sure progress toward freedom and democracy and with her material success, American goals have been partially attained. The Federal Republic has made a notable contribution to the cooperative institutions of Europe and to its diplomatic, military, and scientific development. In foreign policy, Bonn has followed a moderate and constructive line. While constantly mindful of the division of the nation and keeping German interests always in the foreground, it has kept its programs within the framework of NATO and consistently sought the stability and peace of Europe.

THE SOVIET ATTITUDE

Much as they would like to press forward with their ideas and their armies, the Soviets are unlikely to invade West Germany, take over Berlin, or engage in overt aggression in Europe. They know that any such action would put them in danger of severe punishment that would destroy their economic and diplomatic position and would bring the risk of starting a nuclear conflict. Even without a nuclear attack, a sudden and limited encounter on German soil would exact a heavy price. The chances of any Soviet choice of Germany as a battleground are therefore regarded as remote—or even nonexistent. Germany shares a common danger with other European nations and, except for the difference of a few hours' flying time, with the United States. She also shares a common protection. The deterrents that make the Soviets count the risks are not only nuclear; NATO has at its disposal various other measures also. For this reason, American policy rejects disengagement and calls for troops in the forward line. Once these aspects of U.S. security are recognized, there is no room for further doubt of the American position.

Granted that guidance for future policy cannot be found in assumptions concerning future Soviet aggression or past defense strategy, it can still be stated that a rearmed Germany is essential. It is still a deterrent to direct or indirect aggression. For more than a decade the Soviets have taken it for granted that, whatever the cost and whatever the risk, the German leaders would stand with the Allies.[1] They have no expectation that, even to secure reunifica-

[1] See discussion of strategic problems in Robert Endicott Osgood, *NATO*, and in Robert R. Bowie, "Strategy and the Atlantic Alliance," in *Problems of National Strategy*, ed. Henry A. Kissinger (New York: Praeger, 1965), p. 244. The spectre of a Soviet effort to seize Europe while holding the United States at bay with the threat of nuclear holocaust seems fanciful.

tion, West Germany would alter its basic position. They know that for the foreseeable future a break with NATO would be too high a price for Bonn to consider. Over and above this, the German experience during the postwar years is an effective barrier to bargaining with Russia at the expense of the Western Allies.

Any serious possibility of West German desertion of the Western Alliance would entail readjustments in tactics and strategy of a scope difficult to visualize. The Soviets as well as others realize that the loss of West Germany to the democratic cause is in a sense "unthinkable" since it would be followed by the loss of Europe. Such a blow to the present alignment would bring near a possible nuclear confrontation with the Soviets. Although they still use Germany as a bogeyman, under present circumstances the Soviets are no longer, as in the past, in mortal fear of Germany.

THE COST AND THE GAIN

The cost to the United States of maintaining its ties with West Germany does not involve any sacrifice of substance or principle. The Federal Republic shares American aims. It can reinforce American endeavors in third countries and increase the confidence and forward movement of friendly nations. The statesmanship and diplomacy required are of a reasonable order. The outlay of funds, armaments, and diplomatic effort is amply compensated by German military and economic cooperation in the short run and calculated to bring adequate return in the long run.

Reason and tolerance on the part of the United States can allay any unwarranted suspicion on the part of Germany. Both nations have much to gain from genuine cooperation on an equal basis in scientific, economic, and cultural matters, and from the interchange of ideas and programs in areas of mutual concern. The most fruitful collaboration will come when the last vestiges of occupation mentality have been swept away. Writers in the American press could make a useful contribution here by looking to the future rather than to the past and thus fostering a helpful atmosphere.

Americans cannot ignore the difficulties which Germany faces or the darkness of the shadow which the years of Hitler continue to cast over the scene. The past still sets frustrating limits to German policy, both domestic and foreign. Berlin, although an asset, is also a heavy burden and complicates relations with Eastern Europe. The Soviets, still bitter over their war losses, make unreasonable demands. There is misunderstanding and hostility between the extreme wings of the political parties within the Republic that are unwilling to recognize their share in responsibility for the past. These elements in the situation aggravate the difficulties of the United States, the nation that has been more active than any other in seeking the restoration of Germany.

Constructive cooperation with the Federal Republic and support of a strong, free, and united Germany have been an integral part of America's policy of international security. The frontiers of U.S. foreign policy are far from its own shores. Without West Germany as a cornerstone for the structure of European defense and economic cooperation, the United States itself would have been highly vulnerable, while the disposition of troops and position of bases in Europe would have been confined to narrow and unsuitable locations.

If the West had been denied German cooperation, its weakness in recent years might have led to miscalculation in Moscow. The importance the Russians attach to the Western armies may be judged by their maintenance of hundreds of thousands of troops under arms. It is Germany that furnishes the largest contingents to the Western armies. Without the Federal Republic, Washington would have failed to convince Eastern Europe of the determined character of its policy, and the concept of Fortress America would have gained ground at home; much of America's expenditure in time and money under the Marshall Plan and other postwar programs would have rested on foundations undermined by fear; from the Danube to the shores of France, there would have been little certainty; a neutral Austria would have been exposed to danger; and the Communist parties in Italy, France, and elsewhere would have found some support in a troubled Germany.

Through the mutual understanding and coordinated efforts of Germany and the United States the measures taken for reconstruction, aid, and security have accomplished the main purposes for which they were designed. The money extended to fend off collapse and deter aggression has been well spent. The cost has been in billions of dollars, but the economic and military gains are worth many times these sums.

WEAKNESS AND PROBLEMS

In spite of her own efforts and the help she has received from outside, West Germany has notable areas of weakness. These have been mentioned in the sections of chapter 7 that discussed the revolt of youth and the need for educational reform. The press is narrowly controlled by a few publishers and is often demagogic; its handling of the development of the small new rightist party has raised apprehension at home and even more in other countries. The political scene is troubled by arguments over the *Notstandsgesetz*, the law to meet emergency situations, which some consider as opening an avenue to possible dictatorship and others hold to be a wise precaution against unexpected contingencies. The class structure is still too rigid, and the economy tends to monopolistic ownership.

These flaws in a new republic that is still less than twenty-five years old are natural targets for rebellious youth and frequent battlegrounds for liberal reformers. There is no reason to think their efforts will be without result. The stability of economic life, the expansion of production, and the rising standard of living are factors that work in favor of the moderate parties and lessen the impact of the protest groups.

The moral and economic support of the United States has been of major importance to the young republic in gaining new high ground. This support has helped keep alive, even in the darker years, hope for the destiny of the German people, although the obstacles to reunification are formidable and the restoration of greater Berlin is remote. The Germans on their side are concerned about the brain drain and anxious to increase the sophistication of their production. They welcome American ideas and machines; at the same time they fear that there will be too much American corporate control. They still have a sense of dependence on the United States; yet they consider that they must stand on their own and they criticize American policy in Vietnam and in other parts of the world.

If the United States were to withdraw from Europe and bring home its soldiers—even if a few were left in Berlin—Germany would tend to lose faith in American promises. Doubts and disagreements about strategy in Europe are to the interest of neither country.

REUNIFICATION

If reunification were mainly a question of German tradition, sentiment, economics, or prestige, it would be of negligible importance to the Americans who now support it and of limited importance even to the Germans who seek it. But it is those in Germany who think in international terms and focus on the anomaly of two Germanys, each with growing strength, in the center of Europe who feel the urgent need to end the division. The *Ostpolitik* has no great popular appeal. The average German does not perceive the implications of the wider scene for his country's future; some are satisfied with the status quo. Similarly, in other nations it is the architects and planners of institutions of international cooperation who are most aware of the dangers of a divided Germany. The fundamental issues are the security and defense strategy of the Atlantic Community. East Germany's future role in relations between the NATO countries and the Warsaw Pact nations cannot be predicted; but conditions will certainly change, and developments now observable in several East European nations will be of crucial importance.

Washington does not go along with critics who argued that the Federal Republic in its present state is a dependable ally but that a reunified Germany would be too strong and would adversely affect the balance of power. It is well however to examine the alternatives to the American policy. There are dangers in the present division. A highly productive East Germany, held rigidly apart from the Federal Republic, would excite hostility and friction in West Germany. On the other hand, it is possible that at some time the Soviets, also concerned with issues of security and economic development, might try to entice West German politicians and leftist groups by an offer of reunification. This would pose a threat of a different kind. Inside the Federal Republic, some elements would be disaffected, particularly if it were claimed that America was indifferent to Germany's future. In the United States, those who now consider the issue of East-West German relations of minor importance would be confronted with a serious problem. In an extreme case, the West might lose not only East Germany but West Germany also, and NATO would be disrupted.

The interests of the United States are best served by a strong and politically vigorous Federal Republic that is expanding its relations with the east, retaining its position as an active partner in the Atlantic Alliance, trading on a worldwide basis, participating in investment in the less developed countries, and taking as active a part as possible in the councils of the international bodies. There is no early prospect of a German peace treaty, but progress in some directions is possible. The United States cannot wisely shut any doors or deny any reasonable opportunity to a Germany that seeks closer relations both with the nations of the free world and with its eastern neighbors.

With the passage of time and a receding memory of German responsibility for the war and postwar losses, the sense of frustration in Germany grows. Some of the more dynamic groups on the extreme Right and in the new Left are pressing for complete independence of American policy and for a new formulation of German power. These impulses are not yet strong, but they can be restrained only by healthy outlets and normal development of the influence of the Federal Republic both in the East and the West. If there are well-balanced policies and cooperative programs, the moderates in both the major parties will be able to dominate the more explosive intentions of the less disciplined.

THE HOPE OF THE WESTERN ALLIANCE

In the decade ahead America's struggle for stability, security, and a degree of fulfillment in Europe would face impossible dangers if it were not for the fear of atomic destruction in case of conflict; without the nuclear threat the Soviets might take the lesser risk. The United States, looking with apprehension to Europe, sees signs of decline in some of the nations with which it has been closely allied in war and in peace. The sense of doom has spread a psychological pall over the familiar landscape, the ancient cities, the time-honored institutions from which America has drawn its national models, and over societies which were its cultural inspiration. On occasion the situation appears so dark that one wonders whether, even in peace, the Western systems can survive.

The United States however is not without the capacity to meet the danger and develop constructive plans. A restored Europe and the organizations and methods of cooperation developed in earlier years provide a strong foundation for the Western Alliance. The same types of programs, reactivated with a new energy, can help the more disturbed nations to weather the storms that now shake Western Europe, and Eastern Europe as well. American statesmen now face problems as challenging as those of the first years after the war. Even those who have concluded that the Soviets are deterred from aggressive intent by the balance of terror would not be wise to rely on the situation remaining static or to look to the future with complacency.

Germany can be of crucial importance to a United States that is seeking to meet these needs in Europe and elsewhere. In NATO, in the European Economic Community, in international monetary matters, and in the developing countries, the Germans can assist American programs. Joint efforts have led to friendly understanding between individuals, between cities, and between governments. Such qualities as the staunchness of Berlin have convinced Americans of the dependability of the German spirit. In spite of fear, hostility, confusion, and outside interference, the Federal Republic has developed a strong democracy, a vigorous economy, and a spirit of innovation and achievement. These are the realities which can stand us in good stead in our times of trouble.

Chronology, 1944–1969

1944

Nov. 14	European Advisory Commission in London approves revised plan of 12 September defining occupation boundaries for Germany and sector boundaries for Berlin.

1945

Feb. 1	Occupation boundaries are formally approved by Combined Chiefs of Staff at Malta.
Feb. 4–11	Roosevelt, Churchill, and Stalin confer at Yalta.
May 2	All organized resistance in Berlin ends. Soviets complete occupation of city. European Advisory Commission adopts amended version of occupation plan allowing for French participation.
May 8	Surrender ceremony is held in Berlin. Keitel, von Friedensburg, and Strumpf represent the German High Command; Zhukov, Tedder, de Tassigny, and Spaatz the Allies. (Act of military surrender at Rheims on May 7.)
May 17	Soviet Commander in Berlin appoints 16-member *Magistrat* to administer the city.
Jun. 5	First meeting of Allied Control Council (Eisenhower, Montgomery, de Tassigny, and Zhukov) is held in Berlin.
Jun. 10	Soviet occupation authorities in Berlin authorize four political parties: Communist (KPD), Social Democratic (SPD), Christian Democratic Union (CDU), and Liberal Democratic (LDP).
Jun. 21	Truman writes Stalin setting date for withdrawal of Western forces from Soviet Zone.
Jul. 7	Allied Kommandatura is established to govern Berlin.
Jul. 17–Aug. 2	Big Three Conference—Stalin, Truman, Churchill (later Clement Attlee)—at Potsdam prescribes occupation policy for Germany.
Aug. 12	French forces assume responsibility for administration of sector of Berlin.
Nov. 20	Nuremberg trials begin.

1946

Mar. 28	Kommandatura instructs Berlin *Magistrat* to draft a city constitution.
Mar. 31	SPD in Berlin votes against merger with the communists.
Apr. 21	Communist and rump Socialist parties form the Socialist Unity Party (SED) which is under communist domination throughout Soviet-controlled territory.
May 28	Kommandatura recognizes legal functioning in Greater Berlin of both the SED and that portion of the SPD which on March 31 had voted against merger with the communists.
Aug. 13	Draft Constitution for Greater Berlin is accepted by Kommandatura, to become effective following new elections in October.
Sep. 5	Radio in the American Sector (RIAS) is established.
Sep. 6	Secretary of State James Byrnes delivers address in Stuttgart on U.S. involvement in Europe: troops are to remain.
Oct. 20	Results of election in Berlin (the first since the war) for 130 seats in the City Assembly are: SPD 63 seats; CDU 29; SED 26; and LPD 12.
Oct. 21	Temporary constitution for Berlin goes into effect.
Dec. 2	U.S.–U.K. agreement for bizonal fusion.
Dec. 5	Berlin City Assembly elects new 18-member *Magistrat* and Dr. Otto Ostrowski (SPD) as governing mayor.

1947

Mar. 10– Apr. 24	Foreign ministers of U.S., U.K., France, and USSR meet in Moscow.
Mar. 12	President Truman announces Truman Doctrine in message to Congress.
Apr. 11	Berlin City Assembly repudiates pact between Governing Mayor Ostrowski and Soviet authorities.
Apr. 17	Ostrowski resigns. Soviet commandant refuses to recognize resignation.
Jun. 5	Secretary of State Marshall, speaking at Harvard, announces plan for Europe.

Jun. 24 — By 89 votes to 17, Berlin City Assembly elects Professor Ernst Reuter (SPD) governing mayor.

Jun. 27 — Soviet commandant vetoes Reuter's election. Deputy Mayors Louise Schroeder and Ferdinand Friedensburg serve in Reuter's place.

Nov. 25–Dec. 15 — Council of Foreign Ministers meets in London.

Dec. 17 — Western powers reach new version of bizonal agreement.

1948

Feb. 21 — Soviet-sponsored People's Congress of Greater Berlin meets in Soviet Sector.

Feb. 22 — Communists seize power in Czechoslovakia.

Mar. 10 — Soviets impose severe restrictions on Germans traveling from East Zone to Berlin.

Apr. 1 — Soviets impose rail and highway restrictions (known as the Little Blockade) on Allied traffic between Western zones and Berlin. In response, the "Little Airlift" is begun.

Apr. 2 — Soviets announce withdrawal of their representatives from eighteen Kommandatura committees.

Apr. 3 — Soviets close freight routes to Berlin from Munich and Hamburg.

Apr. 20 — Soviets impose additional restrictions on barge traffic to and from Berlin.

Apr. 22 — Draft Berlin Constitution is approved by City Assembly.

May 10 — City Assembly votes to bring University of Berlin under control of Berlin *Magistrat* or to establish new university in West Berlin.

Jun. 9 — Soviets tighten individual travel requirements between Soviet Zone and Berlin.

Jun. 12 — Soviets close highway bridge over Elbe River for repairs.

Jun. 16 — Soviet commandant withdraws from Allied Kommandatura.

Jun. 19 — Soviet authorities suspend all passenger traffic into Berlin.

Jun. 21 — Western powers institute currency reform in Western zones of Germany but not in Berlin.

Jun. 22	Western financial advisors consider problem of currency for Berlin.
Jun. 23	Warsaw conference of Soviet and satellite foreign ministers is held. Soviets order currency reform throughout Soviet Zone and all Berlin. Western powers order own currency reform in Western sectors of Berlin. First Soviet-inspired riot takes place outside Berlin City Hall.
Jun. 24	Soviets impose complete blockade on land traffic into Berlin, alleging "technical difficulties." All electric power flowing from East Berlin and Soviet Zone into Berlin is interrupted. All mail and parcel post service is suspended.
Jun. 26	United States begins airlift of food and essential supplies.
Jun. 29	Berlin City Assembly passes resolution suggesting the United Nations investigate crisis.
Jul. 1	Chief of staff of Soviet forces in Berlin announces that Soviet representatives will no longer take part in Kommandatura meetings.
Jul. 6	Joint U.S., British, and French note protesting blockade is delivered to Moscow.
Jul. 8	Western powers suspend reparation deliveries to Soviet Union.
Aug. 26	Five thousand communist demonstrators storm meeting of Berlin City Assembly in Soviet Sector.
Sep. 1	Parliamentary Council meets in Bonn to draft constitution for West Germany.
Sep. 6	City Assembly moves from Soviet to British Sector because of riots and refusal of Soviet authorities to provide protection.
Sep. 9	Mass meeting of 300,000 in front of Berlin *Reichstag* protests communist actions.
Sep. 14	Western aide-memoire on restrictions on Berlin is delivered to Stalin.
Sep. 18	Soviet reply to Western aide-memoire alleges "technical difficulties."
Sep. 29	Western powers refer Berlin dispute to United Nations.

Oct. 19	Dr. Philip Jessup presents Allied case to UN Security Council.
Oct. 25	UN Security Council resolution on Berlin is vetoed by Soviet Union.
Nov. 10	Free University of Berlin is approved for West Berlin.
Nov. 30	Communists hold "extraordinary session" of City Assembly in East Berlin and establish separate city government. Friedrich Ebert is elected governing mayor of East Berlin.
Dec. 3	Soviet Kommandatura recognizes East Berlin rump government "as the only legal organ of city government" in Berlin.
Dec. 5	Elections in the three Western sectors of Berlin give SPD majority.
Dec. 7	Outgoing City Assembly re-elects Ernst Reuter governing mayor.
Dec. 21	Western commandants reorganize Kommandatura on tripartite basis and extend Soviets an invitation to return at any time.

1949

Jan. 1	Beginning of first (two-year) economic plan in East Zone.
Jan. 30	In an interview with newsman Kingsbury Smith, Stalin states conditions for Berlin settlement.
Feb. 4	West tightens counterblockade. All truck traffic to Soviet Zone is stopped.
Feb. 15–May 5	Philip Jessup and Jacob Malik, U.S. and Soviet delegates to the UN, hold talks on Berlin.
Mar. 2	Western military governors take exception to provision of draft constitution for Federal Republic that would incorporate West Berlin into Federal Republic.
Mar. 19	Communist People's Council approves constitution for East Germany.
Apr. 4	United States signs treaty, becomes a member of North Atlantic Treaty Organization (NATO).
Apr. 8	U.S., British, and French foreign ministers sign agreement in Washington to merge the three zones into Trizonia. Allied High Commission is established and brought into conformity with the provisions of the occupation statutes.

May 4	Four-power representatives to Security Council announce agreement to lift blockade on May 12 (New York Agreement).
May 8	West German Federal Republic adopts Basic Law. Military Government approves law, effective May 12.
May 10	West German Parliamentary Council adopts draft Electoral Law for Germany.
May 12	Blockade is lifted after 10 months and 23 days. Military governors hand over Occupation Statutes to German representatives.
May 14	Three Western commandants in Berlin issue statement of principles granting Berlin a measure of self-government.
May 15	General Lucius D. Clay leaves Germany. Is replaced by John J. McCloy as High Commissioner.
May 16	Elections for delegates to a "German People's Congress" are held in Soviet Zone and Soviet Sector of Berlin.
May 23	Council of Foreign Ministers meets in Paris.
May 30	People's Council adopts constitution for GDR.
Jun. 3	Four Berlin commandants meet for first time since 1948; fail to reach agreement.
Jun. 6–24	American-British Economic Council of bizonal economic area decides to include West Berlin.
Jun. 15	Electoral Law for West Germany allows West Berlin eight nonvoting delegates in the *Bundestag;* five Social Democrats, two Christian Democrats, one Free Democrat are selected.
Jun. 20	Council of Foreign Ministers agrees to abide by May 4, 1949, agreement on Berlin.
Jul. 8	Soviet authorities in East Germany close all principal crossing points between East and West zones and thus limit traffic to one *Autobahn.*
Aug. 6	Three Western commandants recommend inclusion of West Berlin in European Recovery Program under Marshall Plan.
Aug. 14	First *Bundestag* elections are held in Federal Republic.
Sep. 15	Konrad Adenauer is elected Federal chancellor.
Sep. 21	Federal Republic of Germany officially comes into being with entry into force of Occupation Statute for Germany and Charter of Allied High Commission.

Sep. 30	Berlin airlift is terminated.
Oct. 7	GDR is proclaimed by People's Council, with Berlin its capital.
Oct. 8	West Berlin City Assembly denounces GDR and invites Federal Republic to make West Berlin its capital.
Oct. 10	Soviet government announces termination of Soviet military administration in its zone of occupation in Germany and substitutes Soviet Control Commission.
Oct. 11	Provisional GDR government names Pieck president.
Oct. 15	USSR, followed by eight other nations, recognizes GDR.
Oct. 20	*Bundestag* authorizes financial and economic aid program for West Berlin.
Oct. 28	Federal government and Economic Cooperative Administration (ECA) agree to make funds available for Berlin.
Nov. 10	U.S., British, and French Foreign Ministries agree on directive to their high commands regarding cessation of dismantling in Germany and Berlin.
Nov. 12	Soviet Kommandatura in Berlin transfers its administrative functions to East Berlin *Magistrat*.
Dec. 15	West Germany and Berlin are admitted as full members of Marshall Plan. West Berlin is awarded 95,000,000 DM.

1950

Jan. 1	GDR adopts first five-year plan.
Jan. 26	Western commandants protest Soviet slow-down of Western military traffic on Helmstedt *Autobahn* [Slow-down is temporarily lifted but is reimposed January 30, 1950.]
Jan. 27	East German Ministry of Interior announces that all Western traffic into and through the Soviet Zone or Sector of Berlin must obtain special permits from East German police.
Mar. 2	Whitsuntide rally in Berlin of communist Free German Youth (FDJ) is proposed.
May 13	U.S., British, and French Foreign Ministries issue statement on Berlin affirming continued support for their rights and protection for rights of city's inhabitants.
May 24–29	FDJ stages demonstrations.
Jun. 6	East German government announces its acceptance of Oder-Neisse boundary.

Jun. 25	North Korean People's Army invades South Korea.
Jul. 2–3	Soviets impose two-day nuisance restrictions on flow of water and electricity into West Berlin.
Aug. 4	Amended draft constitution is submitted to Berlin Kommandatura.
Aug. 9	Electoral law of East German government permits East Berliners to stand for election to legislature.
Aug. 29	Three Western commandants approve draft constitution for West Berlin on condition that West German law would apply to Berlin only when voted by Berlin City Assembly.
Sep. 19	Foreign ministers of United States, United Kingdom, and France issue communique in New York declaring that Allied governments would treat an "attack on Berlin and The Federal Republic as an attack on themselves."
Sep. 20	Soviet Zone is permitted to join Comecon.
Sep. 21	East Germany shuts off flow of electricity to West Berlin; West Berlin power plant, built under Marshall Plan, assumes load.
Sep. 25	Soviets interrupt barge traffic to West Berlin. In retaliation British hold all barges in British Sector bound for East Berlin.
Sep. 28	Electoral Law is approved for West Berlin.
Oct. 1	New constitution for West Berlin goes into effect.
Oct. 5	Barge traffic is resumed by mutual agreement.
Dec. 3	In election for House of Representatives held in West Berlin, 90.4 percent of eligible voters register their votes. SPD wins 61 seats, CDU 34, and Free Democratic Party (FDP) 32.

1951

Feb. 1	Soviet authorities take over Western enclave of West Staaken. British lodge protest.
Feb. 3	West and East German officials initiate provisional interzonal trade agreement for exchange of goods.
Mar. 7	Allied Kommandatura waives right to review acts of Berlin City Assembly.
Jul. 9	Western powers announce that state of war with Germany is officially ended.

Sep. 1 Soviet authorities impose heavy road tax on vehicles to Berlin.

Sep. 20 East-West German trade agreement is signed. Soviets remove road tax.

Oct. 18 Soviet authorities attempt to take over enclave of Steinstuecken in American Sector. United States files protest.

Oct. 23 Soviet authorities withdraw from Steinstuecken.

Oct. 24 President of United States announces termination of state of war with State of Germany.

Nov. 22 U.S., British, French, and West German foreign ministers meet in Paris to discuss integration of West Germany into Western Europe.

1952

Jan. 9 Economy of West Berlin is incorporated into that of Federal Republic.

Jan. 17 West Berlin nonvoting representation in *Bundestag* is increased from 8 to 19.

Feb. 23 Kommandatura notifies governing mayor of Berlin that the Berlin government can make a group of Federal laws applicable to Berlin by means of a single law—a *Mantelgesetz*.

Mar. 10 Soviets direct draft note to Western powers offering peace treaty.

Mar. 25 Western powers reply that free elections are precondition of any all-German government.

Apr. 9 Soviet authorities deny UN Commission investigating free all-German elections admission to East Berlin; reject control by UN; offer to discuss problem of free German elections.

Apr. 29 Russian MIG-15s attack Air France plane in Berlin corridor. Allies file protest.

May 8 Soviet military authorities deny clearance to American and British vehicles on Berlin-Helmstedt *Autobahn*. (Traffic resumed May 16.)

May 26 United States, United Kingdom, France, and Federal Republic sign Convention on Relations between three powers and Republic to replace Occupation Statute and to confer full sovereignty on Germany, including unification of

Germany. They assure the maintenance of security and welfare of Berlin.

May 27 — European Defense Community treaty is signed in Paris. Communique affirms Germany's participation in the Defense Community and Allied rights in Berlin.
East German authorities cut all telephone service between West Berlin and both East Berlin and the East Zone. Border between East and West Berlin is closed in retaliation for signing of Contractual Agreements.

May 30 — Allies protest to Soviet Union closing of border.

Jun. 19 — Soviet Union rejects Allied note.

Jun. 29 — Secretary of State Dean Acheson visits West Berlin and reaffirms American pledge to remain.

Oct. 8 — Russian MIG-15s buzz and fire at U.S. hospital plane in corridor.

Dec. 3 — East Sector police hold up road traffic into East Berlin searching for "illegal" goods purchased in West Berlin. Allies protest action.

1953

Feb. 18 — James B. Conant, new High Commissioner for Germany, gives address pledging continued support to Berlin.

Feb. 27 — London Debt Agreement is signed by three Western powers and FRG.

Mar. 2 — Climax of refugee exodus from the Soviet Zone—6,000 people ask for asylum in Berlin.

Mar. 5 — Stalin dies.

Mar. 12 — Russian MIG-15s shoot down British Lincoln bomber on routine training flight in corridor. British government protests, announcing that if necessary fighter escort will accompany planes.

Apr. 9 — Chancellor Adenauer and Secretary of State John Foster Dulles exchange notes in Washington on mutual understanding.

May 28 — Decision is made to increase work norms in the GDR. "New Course" is planned.

Jun. 3 — United States and Federal Republic sign agreement concerning application of December 8, 1923, Treaty on Friendship, Commerce, and Consular Rights.

Jun. 9	"New Course" is instituted in East Germany (modified after June 17).
Jun. 16–17	East German uprising starts (and continues for several weeks in the East Zone).
Jul. 10	United States offers to supply food to East Germany. Soviet government rejects U.S. offer.
Jul. 26	Program instituted for issuing food in West Berlin to all those from East Germany who come over to get it (Food Package Program).
Aug. 1	East German government prohibits travel from East Germany to Berlin.
Aug. 26	Three Western High Commissioners ask Soviets to remove all barriers to free movement throughout Germany.
Sep. 1	Soviet reply states that this is a matter for the two German governments to settle.
Sep. 29	Ernst Reuter dies.

1954

Jan. 25–Feb. 18	Council of Foreign Ministers meets in Berlin to discuss German peace treaty and Austrian State Treaty.
Jan. 29	Eden Plan is submitted.
Feb. 4	Soviet Foreign Minister Vyacheslav Molotov puts forward proposal on German question.
Feb. 10	Soviets propose General European Security Agreement.
Feb. 19	Three-power statement reaffirms the 1952 declaration and asserts action to improve conditions in Berlin.
Mar. 25	Soviet Union announces full transfer of sovereignty to East German government.
Mar. 30	East German government states that all military missions operating in East Germany must be accredited to it. (Announcement follows pattern established in Contractual Agreements.)
Apr. 7	*Bundestag* resolution withholds recognition of sovereignty of East German regime.
Jul. 17–20	Electoral college meets in Berlin. Theodor Heuss is reelected president of Federal Republic.
Jul. 30	U.S. Senate passes resolution on restoration of German sovereignty.

Aug. 30	Defeat of European Defense Community by French Parliament.
Sep. 28	Foreign ministers of United States, United Kingdom, and France meeting in London again issue Declaration on Berlin stating that the security and welfare of Berlin are essential.
Oct. 23	Paris Protocol provides for end of occupation and West Germany's admission to NATO. West European Union is established.
Dec. 5	Elections are held in West Berlin. Otto Suhr (SPD) becomes governing mayor.

1955

Mar. 30	Highway tolls on *Autobahn* are increased 1,000 percent. (Do not apply to Allied vehicles.)
May 5	Occupation of West Germany officially ends. Paris Agreement of October 1954 enters into force, resulting in admission of FRG to NATO.
May 9	FRG becomes NATO member.
May 14	Warsaw Pact is signed by Eastern bloc countries (except Yugoslavia).
May 15	Four Allies conclude Austrian State Treaty.
Jul. 18–23	Big Four Summit Conference is held at Geneva. Soviets concur in statement in support of unification by free elections.
Aug. 13	Three Western powers exchange notes on external debts.
Sep. 8–14	Adenauer holds talks with Soviet leaders in Moscow. Diplomatic relations between USSR and FRG are to be established. German prisoners are to be returned by Soviets.
Sep. 20	Soviets transfer to East German government control of all traffic to Berlin, with exception of Allied military traffic (Bolz-Zorin letter on access to Berlin).
Sep. 28	A meeting of Western foreign ministers in New York states that Soviets are still responsible for control of military traffic to Berlin.
Oct. 18	Soviet Union acknowledges responsibility for control over Western military traffic until signing of peace treaty.
Oct. 27–Nov. 16	Meeting of Council of Foreign Ministers in Geneva discusses German problems and European security.

Dec. 9 — Foreign Minister Heinrich von Brentano enunciates Hallstein Doctrine.

1956

Jan. 9 — Second five-year plan starts in East Germany.

Feb. 25 — First Party Secretary Nikita Khrushchev denounces Stalinism in Twentieth Party Congress.

Feb. 29–Mar. 2 — FRG, United Kingdom, France, and United States reach agreement on external debts.

Jun. 28 — Uprising takes place in Poznan, Poland.

Aug. 18 — Communist party is outlawed by Federal Constitutional Court.

Oct. 23 — Hungarians revolt. Uprising takes place in Warsaw.

Oct. 27 — France and FRG agree on incorporation of Saarland into FRG.

1957

Jan. 1 — Saarland is incorporated into FRG.

Mar. 25 — Treaty of Rome lays foundation for European Economic Community and the European Atomic Community.

Sep. 15 — Elections are held in FRG.

Oct. 3 — Plan for a denuclearized zone in Europe is proposed by Polish Foreign Minister Adam Rapacki.

Oct. 4 — USSR launches Sputnik.

Oct. 15 — Yugoslavia recognizes GDR.

Oct. 19 — FRG Embassy in Belgrade is closed (under Hallstein Doctrine).

1958

Jan. 1 — European Common Market is established; FRG is a member.

Feb. 14 — Rapacki Plan is formally presented.

Mar. 27 — Khrushchev succeeds Bulganin as premier of USSR.

May 28 — Rationing ends in East Germany.
General Charles de Gaulle assumes leadership of France.

Nov. 10	Khrushchev's speech in Moscow declares Western Allies must leave Berlin.
Nov. 26	Dulles speculates at news conference about accepting East Germans as agents of the Soviets.
Nov. 27	Khrushchev sends note to United States, United Kingdom, and France containing ultimatum on peace treaty with GDR; Berlin would be a "free city."
Nov. 30	On behalf of President Eisenhower, Dulles rejects Soviet proposal.
Dec. 7	Election is held in Berlin; communists win only 1.9 percent of votes.
Dec. 14	Three Western Allies reject Soviet proposal.
Dec. 16	NATO supports position of Western Allies on Soviet note.

1959

Jan. 27	Dulles holds a news conference in Washington on method of German reunification.
Mar. 4	Khrushchev in East Germany again threatens to sign a peace treaty with GDR.
Mar. 18	Deutschland Plan of SPD for German reunification is submitted.
Mar. 19	In a press conference Khrushchev, in reply to Sanakoyev, states that "U.S., U.K., and France have lawful rights to stay in Berlin."
Mar. 25	De Gaulle in press conference supports reunification, with Oder-Neisse line as boundary.
May 11	Geneva Conference of Foreign Ministers of United States, United Kingdom, France, and USSR considers German question.
May 24	John Foster Dulles dies.
May 26	United States submits Herter Plan at Geneva Conference; contains proposal on German-Berlin question.
Aug. 3	Eisenhower announces forthcoming exchange of visits with Khrushchev.
Aug. 5	Geneva Conference ends in deadlock.
Sep. 15	Khrushchev begins visit to United States.

1960

Jan. 4	At Warsaw Pact meeting in Moscow Soviet plans are announced for separate peace treaty with GDR.
May 17	Paris summit meeting of Big Four breaks up when Khrushchev leaves following U-2 incident.
Aug. 16	East-West German trade agreement is signed.
Aug. 29	Travel restrictions on Germans are imposed by East Zone.
Sep. 30	Bonn cancels trade agreement as countermeasure to East German travel restrictions.
Nov. 8	John F. Kennedy is elected President of United States.
Nov. 22–27	Anderson-Dillon mission goes to Bonn to confer on costs of troops in Germany. (Agreement pending.)
Dec. 29	East-West German trade agreement of August is concluded.

1961

Jan. 20	Kennedy is inaugurated President.
Apr. 17	Bay of Pigs invasion fails.
Jun. 3–4	Kennedy and Khrushchev meet in Vienna. Khrushchev makes new demands.
Jul. 17	Western Allies reject Khrushchev's demands.
Jul. 25	Kennedy delivers major speech on Berlin.
Jul. 30	Senator J. William Fulbright makes statement on GDR border.
Aug. 1	Reports state that 32,000 left GDR in July.
Aug. 2	GDR moves to restrict "border crossers" in Berlin.
Aug. 4	Warsaw Pact countries meet in Moscow.
Aug. 5–7	Western foreign ministers meet in Paris.
Aug. 13	Border in Berlin is closed; Wall is subsequently erected.
Aug. 18	United States announces that Berlin garrison will be increased.

Aug. 19	Vice President Lyndon B. Johnson and General Clay go to Berlin.
Sep. 17	In FRG elections CDU loses absolute majority.
Oct. 23	Offset Agreement is made: U.S. balance of payments is to be helped by German purchases of military equipment in the United States ($3.9 billion between 1961–1966).
Oct. 27	United States-Soviet tank confrontation takes place at Checkpoint Charlie, Berlin.
Nov. 20	Chancellor Adenauer visits Washington to discuss Berlin.

1962

Jan. 2	United States makes diplomatic exploration of Soviet attitude to Berlin.
Feb. 14	Soviets harass planes in air corridors.
Feb. 17	German newspaper reports conversations by Ambassador Hans Kroll in Moscow on German reunification.
Mar. 11	U.S. Secretary of State Dean Rusk and Soviet Foreign Minister Andrei Gromyko discuss German problems at Geneva.
Apr. 12	Khrushchev demands withdrawal of Allied troops from Berlin.
Apr. 16	Rusk and Soviet Ambassador Anatol Dobrynin hold talks in Washington on Berlin.
May 8	Clay leaves Berlin where he was sent on August 19.
Jul. 2	Adenauer begins first state visit to France.
Jul. 10	Khrushchev demands that smaller nations of NATO and Warsaw Pact garrison Berlin and asks that Western Allied troops leave.
Jul. 16	Soviets reject four-power talks on Berlin.
Aug. 17	Peter Fechter is shot and killed at Berlin Wall.
Sep. 5	De Gaulle visits Bonn.
Sep. 14	Twenty-nine East Germans tunnel their escape to West Berlin.
Oct. 22	Kennedy announces presence of Soviet missiles in Cuba and quarantine by United States.
Nov. 7	Khrushchev again demands German peace treaty but this time without ultimatum.

1963

Jan. 12	Cuba recognizes East Germany; Bonn cuts ties with Cuba.
Jan. 14	Khrushchev visits East Germany. De Gaulle in press conference announces his opposition to entry of Great Britain into European Economic Community.
Jan. 20	FRG and France sign treaty of cooperation.
Mar. 7	West German trade representative visits Warsaw.
Apr. 19	De Gaulle announces that France will create nuclear capability.
Apr. 25	Khrushchev demands that Berlin be made neutral under UN.
Jun. 26	Kennedy visits West Berlin; delivers "*Ich bin ein Berliner*" speech.
Jun. 28	Khrushchev visits East Berlin.
Jul. 4	De Gaulle visits West Germany.
Aug. 20	Khrushchev begins 10-day visit to Yugoslavia.
Aug. 30	"Hot line" between Washington and Moscow is established.
Oct. 7	Kennedy signs Nuclear Test Ban Treaty.
Oct. 10	Soviets harass and detain U.S. and British convoys on *Autobahn*.
Oct. 15	Adenauer resigns and is succeeded by Ludwig Erhard.
Nov. 22	Kennedy is assassinated in Dallas.
Dec. 17	First *Passierschein* agreement is made: passes will permit West Berliners to visit relatives in East Berlin.

1964

Jan. 6	New passes are required for West Germans visiting Zone.
Feb. 14–15	Erhard talks with de Gaulle in Paris.
Jun. 1	United States and USSR sign consular convention.
Jun. 12	Soviet-East German treaty of friendship is signed in Moscow. Erhard and President Johnson meet in United States.

Jun. 13	Khrushchev and Party Secretary Walter Ulbricht ask for "free Berlin."
Sep. 23	FRG cabinet approves second *Passierschein* agreement. Khrushchev visits Prague—his last foreign visit as premier and first secretary.
Sep. 24	Willi Stoph succeeds Otto Grotewohl as premier of GDR.
Oct. 15	Khrushchev is replaced by Alexei N. Kosygin as premier and Leonid Brezhnev as first secretary. Chinese test atomic bomb.
Nov. 2	Visits by pensioners (old people) from GDR to West Germany and West Berlin begin.
Nov. 12	Antonin Novotny is re-elected first secretary of the Czech Communist Party. New Economic Model (NEM) is introduced in Czechoslovakia.

1965

Jan. 19–20	De Gaulle and Erhard confer in France.
Feb. 5	Third *Passierschein* agreement is signed.
Feb. 15	FRG announces it will cut aid to the United Arab Republic if Ulbricht is received there.
Feb. 24	Ulbricht arrives in Cairo.
Apr. 6	*Autobahn* to Berlin is blocked for four hours.
Apr. 7	Soviet planes buzz Congress Hall in West Berlin. West Germany pays Israel $75 million (last instalment of $860 million agreed upon).
May 14	China explodes second atomic bomb.
Jun. 15	Rainer Barzel proposal for reunification is made.
Jun. 23	FRG protests helicopter flights by GDR over West Berlin.
Jul. 4	GDR reluctantly acknowledges Allied access rights to Berlin.
Sep. 9	De Gaulle announces he will withdraw from NATO.
Sep. 19	Elections are held in FRG. Erhard defeats Willy Brandt.
Dec. 3	Erich Apel, head of GDR Planning Commission, kills himself.

1966

Feb. 26	Debates proposed by Ulbricht are accepted by SPD but rejected later by GDR.
Mar. 7	Fourth *Passierschein* agreement is signed.
Apr. 4	GDR delays decision on proposed debates. Kurt Georg Kiesinger succeeds Erhard as chancellor of the FRG; Grand Coalition is formed. Czech Thirteenth Party Congress is held.
Oct. 7	President Johnson delivers a speech on relations with Eastern Europe and "building bridges."

1967

Jan. 13	Kiesinger and de Gaulle meet in Paris.
Jan. 27	Romania and FRG agree to exchange ambassadors.
Feb. 8	Foreign Minister Willy Brandt confers with President Johnson in Washington.
Feb. 8–10	Foreign ministers of Warsaw Pact confer on Romania.
Apr. 19	Former Chancellor Adenauer dies in Rhineland home.
Apr. 24	Communist foreign ministers discuss FRG's *Ostpolitik* in Czechoslovakia.
Jun. 2	Benno Ohnesorge is killed in Berlin student riots over visit of Shah of Iran.
Jun. 23	Johnson and Kosygin meet at Glassboro, New Jersey.
Aug. 3	Czechoslovakia and Bonn agree on trade missions.
Aug. 24	Nuclear non-proliferation treaty is sponsored by United States and USSR.
Sep. 15	Fritz Teufel stages student sit-in in City Hall of West Berlin.
Oct. 19	Klaus Schuetz is elected governing mayor of West Berlin replacing Heinrich Albertz.
Dec. 13	NATO ministerial meetings issue communique reasserting Germany's fundamental right to reunite and endorsing Harmel report.

1968

Jan. 3	Alexander Dubcek succeeds Novotny as first secretary of Communist Party of Czechoslovakia.
Jan. 6	Soviet Ambassador Semykon K. Tsarapkin presents secret note on Berlin to Foreign Minister Brandt.
Jan. 12	Bonn and Belgrade agree to exchange ambassadors.
Mar. 7	Warsaw Pact nations open conference in Sofia.
Mar. 18	Foreign Minister Brandt at Nuremberg refers to Oder-Neisse line as Germany's eastern boundary.
Mar. 21	Warsaw students stage sit-in.
Mar. 21–22	Communist allies exert pressure on Czechs at Dresden meeting of Presidium.
Mar. 30	*Bundestag* passes Emergency Law (*Notstandsgesetz*).
Apr. 9	New constitution comes into force in GDR.
Apr. 11	Rudi Dutschke is shot and injured by Josef Bachmann in Berlin.
Apr. 12	GDR issues ordinance forbidding FRG ministers and high officials to pass through East Germany.
Apr. (mid)	During prolonged student riots in Berlin and West Germany many persons are injured and at least one is killed.
Apr. 26	East German guards prevent Mayor Schuetz from passing Babelsberg Checkpoint, Berlin.
Apr. 28	Baden-Wuerttemberg election is held. Students riot in Munich and elsewhere.
Apr. 30	NATO Council states that free access to Berlin is essential.
May 4	U.S. Ambassador George C. McGhee bids farewell in Berlin before leaving Germany.
May 5	Report of Dubcek explanation of democratization in Czechoslovakia and Soviet acceptance of reforms.
May 10	Soviet Ambassador Pyotr A. Abrasimov seeks to justify East German restrictions on travel to Berlin.
May 30	U.S. Ambassador Henry Cabot Lodge, newly appointed to Bonn, visits Berlin.
Jun. 11	East Germany imposes passport and visa requirements for travel to West Berlin.

Jun. 18 — West Germany agrees to allocate $785 million to offset U.S. troop costs.
Foreign Minister Brandt calls on Ambassador Abrasimov in East Berlin.

Jun. 26 — NATO meeting in Iceland calls Berlin travel restrictions a threat to detente.
Secretary Rusk visits Bonn and makes statement on importance of free access to Berlin.

Aug. 21 — Soviet and other Warsaw Pact forces invade Czechoslovakia, but Romania reserves its position.

Sep. 11 — Albert Norden, chief propaganda officer of SED, is reported to have been dismissed.

Sep. 25 — Brezhnev Doctrine is announced in *Pravda.*

Sep. 26 — New communist party (*Deutsche Kommunistische Partei*) is permitted in Federal Republic.

Sep. 29 — Voters in Lower Saxony give low vote to National Democratic Party (NPD).

Oct. 1 — World Communist Summit Conference, scheduled to be held in November, is postponed.

Oct. 3 — As a result of Soviet invasion of Czechoslovakia, NATO reschedules winter meeting of foreign ministers for November 18—a month earlier than arranged.

Oct. 4 — Gromyko makes statement on Brezhnev Doctrine in UN.

Oct. 8 — Gromyko warns Brandt of right to protect socialism even in West Germany (Brezhnev Doctrine).

Oct. 17 — Mayor Schuetz requests Western Allies to ban 400-member rightist party (NPD).

Nov. 10 — United States and FRG negotiate on American troop strength in Germany.

Appendix

RESTATEMENT OF THE UNITED STATES POLICY ON GERMANY

Address of Secretary Byrnes at Stuttgart, Germany, September 6, 1946 (Excerpts) *

It is not in the interest of the German people or in the interest of world peace that Germany should become a pawn or a partner in a military struggle for power between the East and the West. . . .

The working out of a balanced economy throughout Germany to provide the necessary means to pay for approved imports has not been accomplished, although that too is expressly required by the Potsdam Agreement.

The United States is firmly of the belief that Germany should be administered as an economic unit and that zonal barriers should be completely obliterated so far as the economic life and activity in Germany are concerned.

The conditions which now exist in Germany make it impossible for industrial production to reach the levels which the occupying powers agreed were essential for a minimum German peacetime economy. . . .

We favor the economic unification of Germany. If complete unification cannot be secured, we shall do everything in our power to secure the maximum possible unification. . . .

Germany must be given a chance to export goods in order to import enough to make her economy self-sustaining. Germany is a part of Europe, and recovery in Europe, and particularly in the states adjoining Germany, will be slow indeed if Germany with her great resources of iron and coal is turned into a poorhouse. . . .

It is the view of the American Government that the German people throughout Germany, under proper safeguards, should now be given the primary responsibility for the running of their own affairs.

* Reprinted from U.S. Congress, Senate, Committee on Foreign Relations, A *Decade of American Foreign Policy*, Basic Documents, 1941–49, pp. 523–527.

All that the Allied govenments can and should do is to lay down the rules under which German democracy can govern itself. The Allied occupation forces should be limited to the number sufficient to see that those rules are obeyed.

But of course the question for us will be: What force is needed to make certain that Germany does not rearm as it did after the first World War? Our proposal for a treaty with the major powers to enforce for 25 or even 40 years the demilitarization plan finally agreed upon in the peace settlement would have made possible a smaller army of occupation. For enforcement we could rely more upon a force of trained inspectors and less upon infantry.

Security forces will probably have to remain in Germany for a long period. I want no misunderstanding. We will not shirk our duty. We are not withdrawing. We are staying here. As long as there is an occupation army in Germany, American armed forces will be part of that occupation army.

The United States favors the early establishment of a provisional German government for Germany. Progress has been made in the American zone in developing local and state self-government in Germany, and the American Government believes similar progress is possible in all zones. . . .

While we shall insist that Germany observe the principles of peace, goodneighborliness, and humanity, we do not want Germany to become the satellite of any power or powers or to live under a dictatorship, foreign or domestic. The American people hope to see peaceful, democratic Germans become and remain free and independent. . . .

The United States cannot relieve Germany from the hardships inflicted upon her by the war her leaders started. But the United States has no desire to increase those hardships or to deny the German people an opportunity to work their way out of those hardships so long as they respect human freedom and follow the paths of peace.

The American people want to return the government of Germany to the German people. The American people want to help the German people to win their way back to an honorable place among the free and peace-loving nations of the world. . . .

Bibliography

Acheson, Dean. "Withdrawal from Europe? An Illusion." *New York Times Magazine*, December 15, 1963, pp. 7ff.

Adenauer, Konrad. *Erinnerungen, 1953–1955*. Stuttgart: Deutsche Verlagsanstalt, 1966.

———. *Memoirs, 1945–1953*. Chicago: Regnery, 1966.

Apel, Hans. *Ohne Begleiter: 287 Gespraeche jenseits der Zonengrenze*. Cologne: Wissenschaft und Politik, 1965.

———. *Spaltung: Deutschland zwischen Vernunft und Vernichtung*. Berlin: Voltaire Verlag, 1966.

Baerwald, Helmut, and Maerker, Rudolf. *Der SED-Staat: das kommunistische Herrschaftssystem in der Sowjetzone*. Cologne: Wissenschaft und Politik, 1966.

Baring, Arnulf. *Der 17. Juni 1953*. Bonn: Bundesministerium fuer Gesamtdeutsche Fragen, 1957.

Barth, Markus. "Church and Communism in East Germany." *Christian Century* (November 23–30, 1966) 83:1440–3, 1469–72.

Baske, Siegfried, and Englebert, Martha, eds. *Zwei Jahrzehnte Bildungspolitik in der Sowjetzone Deutschlands: Dokumente*. Pt. 1–2, 1945–1965. Heidelberg: Quelle und Meyer in Komm., 1966.

Baylis, Thomas A. "The New Economic System: The Role of Technocrats in the DDR." *Survey* (London, October 1966) 61:139ff.

Die Bemuehungen der deutschen Regierung und ihrer Verbuendeten um die Einheit Deutschlands, 1955–1966. (Weissbuch.) Bonn: Auswaertiges Amt, 1966.

Bender, Peter. *Offensive Entspannung: Moeglichkeit fuer Deutschland*. Cologne: Kiepenheuer und Witsch, 1964.

Berlin, Freie Universitaet, Otto-Suhr-Institut. *Berlin: Pivot of German Destiny*. Translated and edited by Charles B. Robson. Chapel Hill: University of North Carolina Press, 1960.

———. *Die Demokratie im Wandel der Gesellschaft: Vortraege, gehalten im Sommersemester 1962*. Edited by Richard Loewenthal. Berlin: Colloquium Verlag, 1963.

Birrenbach, Kurt. *Die Zukunft der Atlantischen Gemeinschaft: europaeisch-amerikanische Partnerschaft*. Freiburg/Br.: Rombach, 1962

Bluhm, Georg R. *Die Oder-Neisse-Frage*. Hanover: Verlag fuer Literatur und Zeitgeschehen, 1967.

———. *Die Oder-Neisse-Linie in der deutschen Aussenpolitik*. Freiburg/Br.: Rombach, 1963.

Bowie, Robert R. *Shaping the Future: Foreign Policy in an Age of Transition*. New York: Columbia University Press, 1964.

Bowie, Robert R. "Strategy and the Atlantic Alliance." In *Problems of National Strategy: A Book of Readings*, edited by Henry A. Kissinger, pp. 237–63, New York: Praeger, 1965.

Bradley, Omar N. *A Soldier's Story*. New York: Henry Holt, 1951.

Brandt, Willy. *Aussenpolitik, Deutschlandpolitik, Europapolitik: Grundsaetzliche Erklaerungen waehrend des ersten Jahres im Auswaertigen Amt*. Berlin: Berlin-Verlag, 1968.

———. *Friedenspolitik in Europa*. Frankfurt: Fischer, 1968.

———. *The Ordeal of Coexistence*. Cambridge, Mass.: Harvard University Press, 1963.

———. *A Peace Policy for Europe*. New York: Holt, Rinehart and Winston, 1968.

Brandt, Willy, and Lowenthal, Richard. *Ernst Reuter, ein Leben fuer die Freiheit: eine politische Biographie*. Munich: Kindler, 1957.

Brant, Stefan [pseud.]. *The East German Rising, 17 June, 1953*. New York: Praeger, 1957.

Braunthal, Gerard. *The Federation of German Industry in Politics*. Ithaca, N.Y.: Cornell University Press, 1965.

Brecht, Arnold. *Wiedervereinigung. Drei Vorlesungen, gehalten auf Einladung der Juristischen Fakultaet an der Universitaet Heidelberg im Juli 1957*. Munich: Nymphenburger Verlagshandlung, 1957.

Brentano, Heinrich von. *Germany and Europe: Reflections on German Foreign Policy*. New York: Praeger, 1964.

Bromke, Adam, ed. *The Communist States at the Crossroads Between Moscow and Peking*. New York: Praeger, 1965.

Brown, James F. *The New Eastern Europe: The Khrushchev Era and After*. New York: Praeger, 1966.

Brundert, Willi. "Gedanken zum Thema Deutsche Wiedervereinigung und europaeische Mitte." In *Osteuropa und die Hoffnung auf Freiheit* edited by Alfred Domes.

Brzezinski, Zbigniew K. *Alternative to Partition: For a Broader Conception of America's Role in Europe*. New York: McGraw-Hill, 1965.

Bundesministerium fuer Gesamtdeutsche Fragen. *SBZ von A-Z: Ein Taschen- und Nachschlagebuch ueber die Sowjetische Besatzungszone Deutschlands*. Bonn: Deutscher Bundes-Verlag, 1966.

———. *Vierter Taetigkeitsbericht 1961–1965*. Bonn: Deutscher Bundes-Verlag, 1965.

Byrnes, Robert F., ed. *The United States and Eastern Europe*. Englewood Cliffs, N.J.: Prentice-Hall, 1967.

Cameron, James. "A Shadow No Larger Than a Crooked Cross." *New York Times Magazine*, September 11, 1966, pp. 94–6ff.

Campbell, John C. "East Europe, Germany, and the West." *Annals of the American Academy of Political and Social Science* (May 1958) 317: 153–63.

Charlesworth, James C., ed. "Realignments in the Communist and Western Worlds." *Annals of the American Academy of Political and Social Science*, July 1967.

Childs, David. "The East German Elite: The Red Jesuits and Others." *The World Today* (January 1966) 22:32–41.

Churchill, Sir Winston L. S. *Triumph and Tragedy*. Boston: Houghton Mifflin, 1953.

Clay, Lucius D. "Berlin." *Foreign Affairs* (October 1962) 41:47–58.

———. *Decision in Germany*. Garden City, N.Y.: Doubleday, 1950.

Collier, David S., and Glaser, Kurt, eds. *Berlin and the Future of Eastern Europe*. Chicago: Regnery, 1963.

Conant, James B. *Federal Republic of Germany: Our New Ally. A Lecture Delivered at the University of Minnesota on February 24, 1957*. Minneapolis: University of Minnesota Press, 1957.

———. *Germany and Freedom: A Personal Appraisal*. Cambridge: Harvard University Press, 1958.

Conze, Werner. *Das deutsch-russische Verhaeltnis im Wandel der modernen Welt*. Goettingen: Vandenhoeck und Ruprecht, 1967.

———. *Die Deutsche Nation: Ergebnis der Geschichte*. Goettingen: Vandenhoeck und Ruprecht, 1965.

Cornides, Wilhelm. "President Kennedy's Engagement in Berlin." *Europa Archiv* (June 25, 1963) 18:427–44.

———. *Die Weltmaechte und Deutschland: Geschichte der juengsten Vergangenheit, 1945–1955*. Tuebingen: Wunderlich, 1957.

Craig, Gordon A. *From Bismarck to Adenauer: Aspects of German Statecraft*. Baltimore: Johns Hopkins Press, 1958.

Dahrendorf, Ralf. *Gesellschaft und Demokratie in Deutschland*. Munich: Piper, 1965.

———. "The New Germanies: Restoration, Revolution, Reconstruction." *Encounter* (April 1964) 22:50–8.

Davison, W. Phillips. *The Berlin Blockade*. Princeton: Princeton University Press, 1958.

Deutsch, Karl W., and Edinger, Lewis J. *Germany Rejoins the Powers: Mass Opinion, Interest Groups, and Elites in Contemporary German Foreign Policy*. Stanford, Calif.: Stanford University Press, 1959.

Doenhoff, Marion, Graefin; Leonhardt, Rudolf Walter; and Sommer, Theo. *Reise in ein fernes Land: Bericht ueber Kultur, Wirtschaft und Politik in der DDR*. Hamburg: Nannen Verlag, 1964.

Domes, Alfred, ed. *Osteuropa und die Hoffnung auf Freiheit*. Cologne: Wissenschaft und Politik, 1967.

Duebel, Siegfried, ed. *Dokumente zur Jugendpolitik der SED*. Munich: Juventa Verlag, 1966.

Dulles, Allen W. "Alternatives for Germany." *Foreign Affairs* (April 1947) 25:421–32.

Dulles, Allen W. *The Secret Surrender*. New York: Harper and Row, 1967.

Dulles, Eleanor Lansing. *American Foreign Policy in the Making*. New York: Harper and Row, 1968.

———. *Berlin: The Wall Is Not Forever*. Chapel Hill, N.C.: University of North Carolina Press, 1967.

———. *Berlin und die Amerikaner*. German translation of *Berlin: The Wall Is Not Forever*. Cologne: Wissenschaft und Politik, 1967.

———. *John Foster Dulles: The Last Year*. New York: Harcourt, Brace and World, 1963.

Dulles, Eleanor Lansing, and Crane, Robert Dickson, eds. *Détente: Cold War Strategies in Transition*. New York: Praeger, 1965.

Eckardt, Felix. *Ein unordentliches Leben*. Duesseldorf/Vienna: Econ-Verlag, 1967.

Eden, Sir Anthony. *Full Circle: Memoirs, 1951–1957*. London: Cassell, 1960.

Eisenhower, Dwight D. *Crusade in Europe*. Garden City, N.Y.: Doubleday, 1948.

———. *Mandate for Change, 1953–1956: The White House Years*. Garden City, N.Y.: Doubleday, 1963.

———. *Waging Peace, 1956–1961: The White House Years*. Garden City, N.Y.: Doubleday, 1965.

Elias, Zdenek, and Netik, Jaromir. "Czechoslovakia." In *Communism in Europe*, edited by William E. Griffith, v. 2, pt. 2, 1966.

Engelhardt, Gerhard. *Die Leibeserziehung an den Schulen in der sowjetischen Besatzungszone: Zielsetzung und Entwicklung*. Bonn: Bundesministerium fuer Gesamtdeutsche Fragen, 1965.

Erler, Fritz K. G. "The Struggle for German Reunification." *Foreign Affairs* (April 1956) 34:380–93.

———. *Ein Volk sucht seine Sicherheit: Bemerkungen zur deutschen Sicherheitspolitik*. Frankfurt/M.: Europaeische Verlagsanstalt, 1961.

Eschenburg, Theodor. "A Definition of Self-Determination: Confusion of Terms Used in Discussions of German Problem." *The German Tribune*, May 2, 1964, p. 4.

———. *Die Deutsche Frage: die Verfassungsprobleme der Wiedervereinigung*. 3d ed. Munich: Oldenbourg, 1960.

———. *Die improvisierte Demokratie: gesammelte Aufsaetze zur Weimarer Republik*. Munich: Piper, 1963.

———. *Staat und Gesellschaft in Deutschland*. Stuttgart: Schwab, 1956.

Feis, Herbert. *Churchill, Roosevelt, Stalin: The War They Waged and the Peace They Sought*. Princeton, N.J.: Princeton University Press, 1957.

Fischer, Fritz. *Griff nach der Weltmacht: die Kriegszielpolitik des kaiserlichen Deutschland, 1914–18*. Duesseldorf: Droste, 1962.

Fischer, Ruth. *Stalin and German Communism: A Study in the Origins of the State Party*. Cambridge, Mass.: Harvard University Press, 1948.

Flechtheim, Ossip K. *Weltkommunismus im Wandel*. Cologne: Wissenschaft und Politik, 1965.

Floyd, David. *Rumania: Russia's Dissident Ally*. London, Eng.: Pall Mall Press, 1965.

Forster, Thomas M. *NVA-Die Armee der Sowjetzone*. 3d rev. ed. Cologne: Markus Verlag, 1966/67.

Fraenkel, Ernst. *Die repraesentative und die plebiszitaere Komponente im demokratischen Verfassungsstaat*. Tuebingen: Mohr, 1958.

Fraenkel, Ernst, and Bracher, Karl Dietrich, eds. *Staat und Politik*. Frankfurt/M.: Fischer Buecherei, 1964.

Freund, Gerald. *Germany Between Two Worlds*. New York: Harcourt, Brace, 1961.

Friedrich, Carl Joachim. *Der Verfassungsstaat der Neuzeit*. Berlin: Springer, 1953.

Friedrich, Paul J. "Germany: Reunification Through Détente?" *Western Politica* (Winter 1967) 1:22–31.

Fulbright, James William. *Old Myths and New Realities, and Other Commentaries*. New York: Random House, 1964.

Gablentz, Otto Martin von der. *Die Berlin-Frage in ihrer weltpolitischen Verflechtung, 1944–1963. Eine Einfuehrung*. Munich: Oldenbourg, 1963.

———. *Documents on Berlin, 1943–1963*. (2d. rev. and enl. ed.) Selected and edited by Wolfgang Heidelmeyer and Guenter Hindrichs. Munich: Oldenbourg, 1963.

———. *Dokumente zur Berlin-Frage, 1944–1962*. (2d. rev. and enl. ed.) Edited by Wolfgang Heidelmeyer and Guenter Hindrichs. Munich: Oldenbourg, 1962.

Gallois, Pierre M. "Nuclear Strategy: A French View." In *Détente: Cold War Strategies in Transition*, edited by Eleanor Lansing Dulles and Robert Dickson Crane.

Gaus, Guenter. *Staatserhaltende Opposition: oder: hat die SPD kapituliert? Gespraeche mit Herbert Wehner*. Reinbeck bei Hamburg: Rowohlt, 1966.

Gerson, Louis L. *John Foster Dulles*. New York: Cooper Square Publishers, 1967.

Gleitze, Bruno, et al. *Der Osten auf dem Wege zur Marktwirtschaft*. Berlin: Duncker und Humblot, 1967.

Gniffke, Erich W. *Jahre mit Ulbricht*. Cologne: Wissenschaft und Politik, 1966.

Goergey, Laszlo. "Emerging Patterns in West German—East European Relations." *Orbis* (Fall 1966) 10:911–29.

Goetting, Gerald. *Christians and Politics in the German Democratic Republic*. Berlin: Union Verlag, 1966.

Goold-Adams, Richard John Morton. *The Time of Power: A Reappraisal of John Foster Dulles*. London: Weidenfeld and Nicolson, 1962.

Gottlieb, Manuel. *The German Peace Settlement and the Berlin Crisis*. New York: Paine-Whitman, 1960.

Grewe, Wilhelm G. *Deutsche Aussenpolitik der Nachkriegszeit*. Stuttgart: Deutsche Verlagsanstalt, 1960.

Griffith, William E., ed. *Communism in Europe: Continuity, Change, and the Sino-Soviet Dispute*. v. 1–2. Cambridge, Mass.: MIT Press, 1964–66.

Grosser, Alfred. *Die Bonner Demokratie: Deutschland von draussen gesehen*. Duesseldorf: Rauch, 1960.

———. "France and Germany: Divergent Outlooks." *Foreign Affairs* (October 1965) 44:26–36.

Guttenberg, Karl Theodor, Freiherr zu. *Wenn der Westen will: Plaedoyer fuer eine mutige Politik*. 2d ed. Stuttgart-Degerloch: Seewald, 1965.

Haffner, Sebastian. "Germany, Russia and the West." *Encounter* (October 1961) 17:62–7.

Hamel, Hannelore. *Das sowjetische Herrschaftsprinzip des demokratischen Zentralismus in der Wirtschaftsordnung Mitteldeutschlands*. Berlin: Duncker und Humblot, 1966.

Hammarskjoeld Forum. *The Issues in the Berlin-German Crisis: The Background Papers and Proceedings of the First Hammarskjoeld Forum Organized by the Association of the Bar of the City of New York, 1962*. New York: Oceana Publications, 1963.

Hangen, Welles. *The Muted Revolution: East Germany's Challenge to Russia and the West*. New York: Knopf, 1966.

———. "New Perspectives Behind the Wall." *Foreign Affairs* (October 1966) 45:135–47.

Hartl, Hans, and Marx, Werner. *Fuenfzig Jahre sowjetische Deutschlandpolitik*. Boppard a. Rh.: Boldt, 1967.

Hartmann, Frederick H. *Germany Between East and West: The Reunification Problem*. Englewood Cliffs, N.J.: Prentice-Hall, 1965.

Havemann, Robert. *Dialektik ohne Dogma? Naturwissenschaft und Weltanschauung*. Reinbek bei Hamburg: Rowohlt, 1965.

Healey, Denis. "The Case for Berlin Negotiations." *New Leader* (September 18, 1961) 44:6–8.

———. *A Neutral Belt in Europe?* London, Eng.: Fabian Society, 1958.

Heil, Karolus Heinz. *Das Fernsehen in der sowjetischen Besatzungszone Deutschlands, 1953–1963*. Bonn: Bundesministerium fuer Gesamtdeutsche Fragen, 1967.

Heller, Deane and David. *The Berlin Wall*. New York: Walker, 1962.

Hermann, Friederich-Georg. *Der Kampf gegen Religion und Kirche in der Sowjetischen Besatzungszone Deutschlands*. Stuttgart: Quell-Verlag, 1966.

Hillgruber, Andreas. *Deutschlands Rolle in der Vorgeschichte der beiden Weltkriege*. Goettingen: Vandenhoeck und Ruprecht, 1967.

Hiscocks, Richard. *The Adenauer Era*. Philadelphia: Lippincott, 1966.

Hoffmann, Joachim. *Zentralverwaltungswirtschaft am Beispiel der SPD*. Frankfurt/M., Berlin: Diesterweg, 1966.

Holbik, Karel, and Myers, Henry. *Postwar Trade in Divided Germany*. Baltimore: Johns Hopkins Press, 1964.

Hoover Institution on War, Revolution and Peace. *Yearbook on International Communist Affairs, 1966*. Milorad M. Drachkovitch and L. H. Gann, eds. Stanford, Calif.: The Institution, 1967.

———. *Yearbook on International Communist Affairs, 1968*. Richard V. Allen, ed. Stanford, Calif.: The Institution, 1969.

Hubatsch, Walther et al., eds. *The German Question*. New York: Herder Book Center, 1967.

Institut zur Foerderung Oeffentlicher Angelegenheiten, Frankfurt am Main. *Bundesrecht und Bundesgesetzgebung: Bericht ueber die Weinheimer Tagung des Instituts . . . am 22. und 23. Oktober 1949*. Referate: Wilhelm Grewe, Richard Ringelmann, und Georg A. Zinn; Diskussion und Ergebnisse. Frankfurt/M.: Metzner, 1950.

Institute for Strategic Studies. *The Military Balance, 1968–1969*. London: The Institute, 1968.

Jaenicke, Martin. *Der Dritte Weg: die antistalinistische Opposition gegen Ulbricht seit 1953*. Cologne: Neuer Deutscher Verlag, 1964.

Jaksch, Wenzel. *Westeuropa, Osteuropa, Sowjetunion: Perspektiven wirtschaftlicher Zusammenarbeit; eine politisch-wirtschaftliche Studie*. New York: Atlantic-Forum, 1965.

Jaspers, Karl. *Freiheit und Wiedervereinigung; ueber Aufgaben deutscher Politik*. Munich: Piper, 1960.

Johnson, Lyndon B. "Making Europe Whole: An Unfinished Task." Address delivered before the National Conference of Editorial Writers in New York, October 7, 1966. *Department of State Bulletin* (October 24, 1966) vol. 55, no. 1426, pp. 622–4.

Kapsa, Lothar, comp. *Zusammenstellung der von der "Deutschen Demokratischen Republik" seit deren Gruendung, 7. Okt. 1949, abgeschlossenen internationalen Vertraege und Vereinbarungen*. 4th ed. Processed. Bonn: Archiv fuer Gesamtdeutsche Fragen, 1965.

Kellen, Konrad. "Adenauer at Ninety." *Foreign Affairs* (January 1966) 44:275–90.

Keller, John W. *Germany, the Wall and Berlin: Internal Politics During an International Crisis*. New York: Vantage Press, 1964.

Kelsen, Hans. "The Legal Status of Germany According to the Declaration of Berlin." *American Journal of International Law* (July 1945) 39: 518–26.

———. *Reine Rechtslehre*. 2d rev. and enl. ed. Vienna: Deuticke, 1960.

Kennan, George Frost. *Memoirs, 1925–1950.* Boston: Little, Brown, 1967.

———. "Polycentrism and Western Policy." *Foreign Affairs* (January 1964) 42:171–83.

Kennedy, John F. *The Strategy of Peace.* Edited by Allan Nevins. New York: Harper, 1960.

Kersten, Heinz. *Das Filmwesen in der sowjetischen Besatzungszone Deutschlands.* Pts. 1–2. 2d rev. and enl. ed. Bonn: Bundesministerium fuer Gesamtdeutsche Fragen, 1963.

Kertesz, Stephen D. *The Fate of East Central Europe: Hopes and Failures of American Foreign Policy.* Notre Dame, Ind.: University of Notre Dame Press, 1956.

[Kiesinger, Kurt Georg] "Chancellor's Statement Paints None too Rosy a Picture; Common Sense and Action in the Right Place Could Achieve Much." *The German Tribune,* March 23, 1968, p. 2.

Kirchheimer, Otto. *Politische Justiz: Verwendung juristischer Verfahrensmoeglichkeiten zu juristischen Zwecken.* Rev. ed. Neuwied and Berlin: Luchterhand, 1965.

Kissinger, Henry A. *The Necessity for Choice: Prospects of American Foreign Policy.* New York: Harper, 1961.

———. "Strains on the Alliance." *Foreign Affairs* (January 1963) 41: 261–85.

Kitzinger, Uwe W. *German Electoral Politics: A Study of the 1957 Campaign.* Oxford: Clarendon Press, 1960.

Kluke, Paul. *Selbstbestimmung: vom Weg einer Idee durch die Geschichte.* Goettingen: Vandenhoeck und Ruprecht, 1963.

Knoll, Joachim H., and Siebert, Horst. *Erwachsenenbildung, Erwachsenenqualifizierung: Darstellung und Dokumente der Erwachsenenbildung in der DDR.* Heidelberg: Quelle und Meyer, 1968.

Koch, Hans-Gerhard. *Neue Erde ohne Himmel: der Kampf des Atheismus gegen das Christentum in der "DDR." Modell einer weltweiten Auseinandersetzung.* Stuttgart: Quell Verlag, 1963.

Koehne, Edda. *Die Preisbildung in der sowjetischen Besatzungszone Deutschlands.* Bonn: Deutscher Bundes-Verlag, 1966.

Kogon, Eugen. *Die unvollendete Erneuerung: Deutschland im Kraeftefeld, 1945–1963. Politische und gesellschaftspolitische Aufsaetze aus zwei Jahrzehnten.* Frankfurt a.M.: Europaeische Verlagsanstalt, 1964.

Krengel, Rolf. *Die Bedeutung des Ost-West-Handels fuer die Ost-West-Beziehungen.* Goettingen: Vandenhoeck und Ruprecht, 1967.

Krippendorff, Ekkehart. *Die Liberal-demokratische Partei Deutschlands in der sowjetischen Besatzungszone, 1945/48: Entstehung, Struktur, Politik.* Duesseldorf: Droste, 1961.

Krumholz, Walter; Lutze, Wilhelm; Hoepfner, Richard, et al. *Berlin-ABC.* Berlin: Presse und Informationsamt des Landes Berlin, 1965.

Kuby, Erich. *Das ist des Deutschen Vaterland: 70 Millionen in zwei Wartesaelen*. Stuttgart: Scherz und Goverts, 1957.

Kuehnl, R. "Neofascism on the Rise: An Analysis of the Structure and Programme of the National-Democratic Party in the German Federal Republic." *Review of International Affairs* (Belgrade), vol. 18, no. 405, pp. 11–13, and vol. 18, no. 406, pp. 8–11.

Laqueur, Walter. *Russia and Germany: A Century of Conflict*. Boston: Little, Brown, 1965.

Lauret, René. *France and Germany: The Legacy of Charlemagne*. Chicago: Regnery, 1964.

Legien, Rudolf. *The Four Power Agreements on Berlin: Alternative Solutions to the Status Quo?* Berlin: Heymann, 1961.

Leonhardt, Rudolf Walter. *This Germany: The Story Since the Third Reich*. Greenwich, Conn.: New York Graphic Society, 1964.

Leonhard, Wolfgang. *Child of the Revolution*. Chicago: Regnery, 1958.

———. *Die Revolution entlaesst ihre Kinder*. Cologne: Kiepenheuer und Witsch, 1955.

Lipgens, Walter. *Europa-Foederationsplaene der Widerstandsbewegungen 1940–1945*. Munich: Oldenbourg, 1968.

Lowenthal, Richard. "Can We Make Common Cause With Russia?" *New York Times Magazine*, November 21, 1965, p. 34ff.

———. "The Germans Feel Like Germans Again." *New York Times Magazine*, March 6, 1966, p. 36ff.

———, ed. *Die Demokratie im Wandel der Gesellschaft: Vortraege, gehalten im Sommersemester 1962*. Berlin: Colloquium Verlag, 1962.

Ludz, Peter Christian, ed. *Studien und Materialien zur Soziologie der DDR*. Cologne: Westdeutscher Verlag, 1964.

Mackintosh, Malcolm. "Three Détentes: 1955–1964." In *Détente: Cold War Strategies in Transition*, edited by Eleanor Lansing Dulles and Robert Dickson Crane. New York: Praeger, 1965.

Macridis, Roy C., ed. *Foreign Policy in World Politics*, 2d ed. Englewood Cliffs, N.J.: Prentice-Hall, 1962.

Maier, Hans. *NPD: Struktur und Ideologie einer nationalen Reichspartei*. Munich: Piper, 1967.

Majonica, Ernst. *Deutsche Aussenpolitik: Probleme und Entscheidungen*. Stuttgart: Kohlhammer, 1965.

Mampel, Siegfried. *Die Entwicklung der Verfassungsordnung in der Sowjetzone Deutschlands von 1945 bis 1963*. Tuebingen: Mohr, 1964.

———. *The Political Structure of the Soviet Sector and Its Relationship to the Soviet Zone*. Berlin: Colloquium Verlag, 1966.

———. *Das Recht in Mitteldeutschland: Staats- und Rechtslehre, Verfassungsrecht*. Cologne, Berlin: Heymann, 1966.

———. *Der Sowjetsektor von Berlin*. Frankfurt/M.: Metzner, 1963.

Mampel, Siegfried. *Die Verfassung der sowjetischen Besatzungszone Deutschlands: Text und Kommentar.* Frankfurt/M.: Metzner, 1962.

———. *Die volksdemokratische Ordnung in Mitteldeutschland: Texte zur verfassungsrechtlichen Situation.* Frankfurt/M.: Metzner, 1966.

Mander, John. *Berlin: Hostage for the West.* Baltimore: Penguin Books, 1962.

Mann, Golo. "Rapallo: The Vanishing Dream." *Survey* (London, October 1962) 44/45:74–88.

Maser, Werner. *Der Kampf der SED gegen die Kirche.* 2d ed. Mannheim: Pesch-Haus, 1962.

Mason, Edward S. "Has our Policy in Germany Failed?" *Foreign Affairs* (July 1946) 24:579–90.

Mehnert, Klaus. *Der deutsche Standort.* Stuttgart: Deutsche Verlagsanstalt, 1967.

Meier, Viktor. *Neuer Nationalismus in Suedosteuropa.* Opladen: Leske, 1968.

Meier, Viktor. "Yugoslav Communism." In *Communism in Europe*, edited by William E. Griffith, vol. 1.

Meissner, Boris. *Russland, die Weltmaechte und Deutschland: die sowjetische Deutschlandpolitik, 1943–1953.* Hamburg: Noelke, 1953.

———. "Sowjetdemokratie und bolschewistische Parteidiktatur." In Berlin, Freie Universitaet, Otto-Suhr-Institut, *Die Demokratie im Wandel der Gesellschaft.*

———. "Das Verhaeltnis von Partei und Staat im Ostblock." In *Die Sowjetunion in Europa: Vortraege.* Wiesbaden: Harrassowitz, 1962.

Merkel, Konrad, and Schuhans, Eduard. *Die Agrarwirtschaft in Mitteldeutschland: Sozialisierung und Produktionsergebnisse.* 2d ed. Bonn: Bundesministerium fuer Gesamtdeutsche Fragen, 1963.

Merkl, Peter H. *The Origin of the West German Republic.* New York: Oxford University Press, 1963.

Miller, Dorothy, and Trend, Harry G. "Economic Reforms in East Germany." *Problems of Communism* (March/April 1966) 15.

Moras, Joachim, and Paeschke, Hans, eds. *Deutscher Geist zwischen gestern und morgen: Bilanz der kulturellen Entwicklung seit 1945.* Stuttgart: Deutsche Verlagsanstalt, 1954.

Morgenthau, Hans J. "Germany Gives Rise to Vast Uncertainties." *New York Times Magazine*, September 8, 1963, p. 21ff.

———. "The Problem of German Reunification." *Annals of the American Academy of Political and Social Science* (July 1960) 330:124–32.

Morgenthau, Hans Joachim, ed. *Germany and the Future of Europe.* Chicago: University of Chicago Press, 1951.

Morgenthau, Henry, Jr. *Germany Is Our Problem.* New York: Harper, 1945.

Mosely, Philip E. "Dismemberment of Germany." *Foreign Affairs* (April 1950) 28:487–98.

Murphy, Robert Daniel. *Diplomat Among Warriors*. Garden City, N.Y.: Doubleday, 1964.

Nawrocki, Joachim. *Das geplante Wunder: Leben und Wirtschaften im anderen Deutschland*. Hamburg: Wegner, 1967.

Neal, Fred Warner. "The Unsolved German Settlement." *Annals of the American Academy of Political and Social Science* (January 1964) 351: 148–56.

Nesselrode, Franz von. *Germany's Other Half: A Journalist's Appraisal of East Germany*. London and New York: Abelard-Schuman, 1963.

Norden, Albert; Matern, Hermann; and Ebert, Friedrich. *Zwei deutsche Staaten: die nationale Politik der DDR*. Vienna: Europa Verlag, 1967.

Organski, A. F. K. "Berlin and Two Germanies." *Current History* (April 1959) 36:200–204.

Osgood, Robert Endicott. *NATO: The Entangling Alliance*. Chicago: University of Chicago Press, 1962.

Picht, Georg. *Die deutsche Bildungskatastrophe: Analyse und Dokumentation*. Olten und Freiburg/B.: Walter, 1964.

Planck, Charles R. *The Changing Status of German Reunification in Western Diplomacy, 1955–66*. Baltimore: Johns Hopkins Press, 1967.

———. *Sicherheit in Europa*. Munich: Oldenbourg, 1968.

Plischke, Elmer. *Contemporary Government of Germany*. Boston: Houghton Mifflin, 1961.

———. *Government and Politics in Contemporary Berlin*. The Hague: Nijhoff, 1963.

———. "Integrating Berlin and the Federal Republic of Germany." *Journal of Politics* (February 1965) 27:35–65.

Pollock, James K. "The Electoral System of the Federal Republic of Germany: A Study in Representative Government." *American Political Science Review* (June 1952) 46: 1056–68.

———. "The West German Electoral Law of 1953." *American Political Science Review* (March 1955) 49:107–30.

Pounds, Norman J. G. *Divided Germany and Berlin*. Princeton, N.J.: Van Nostrand, 1962.

Prinzipien der Verfassungsinterpretation. Gefaehrdungshaftung im oeffentlichen Recht. Berichte von Peter Schneider [and others] und Aussprache zu den Berichten in den Verhandlungen der Tagung der deutschen Staatsrechtslehrer zu Freiburg vom 4.–7. Oktober 1961. Berlin: de Gruyter, 1963.

Rasch, Harold. *Die Bundesrepublik und Osteuropa: Grundfragen einer kuenftigen deutschen Ostpolitik*. Cologne: Pahl-Rugenstein, 1963.

Richards, Fred H. *Die NPD, Alternative oder Wiederkehr?* Munich: Olzog, 1967.

Richert, Ernst. *Die DDR Elite, oder unsere Partner von Morgen*. Hamburg: Rowohl, 1968.

Richert, Ernst. *Macht ohne Mandat: der Staatsapparat in der sowjetischen Besatzungszone Deutschlands*. Cologne: Westdeutscher Verlag, 1958.

———. *Sozialistische Universitaet. Die Hochschulpolitik der SED*. Berlin: Colloquium Verlag, 1967.

Rittner, Fritz, et al., eds. *Die Lage des Rechts in Mitteldeutschland*. Karlsruhe: Mueller, 1965.

Roberts, Henry L. *Russia and America: Dangers and Prospects*. New York: Harper, 1956.

Robson, Charles B. *Berlin and the German Question*. Munich: Kopernikus, 1962.

Robson, Charles B., and Zohlnhoefer, Werner. "Berlinproblem und 'Deutsche Frage' im Spiegel des Englischsprachigen Schrifttums der Nachkriegszeit: Ein Literaturbericht." In *Jahrbuch fuer die Geschichte Mittel- und Ostdeutschlands*, pp. 297–323. Berlin: de Gruyter, 1962.

Rolfe, Sidney E. *Capital Markets in the Atlantic Economic Relationships*. Boulogne-sur-Seine: Atlantic Institute, 1967.

Schack, Alard von. "The Next Stage in Federal Republic Eastern Policy." *The German Tribune: A Selection from German Periodicals*, no. 1 (May 4, 1968); Quarterly Supplement to the weekly edition of *The German Tribune*.

Schenk, Fritz. *Im Vorzimmer der Diktatur: 12 Jahre Pankow*. Cologne: Kiepenheuer und Witsch, 1962.

Schiller, Karl. *Berliner Wirtschaft und deutsche Politik*. Stuttgart-Degerloch: Seewald, 1964.

Schlesinger, Arthur M. *A Thousand Days: John F. Kennedy in the White House*. Boston: Houghton Mifflin, 1965.

Schlueter, Hilmar Werner. *Die Wiedervereinigung Deutschlands: ein zeitgeschichtlicher Leitfaden*. 5th ed., rev. and enl. Bad Godesberg: Hohwacht Verlag, 1964.

Scholz, Arno and Orton, Peter K. *Outpost Berlin*. London: Orton-Press.

Schroeder, Gerhard. "Germany Looks at Eastern Europe." *Foreign Affairs* (October 1965) 44:15–25.

Schuetz, Wilhelm W. *Modelle der Deutschlandpolitik: Wege zu einer neuen Aussenpolitik*. Cologne: Kiepenheuer und Witsch, 1966.

———. *Reform der Deutschlandpolitik*. Cologne: Kiepenheuer und Witsch, 1966.

———. *Rethinking German Policy: New Approaches to Reunification*. New York: Praeger, 1967.

———. *Unteilbare Freiheit*. Goettingen: Vandenhoeck und Ruprecht, 1964.

Schulz, Eberhard. *An Ulbricht fuehrt kein Weg mehr vorbei! Provozierende Thesen zur deutschen Frage*. Hamburg: Hoffman und Campe, 1967.

Schulz, Eberhard, and Dieter, Hans. *Braucht der Osten die DDR?* Opladen: Leske, 1968.

Schuster, Rudolf. *Deutschlands staatliche Existenz im Widerstreit politischer und rechtlicher Gesichtspunkte, 1945–1963.* Munich: Oldenbourg, 1963.

Sethe, Paul. *Deutsche Geschichte im letzten Jahrhundert.* Frankfurt/M.: Scheffler, 1960.

Shell, Kurt L. *Bedrohung und Bewaehrung: Fuehrung und Bevoelkerung in der Berlin-Krise.* Cologne, Opladen: Westdeutscher Verlag, 1965.

Shulman, Marshall D. *Stalin's Foreign Policy Reappraised.* Cambridge, Mass.: Harvard University Press, 1963.

Siegler, Heinrich, Freiherr von, ed. *Wiedervereinigung und Sicherheit Deutschlands: eine dokumentarische Diskussionsgrundlage.* 5th ed., enl. Bonn: Siegler, 1964.

Smith, Jean Edward. *The Defense of Berlin.* Baltimore: Johns Hopkins Press, 1963.

———. "The German Democratic Republic and the West." *International Journal* (Spring 1967) 22:231–52.

———. "Red Prussianism." *Bulletin of the Atomic Scientists* (May 1967) 23:24–30.

Snell, John L., ed. *The Meaning of Yalta: Big Three Diplomacy and the New Balance of Power.* Baton Rouge: Louisiana State University Press, 1956.

Solberg, Richard W. *God and Caesar in East Germany: The Conflicts of Church and State in East Germany Since 1945.* New York: Macmillan, 1961.

Sontheimer, Kurt. *Politische Wissenschaft und Staatsrechtslehre.* Freiburg/B.: Rombach, 1963.

Die soziale Sicherung in der Bundesrepublik Deutschland, bisherige und kuenftige Entwicklung. Stand: 1. Maerz 1967. Bonn: Stollfuss (in Komm.) 1967.

Sozialistische Einheitspartei Deutschlands, Zentralkomitee. *Deutschlandplan der SPD: Kommentare, Argumente, Begruendungen.* Bonn: Vorstand der Sozial-Demokratischen Partei, 1959.

Speier, Hans. *Divided Berlin: The Anatomy of Soviet Political Blackmail.* New York: Praeger, 1961.

———. *German Rearmament and Atomic War: The Views of German Military and Political Leaders.* Evanston, Ill.: Row, Peterson, 1957.

Speier, Hans, and Davison, W. Phillips, eds. *West German Leadership and Foreign Policy.* Evanston, Ill.: Row, Peterson, 1957.

Spittmann, Ilse. "Soviet Union and DDR." *Survey* (London, October 1966) 61:165–76.

Staatliche Zentralverwaltung fuer Statistik. *Statistisches Jahrbuch der Deutschen Demokratischen Republik, 1955–1958.* Berlin: Deutscher Zentralverlag. Published annually.

Stahl, Walter, ed. *Education for Democracy in West Germany: Achievements, Shortcomings, Prospects.* New York: Praeger, 1961.

Starlinger, Wilhelm. *Grenzen der Sowjetmacht im Spiegel einer West-Ostbegegnung hinter Palisaden von 1945–1954*. Kitzingen/M.: Holzner, 1954.

Statistisches Bundesamt. *Statistisches Jahrbuch fuer die Bundesrepublik Deutschland*. Wiesbaden: Kohlhammer. Published annually.

Statistisches Landesamt Berlin. *Statistisches Jahrbuch Berlin, 1956–1968*. Berlin: Kulturbuch. Published annually.

Stehle, Hansjakob. "Polish Communism." In *Communism in Europe*, edited by William E. Griffith, vol. 2.

Stern, Carola. "East Germany." In *Communism in Europe*, edited by William E. Griffith, vol. 2.

———. *Portraet einer bolschewistischen Partei: Entwicklung, Funktion und Situation der SED*. Cologne: Verlag fuer Politik und Wirtschaft, 1957.

———. *Ulbricht*. Cologne/Berlin: Kiepenheuer und Witsch, 1963.

Stolper, Wolfgang F. *Germany Between East and West*. Washington, D.C.: National Planning Association, 1960.

Stolper, Wolfgang F., and Roskamp, Karl W. *The Structure of the East German Economy*. Cambridge, Mass.: Harvard University Press, 1960.

Stolze, Diether, ed. *Perspektive 1980. Deutschland: Industriestaat ohne Zukunft?* Hamburg: Wegner, 1967.

Storbeck, Dietrich. *Soziale Strukturen in Mitteldeutschland: eine sozialistische Bevoelkerungsanalyse im gesamtdeutschen Vergleich*. Berlin: Duncker und Humblot, 1964.

Strauss, Franz Josef. *The Grand Design: A European Solution to German Reunification*. New York: Praeger, 1966.

Strauss, Harold. *The Division and Dismemberment of Germany: From the Casablanca Conference, January 1943, to the Establishment of the East German Republic, October 1949*. Thesis No. 86, Geneva University. Ambilly: Les Presses de Savoie, 1952.

Tauber, Kurt P. *Beyond Eagle and Swastika: German Nationalism Since 1945*. 2 vols. Middletown, Conn.: Wesleyan University Press, 1967.

Thalheim, Karl C. *Die Wirtschaft der Sowjetzone in Krise und Umbau*. Berlin: Duncker und Humblot, 1964.

Thayer, Charles Wheeler. *The Unquiet Germans*. New York: Harper, 1957.

Thomas, Stephan. "Beyond the Wall." *Survey* (London, October 1962) 44/45:54–65.

Toennis, Norbert, ed. *Gibt es noch Wege zur Wiedervereinigung? Eine* Untersuchung von Johann Baptist Gradl [and others]. Bonn: Antares Verlag, 1960.

Ulbricht, Walter. *Die Entwicklung des deutschen volksdemokratischen Staates, 1945–1958*. Berlin: Dietz, 1958.

Uschakow, Alexander, ed. *Das sowjetische internationale Privatrecht, 1917 bis 1962: eine bibliographische Dokumentation*. Cologne: Wissenschaft und Politik, 1964.

U.S. Congress, Senate, Committee on Foreign Relations. *A Decade of American Foreign Policy: Basic Documents, 1941–1949*. Washington, D.C.: Government Printing Office, 1950.

———. *Documents on Germany, 1944–1961*. Washington, D.C.: Government Printing Office, 1961.

U.S. Department of State, Historical Division. *American Foreign Policy: Basic Documents, 1950–1955*. 2 vols. Department of State Publication No. 6446. Washington, D.C.: Government Printing Office, 1957.

———. *Documents on Germany, 1944–1959*. Background documents on Germany, 1944–1959, and a chronology of political developments affecting Berlin, 1945–1956. Washington, D.C.: Government Printing Office, 1959.

U.S. Department of State, Historical Office. *American Foreign Policy: Current Documents*. Washington, D.C.: Government Printing Office. Published annually, starting 1956.

U.S. Embassy, Bonn, Economic Affairs Section. *Handbook of Economic Statistics: Federal Republic of Germany and Western Sectors of Berlin*. Bad Godesberg: U.S. Department of State. Published quarterly.

Vali, Ferenc A. *The Quest for a United Germany*. Baltimore: Johns Hopkins Press, 1967.

———. *Rift and Revolt in Hungary: Nationalism versus Communism*. Cambridge, Mass.: Harvard University Press, 1961.

Vicker, Ray. "Eager Satellite: East Germany Leads Way in Red Scramble for Economic Reform." *Wall Street Journal*, October 4, 1965.

Vogt, Hartmut. *Bildung fuer die Zukunft. Entwicklungstendenzen im deutschen Bildungswesen in West und Ost*. Goettingen: Vandenhoeck und Ruprecht, 1967.

Wagner, Wolfgang. *The Partitioning of Europe*. Stuttgart: Deutsche Verlagsanstalt, 1959.

Wallich, Henry C. *Mainsprings of the German Revival*. New Haven, Conn.: Yale University Press, 1955.

Wehner, Herbert. *Gespraeche mit. . . . See* Gaus, Guenter. *Staatserhaltende Opposition*.

Wenger, Paul W. *Wer gewinnt Deutschland? Kleinpreussische Selbstisolierung oder mitteleuropaeische Foederation*. Stuttgart: Seewald, 1959.

Wettig, Gerhard. *Entmilitarisierung und Wiederbewaffnung in Deutschland 1943–1955*. Munich: Oldenbourg, 1967.

Wheeler-Bennet, John. *The Nemesis of Power: The German Army in Politics, 1918–1945*. New York: St. Martin's Press, 1953.

Wighton, Charles. *Adenauer, Democratic Dictator: A Critical Biography*. London: Muller, 1963.

Wissenschaftsrat zum Ausbau der Wissenschaftlichen Einrichtungen. *Empfehlungen des Wissenschaftsrates zum Ausbau der wissenschaftlichen Hochschulen bis 1970*. Tuebingen: Mohr, 1967.

Wolfe, James H. *Indivisible Germany: Illusion or Reality?* The Hague: Nijhoff, 1963.

Windsor, Philip. *City on Leave: A History of Berlin, 1945–1962.* New York: Praeger, 1963.

Wollenberg, Erich. *Der Apparat: Stalins fuenfte Kolonne.* Bonn: Bundesministerium fuer Gesamtdeutsche Fragen, 1951.

Wright, Quincy. "Some Legal Aspects of the Berlin Crisis." *American Journal of International Law* (July 1961) 55:959–65.

Index